PREEMINENT STRATEGIST

PREEMINENT STRATEGIST

General Joseph Eggleston Johnston, The Confederacy's Most Agile General

F. GREGORY TORETTA

CASEMATE
Pennsylvania & Yorkshire

Published in the United States of America and Great Britain in 2026 by
CASEMATE PUBLISHERS
1950 Lawrence Road, Havertown, PA 19083, USA
and
47 Church Street, Barnsley, S70 2AS, UK

Hardcover Edition: ISBN 978-1-63624-596-6
Digital Edition: ISBN 978-1-63624-597-3

A CIP record for this book is available from the British Library

Printed and bound in the United Kingdom by CPI Group (UK) Ltd, Croydon, CR0 4YY
Typeset in India by DiTech Publishing Services

For a complete list of Casemate titles, please contact:

CASEMATE PUBLISHERS (US)
Telephone (610) 853-9131
Fax (610) 853-9146
Email: casemate@casematepublishers.com
www.casematepublishers.com

CASEMATE PUBLISHERS (UK)
Telephone (0)1226 734350
Email: casemate@casemateuk.com
www.casemateuk.com

Cover image: Joseph Eggleston Johnston (1807–91). (National Archives)

The Publisher's authorised representative in the EU for product safety is Authorised Rep Compliance Ltd., Ground Floor, 71 Lower Baggot Street, Dublin D02 P593, Ireland.
www.arccompliance.com

Contents

Acknowledgments vii
Prologue ix

1 Lineage, Parentage, and West Point 1
2 Early Military Career 5
3 War with Mexico 13
4 Promotion and Resignation 25
5 First Manassas 29
6 Technological Changes and Northern Advantages 37
7 Feud Over the General's Rank 41
8 Johnston Falls Back Behind the Rapidan and Rappahannock Rivers 49
9 The Peninsula 53
10 Williamsburg 61
11 Guarding Richmond 71
12 Seven Pines 75
13 Geographical Command 95
14 Vicksburg 107
15 Condemnation over the Surrender of Vicksburg 129
16 The Army of Tennessee 139
17 Dalton Realities and Richmond's Castles in the Air 149
18 Opposing Sherman's Campaign to Atlanta 161
19 Chattahoochee River 191
20 Relieved of Command 199
21 Recalled to Service 211
22 Surrender 221
23 Private Citizen 227
24 Death and Funeral 231

Conclusion 233

Endnotes 241
Bibliography 251
Index 253

Acknowledgments

I want to give special thanks to my wife, Joan, whose love and devotion sustained me in writing this manuscript. Also, a special thanks to my sons, George, Stephen, and Philip, who helped me with technical computer support and purchased a new computer for me when the old one ceased to function.

Prologue

When naming the best generals of the Confederate states, the names of Robert E. Lee, "Stonewall" Jackson, and Albert Sidney Johnston are mentioned, but few think of Joseph Eggleston Johnston among this exalted group. In fact, although never utilized to his full potential, Joseph E. Johnston (1807–91) was preeminent among all the others. He understood the impact that the technological changes developed prior to the American Civil War in weaponry (rifled musket and cannon), communications (telegraph), and logistics (railroad) would have on the battlefield and adjusted his planning accordingly. He realized the South must husband its resources and manpower to offset the great disparity in population and industrial capacity the North possessed. Johnston believed that the South's best resource was its manpower, which he considered more important than its land or cities. He modified his tactics and strategy to accommodate these circumstances. President Jefferson Davis and many other Southern generals could not make this adaptation. The famous British war correspondent, Sir William Howard Russell, wrote in his journal in the fall of 1861: "Johnston is their best strategist."

Johnston attended West Point, one of the most prestigious engineering schools of the 19th century and one of the best military institutions in the world. He served on the frontier in the West and with General Winfield Scott in the Mexican War.

When his state of Virginia seceded from the Union, he resigned his commission and aligned with the Confederate States of America. General Joseph Eggleston Johnston was the highest-ranking United States officer to resign and serve the Confederacy. Johnston was the first to receive the rank of brigadier general in the regular Confederate Army. However, he was slighted by President Jefferson Davis when selections were made under a law passed by the Confederate government for five full generals in the Confederacy, Johnston being ranked fourth even though he was the most senior U.S. Army officer to join the Southern states. This affront stemmed from Johnston's appointment as quartermaster general in the old army against the wishes of Jefferson Davis, then chairman of the Senate Military Affairs Committee, who wanted another general for the position. Their relationship soured throughout the war, culminating in General Johnston's controversial removal as commander of the Army of Tennessee at Atlanta after he had conducted a masterful defense against General Sherman's campaign in 1864. There is every indication that had Johnston been adequately and properly supported by President Davis and the Confederate government during the Atlanta campaign, the South would have obtained a favorable outcome in the war.

After the war, Johnston wrote a detailed memoir, *Narrative of Military Operations* (1874), a fulsome account of the conflict and his part in it, in which he stated: "I offer these pages as my contribution of materials for the use of the future historian of the War between the States." Yet the *Narrative* was also to defend his reputation and war record against calumny from Jefferson Davis and others. Johnston served the South throughout the war, from its first victory at Manassas in July 1861 to its last at Bentonville, North Carolina, in April 1865, and was one of the last generals to surrender at the end of the struggle.

The object of this biography is to present the facts and unearth the truth, as every good historian hopes to achieve. Its goal is to present relevant insights as to Johnston's strategic genius and superior military skill.

General Joseph Eggleston Johnston, whose motto was "Let the place go, and save the garrison," was the Confederacy's preeminent strategist and tactician. He was regarded as the Confederacy's best general by both Ulysses S. Grant and William Tecumseh Sherman.

Let the reader decide.

CHAPTER I

Lineage, Parentage, and West Point

Joseph Eggleston Johnston (1807–91) was a West Point graduate and served in the Mexican–American War and Seminole Wars. During the American Civil War, he was one of the most senior general officers in the Confederate States Army. (National Archives)

Joseph Eggleston Johnston was born on February 3, 1807, in Farmville, Virginia, to Peter Johnston and Mary Valentine Wood Johnston. He was the grandson of Peter Johnston, who was born in Annan, Scotland, in 1710 and had emigrated from Edinburgh, Scotland, to Virginia in 1727, settling on the James River at Osborne's Landing, where he prospered in the merchant trade. At the age of 51, having spent many years absorbed in his business, Peter Johnston decided it was time to marry. He courted and married a widow, Mrs. Martha Rogers, on March 19, 1761. She was the daughter of a fellow merchant, Mr. John Butler, who resided on the Appomattox River just below Petersburg. In 1765, after the French and Indian War, he moved to the county of Prince Edward in the Piedmont section of the Virginia colony, and settled on an estate near Farmville which they named Cherry Grove. During the American Revolution, he sided with the Patriot cause. His eldest son, also named Peter, was born at Osborne's Landing on January 6, 1763. The younger Peter left home at the age of 17 to join the cavalry legion of "Light Horse Harry" Lee, the father of Robert E. Lee, for campaigns in the Carolinas, where he attained the rank of lieutenant. In 1788, after the war, Lieutenant Peter Johnston married Mary Valentine Wood, daughter of Colonel Valentine Wood of Goochland County and niece of Virginia patriot Patrick Henry. He brought her to the family estate, which Peter inherited at the death of his father in accordance with the English custom of primogeniture. Their first child, named Martha, died in infancy; however, they had nine more healthy children, all boys. Joseph Eggleston was their seventh son, being named after Peter's captain and squad commander under whom he had served during the Revolution.

Panecillo

Peter Johnston, whose political affiliations were with the Republican Party—adherents of the school of Thomas Jefferson—entered politics and was a member of the Virginia State Assembly for 13 terms, twice being chosen speaker of the House of Delegates. He served on the commission to settle the boundary dispute between Tennessee and Virginia, and in 1811 was elected judge of the Virginia General Court, assigned to a circuit in central Virginia. He traded circuits with Judge William Brokenbrough and took up residence at Panecillo, a two-story log house he constructed in Abingdon, Virginia, more conveniently located for Peter to serve the southwest Virginia circuit. Abingdon, a small frontier town in the mountains of Virginia, was a half-dozen miles from the Tennessee border and 300 miles from the nearest city. Judge Peter Johnston was invited to join the board of trustees of the Abingdon Academy, where his sons would receive their education. At a very young age, Joseph Johnston took a keen interest in military leaders and military history, especially the battle of King's Mountain in 1780, where the Patriots crushed the Tory forces of Major Patrick Ferguson, which started Cornwallis on a path leading to his surrender at Yorktown. Peter noticed Joseph's interest in the military and presented him with the sword he had carried in the Revolution, even though Joseph was just aged eight at the time and six older brothers stood ahead of him for the inheritance. Joseph cherished the sword his whole life.

The Colonel

After attending the Abingdon Academy, Joseph, at age 18, wished to enroll in the United States Military Academy at West Point. Judge Johnston secured Joseph an appointment on February 21, 1825, through the influence of a political friend, James Barbour, United States senator from Virginia, and a nomination by Secretary of War John C. Calhoun under President John Quincy Adams, which Joseph received on March 3. Joseph was one of 105 young men who had received appointments to the class of 1829. All appointments, including Johnston's, were conditional upon passing a preliminary exam in June. The exam consisted of reading a few sentences from a history book to ensure literacy and solving a simple arithmetic problem. On June 28, Johnston assembled in front of the cadet barracks with the other 86 who had successfully passed, and they took the formal oath on July 1. At West Point, Johnston studied civil engineering, learning how to build bridges, tunnels, railroads, and fortifications, and how to successfully utilize artillery. He was taught mathematics and science, which he struggled with, but excelled at battle tactics and strategy. French was required so that the students could learn from the writings of Napoleon Bonaparte, considered one of the greatest military minds in history; Joseph was skillful at this language, speaking it well, reading its literature and translating some works into English. Johnston received the sobriquet "The Colonel" from some of the cadets because he was so proper, quiet, and serious.

During his first year at West Point, he experienced a personal loss in November when he learned his mother had passed on. "How is it possible," he wrote in his melancholy, "for me to bear the loss of such a mother, the best, the tenderest, and the most virtuous, with other than the greatest anguish?"[1]

Johnston did moderately well in his studies, ranking 27th out of 85 who remained at the end of the year; his grades improved every year after. He became best friends with his classmate Robert E. Lee. They had much in common: both were from Virginia, were intelligent and ambitious, and were serious students who avoided activities that earned demerits. Johnston's father had served under Lee's father in the American Revolution. Later in life, Johnston admitted to a friend: "In youth and early manhood I loved and admired him more than any man in the world."[2] Johnston wrote years later about their companionship:

> We had the same intimate associates, who thought, as I did, that no other youth or man so united the qualities that win warm friendship and command high respect. For he was full of sympathy and kindness, genial and fond of gay conversation, and even of fun, that made him the most agreeable of companions, while his correctness of demeanor and language and attention to all duties, personal and official, and a dignity as much a part of himself as the elegance of his person, gave him a superiority that everyone acknowledged in his heart. He was the only one of all the men I have known who could laugh at the faults and follies of his friends in such a manner as to make them ashamed without touching their affection for him, and to confirm their respect and sense of his superiority.[3]

CHAPTER 2

Early Military Career

In June 1829, Joseph Johnston completed his four years as a cadet and became a commissioned officer on July 1 that year. Johnston ranked thirteenth out of 46 graduates and was appointed to the artillery division of the United States Army. He was not eligible for the prestigious Army Corps of Engineers, which only accepted the top two cadets that year—Charles Mason, who graduated first, and Robert E. Lee.

The regular army had only four regiments of artillery in the 1830s, whose job was to garrison the forts along the seacoast. As a second lieutenant in Company C of the 4th U.S. Artillery, Johnston's first duty was to man Fort Columbus on Governor's Island in New York Harbor, a post in which he served for two years until the summer of 1831. In the early fall of 1831, Johnston's Company C was one of five sent to Fort Monroe, on the coast in southeastern Virginia, to reinforce the garrison there. The reinforcement was needed due to enslaved Black abolitionists—led by Nat Turner, an enslaved preacher and freedom fighter—who had marched throughout Virginia's Southampton County that August, close to Johnston's birthplace. Known as Nat Turner's Rebellion, this event—the only effective and sustained fight for freedom by enslaved people in U.S. history—left 60 white and over two hundred enslaved Black people dead before it was suppressed by white authorities. Johnston found Robert E. Lee stationed there as an engineer assigned to construction work at the fort. The two resumed their West Point friendship and engaged in the social activities of the garrison together.

Army of the Frontier

Another conflict erupted when Black Hawk, a Sauk leader, left the Iowa Indian Territory with a contingent of Sauks, Meskwakis, and Kickapoos—known as the "British Band"—crossed the Mississippi River and headed into the state of Illinois on April 5, 1832. They had become known as the British Band for sometimes flying the British flag in defiance of claims of United States sovereignty. The group consisted of some five hundred warriors and six hundred noncombatants. They wished to resettle on the tribal land ceded to the United States in the 1804 Treaty of St. Louis, which the tribes disputed. Commanded by Brigadier General Henry Atkinson, a force of 450 regular army infantrymen and 2,100 mounted militia—dubbed the "Army of the Frontier"—started in pursuit of the British Band in June 1832, but were unable to locate them. On June 15, President Andrew Jackson, who was disappointed in the progress of the campaign, appointed Gen. Winfield Scott to take command from Atkinson. On June 28, Scott arrived at Fort Monroe to take over the expedition. He had summoned nine companies of regular artillery for infantry service; Johnston's Company C of the 4th Regiment was one of those chosen. Johnston's company travelled by sea to New York then up the Hudson River to West Point, where nearly the entire graduating class of 1832 joined the expedition. The expedition proceeded to Albany then via the Erie Canal to Buffalo on Lake Erie, where four lake steamers awaited them to carry them to Detroit. During the journey across the Great Lakes, Asiatic cholera broke out, decimating the expedition. By the time the vessels finally landed at Fort Dearborn in Chicago, Scott had only about 350 effective soldiers left of the almost 850 men who were transported. Apparently, Johnston did not contract the disease, but 81 of the 372 artillerymen en route died, nearly a fourth of their number. Scott moved on ahead of his troops, while Johnston stayed behind in Chicago. However, the Black Hawk War had ended, as General Atkinson and the militia caught up with the British Band on July 21 and defeated them in the battle of Wisconsin Heights. The Americans resumed the pursuit and annihilated the remnants of Black Hawk's band at the battle of Bad Axe on August 1 and 2. Black Hawk was captured and sent to Jefferson Barracks, Missouri. The minor chiefs were taken to Fort Armstrong on Rock Island in the Mississippi River, where they signed a treaty on September 21 foreswearing all rights to land east of the Mississippi. Johnston signed the treaty as a formal witness. He turned around and returned to Norfolk on the steamer *Potomac* on November 11, having never seen any action.

However, another crisis of national proportions erupted when a state convention in South Carolina adopted the Ordinance of Nullification on November 24, 1832, declaring the Tariff of 1832—signed by President Andrew Jackson on July 14 that year—null and void within the state boundaries after February 1, 1833. The Force Bill was passed by Congress on March 1, 1833, authorizing the President to use military force against South Carolina. Military preparations were initiated by South Carolina to resist Federal enforcement. Johnston again left Fort Monroe with Company C in November 1832, heading to Charleston, South Carolina, to augment the garrison there. Confrontation was avoided because Congress had enacted the Compromise Tariff of 1833, which was satisfactory to South Carolina, the same day that the Force Bill was adopted. The South Carolina convention reconvened on March 15, 1833, and repealed the Ordinance of Nullification. It is ironic that three of Johnston's brothers—who lived in Columbia, South Carolina, at the same time—were drilling with the state's militia.

Again, Johnston returned to Fort Monroe in the spring of 1833. On occasions, Lee and Johnston took a boat across the James River to Norfolk for formal socializing. Lee wrote to a mutual friend that "from occasionally accompanying me over the river, 'The Colonel' is in some danger of being caught by a pair of black eyes," but Johnston's affair with a local woman was transient. When his sister-in-law, Louisa, accused him of being in love, Johnston wrote to her: "No I am not. Never was, more than a philosopher should be. I am 24—too old to believe in romance and sentimentality & too much a philosopher to be under their influence even if they really existed."[1]

After serving in the Creek Nation in central Alabama to help keep peace between Creeks and whites on the frontier from December 18, 1833 until early 1834, Johnston returned to Virginia and then took up duty in Washington, D.C. Johnston was assigned to the Topographical Engineers to draft maps of the Ohio Territory. He lived at this time at Mrs. Ulrich's boardinghouse, sharing meals with prominent cabinet members, congressmen, and military men who resided there. Lee, stationed in Washington as assistant to the Chief of Engineers, would occasionally dine there when unable to go to his home in Arlington. In the summer of 1834, Johnston contacted "a bilious fever" due to the unhealthy climate in the nation's capital, but fully recovered.

Seminole War

Another serious Indian war erupted in Florida in June 1835, in which Johnston became embroiled. President Jackson had called for an Indian Removal Act in his 1829 State of the Union address. This was passed by Congress on May 26, 1830, and signed by Jackson two days later. The Act required that all Indians who lived in the eastern states move west across the Mississippi River. In March 1835, the chiefs of the Seminole Indians in Florida were in tough negotiations with the United States to relocate. When the chiefs could not be brought to terms, Wiley Thompson, the new U.S. Indian agent to the Seminoles, had Osceola, the most obstinate Seminole chief, seized and clapped in irons, a direct violation of the truce. Osceola, humiliated and bitter, signed the treaty the next day to obtain his release, but his compliance was only a deception. Soon after, the Seminoles, along with Black Seminoles (a group of the previously enslaved, and the enslaved who had sought freedom)—in all about four thousand strong—launched coordinated attacks raiding farms and settlements. A column of two companies on their way to Fort King, 110 United States soldiers, under the command of Major Francis Dade were ambushed and annihilated on December 28; only three survived. On the same day, Wiley Thompson and his dinner guest were shot and killed as they took their evening walk, as well as six others outside of Fort King. Thus, the Second Seminole War was started, lasting from 1835 to 1842. In January 1836, money for a full-scale war was appropriated by Congress.

Major General Winfield Scott was called upon to conduct a campaign to crush the Seminoles. Second Lieutenant Joseph E. Johnston was appointed to Winfield Scott's staff as an aide-de-camp. Scott's plan was for a three-pronged simultaneous offensive, totaling five thousand men, to converge on the Cove of the Withlacoochee, an irregularly shaped inland lake surrounded by heavy forest and dotted with small islands; it was the heart of the Seminole nation. Scott had to assemble supplies and recruit volunteer militia, which made up the bulk of his army, to implement his campaign.

On January 23, Johnston left Washington and stopped briefly at Columbia, South Carolina, to meet with some of his brothers, then rode to Augusta and Savannah. While there, he was "employed in correspondence with 4 Governors & divers generals & colonels, not to mention Qr. Masters & commissaries, on all matters pertaining to arming & equipping militia & subduing Indians," as he indicated in a letter dated February 18, 1836, to his brother, Beverly Johnston.[2]

On March 9, 1836, Johnston, together with Scott and the rest of his staff, started on a 50-mile journey from Picolata on the St. Johns River south of St. Augustine to Fort Drane. From Fort Drane, Scott would accompany a column of two thousand men under the command of Brigadier General Duncan L. Clinch moving south toward the Cove. A second column of some fourteen hundred men, commanded by Brigadier General Abraham Eustis, would travel southwest from Volusia, a town at Mosquito Inlet on the St. Johns River. Finally, a third column (1,250 men) under Colonel William Lindsay would move north and east from Fort Brooke (Tampa). Scott's orders called for Eustis and Lindsay to be in place by March 25. They would form an anvil upon which Clinch's force, constituting the hammer, would drive the Seminoles.

Eustis and Lindsay would communicate their locations to each other by firing an evening and morning gun. However, the plan fell apart as all three columns were delayed. Eustis was two days late in departing Volusia due to an attack by the Seminoles, and did not arrive until March 30. Lindsay's column reached their position on March 28 but received no reply after firing their cannon. Clinch's men left Fort Drane on March 26, marching along such a marshy road that required them to cut down trees and lay logs so the wagons could pass. On March 28, Clinch crossed the Withlacoochee to attack the Cove, but the villages were empty. On March 31, all three commanders, running dangerously low on supplies, headed for Fort Brooke. The campaign ended in failure. Nevertheless, Johnston received a promotion to first lieutenant in July 1836. He continued to serve in Florida under new commanders, first under the newly appointed Governor of the Territory of Florida (March 16, 1836), Richard Keith Call, until December; then under Major General Thomas S. Jesup until the spring. There is only a brief mention in his book of his involvement in active campaigning against the Seminoles at the battle of Wahoo Swamp on November 21, 1836.

Resignation

Johnston, dissatisfied with his slow promotion, decided to resign in May 1837; the department accepted his resignation on May 31. He explained in a letter to his brother, Beverly: "[F]rom the rules of our service, of promotion by regiments, many of my juniors who had the luck to be assigned to regiments in which promotion was less slow than in that to which I belonged had got before me on the army list."[3]

The pay of a second lieutenant in the 1830s was less than $800 a year, while as a civilian engineer his engineering skills could command multiple times that salary. But Johnston could not have picked a worse time to enter the civilian workforce; the Panic of 1837 was in full swing. The recession that ensued lasted from 1837–44, a period of deflating wages and prices, when unemployment may have reached 25 percent in some areas. This crisis was preceded by a period of economic expansion from 1834–36, with an increase in construction projects—bridges, canals, and railroads—creating high-paying jobs for engineers. There was rampant speculation in public lands after the Indian Removal Act of May 28, 1830, with the sale of public lands increasing five times from 1834–36. The speculators were paying for their land with paper money from state banks not backed by hard currency. President Andrew Jackson contributed to this practice when, in July 1832, he vetoed the bill to re-charter the Second Bank of the United States, fiscal agent and central bank for the United States. Federal revenues were placed in "pet" banks across the country, many of which were in western regions as a result of the Deposit and Distribution Act of 1836. The effect was to transfer specie away from the large commercial banks on the East Coast, causing them to curtail their loans. Meanwhile, state-chartered banks in the West and the South—the "pet" banks—were printing banknotes and lending funds without restraint, with risky reserve ratios of specie.

Government law required that land purchases be completed with specie or paper notes from specie-backed banks. To curb the use of soft currency, President Jackson issued a presidential executive order on July 11, 1836, requiring the implementation of the Specie Circular by Secretary of the Treasury Levi Woodbury. The government would not take anything but gold and silver specie in exchange for public lands after August 15. All these factors led to a real estate and commodity crash, with a decline in cotton prices by 25 percent in February and March 1837. The New York banks scaled back on lending and there was a severe contraction of credit by all financial institutions, forcing the cancellation or suspension of new construction projects.

Second Seminole War

Johnston couldn't find work in engineering. Instead, he applied for a job with the government's Topographical Bureau in Washington. In the late summer, Secretary of War Poinsett appointed him Adjutant and Topographical Engineer, without military rank, and assigned him as a surveyor in an expedition under Lieutenant Levin M. Powell of the U.S. Navy. They were ordered to explore and survey the 450-mile stretch of coastline and rivers from St. Augustine to Key West, in cooperation with the Army, to recommend sites for depots and forts. On January 15, 1838, the expedition encountered a band of Seminole Indians as they entered the Jupiter inlet of the Indian River, which the Seminoles named Locha Hatchee. Powell left two dozen men behind to guard the boats and led 55 sailors and 25 soldiers in pursuit of the Seminoles to their camp, Johnston accompanying them. They came "within sight of a large camp from which the warriors hastened to meet us," according to Johnston. In the ensuing engagement, every officer received incapacitating wounds, and the naval recruits fell back in near panic to the boats. Johnston took command of the regular soldiers to cover the retreat ordered by Powell. Johnston later recalled: "[T]he little rearguard, less than thirty, disputed every yard of ground. I placed them in ambuscade hoping to check the advancing Indians by their fire and encourage our retreating poltroons." Johnston was in the thick of the fighting; he later claimed to have counted 30 bullet holes in his clothing, two of which were in his cap. One of the bullets grazed his forehead, leaving a permanent scar. Powell mentioned Johnston in his formal report: "[T]o the steady courage and conduct of this officer, we are mainly indebted for the comparative security in which we returned to our boats."[4] In March 1838, Powell took another expedition into the still-unexplored Everglades of Florida, starting from Fort Dallas (Miami). Johnston went with the surveying party and became one of the first white men to enter the Everglades.

Johnston's involvement in the Second Seminole War rekindled his desire to pursue a military career, and on July 7, 1838, he secured a reappointment to the Army in the newly formed Corps of Topographical Engineers with the rank of first lieutenant. He was given the rank of "brevet captain" on the same day "for gallantry on several occasions in the war against the Florida Indians." He was involved in surveying assignments along the international boundary between the United States and Canada in 1840, and on the Sabine River on the Texas–Louisiana border in 1841. In 1842, he served on the staff of General William A. Worth as Assistant Adjutant General in Florida. Robert E. Lee wrote to a friend saying: "Joe Johnston is playing Adjt. Genl. in Florida to his heart's content. His plan is good, he is working for promotion. I hope he will succeed." Worth brought the Seminoles to gradual capitulation and peace by promoting an active campaign year-round, focusing on the destruction of Indian towns and fields. Johnston had great admiration for Worth, who had been the commandant at West Point during his first three years there. He reported to his nephew, Preston Johnston: "Genl. Worth is my earliest admiration as a military man & has always shown the kindest disposition for me, & then, Pres, his family is such a one as nobody else can boast of. These things together make the position of Adjt. Genl. more agreeable in his staff than that of any other general."[5]

Lydia

Johnston was accompanied by two other officers during his survey of the international boundary between the United States and Canada: Captain Augustus Canfield and Second Lieutenant Robert McLane. Johnston struck up a friendship with McLane, who was 10 years younger than him. In 1840, McLane invited Johnston to his home in Baltimore, Maryland, for the Christmas holidays. There, Johnston met Robert's family: his invalid mother, Kitty, his four brothers and three sisters, and his prominent father,

Louis McLane. Louis had served in both the House of Representatives and the United States Senate, as well as in Jackson's Cabinet. He had been the minister to England, Secretary of the Treasury, and Secretary of State; many thought he would run for president of the United States. In 1837, he became president of the Baltimore and Ohio Railroad. But Joseph Johnston was especially attracted to Robert's 18-year-old sister, Lydia Mulligan Sims McLane (1822–87). Lydia had dark hair and eyes, a long straight nose, a strong chin, and a firm mouth with a mischievous smile; she was considered more handsome than pretty by observers. She was a gentile young woman, warm and friendly, with a genuinely sweet disposition and endearing wit. Joseph and Lydia had great affection for each other, and for five years they kept in touch through long letters and brief visits. On July 10, 1845, they were married in Baltimore by the Reverend William E. Wyatt at St. Paul's Episcopal Church. Joseph was 38 and Lydia 23. They were devoted and supportive of each other throughout their marriage, only being parted by her death. Johnston finished his letters to his wife with: "Good night my love, my life, my soul." Unfortunately, although Johnston wanted to be a father, the marriage produced no offspring.

CHAPTER 3

War with Mexico

On the morning of April 25, 1846, Captain Seth Thornton, with a patrol of 63 dragoons, was ambushed by Mexican cavalry on the north bank of the Rio Grande. Eleven of the troopers were killed and six wounded, with all the rest, including the commander, captured. They had been sent by Major General Zachary Taylor to investigate a report that Mexican forces had crossed the north bank of the Rio Grande. Indeed, on April 23, some sixteen hundred Mexican cavalrymen, commanded by General Anastasio Torrejon, had crossed over the mighty river. General Taylor and his command had been sent to support American territorial claims in Texas. The Republic of Texas, which had won its independence from Mexico in 1836, was annexed by the United States in 1845. The two nations disputed the area enclosed by the Rio Grande and Nueces River. News of Thornton's entrapment reached President James K. Polk, who asked Congress for a declaration of war, stating American blood had been shed on American soil. That the soil was in contention did not seem to matter; Congress passed a war bill on May 13.

Initially, Zachary Taylor's army advanced on the Mexicans, winning the battles of Palo Alto (May 8, 1846), Resaca de la Palma (May 9, 1846), Monterey (September 19–24, 1846), and Buena Vista (February 23, 1847). However, Gen. Winfield Scott, doubtful whether Taylor could approach Mexico City from his position in Monterey, proposed an alternative in October 1846, a landing at Vera Cruz and marching on the capital from there. President Polk approved the plan and Scott started putting together a joint sea and land operation. When Johnston heard of this development, he applied for active duty and was ordered to the Brazos, just north of where the Rio Grande enters the Gulf of Mexico. As he joined in Scott's invasion, he transferred from the Topographical Engineers to a regiment of gray-coated *voltigeurs* who were trained as expert skirmishers.

Johnston took the wooden steamer *Massachusetts*, General Scott's command vessel, south from New Orleans, sharing a cabin with Captain Robert E. Lee. Prone to seasickness, Johnston suffered horribly from the movement of the vessel. The expedition arrived off Vera Cruz on March 5. The fleet sailed behind Sacrificios Island, which provided shelter from "northers," winds or storms from the north. On March 9, the troops were loaded on flatboats, 70 soldiers to a scow, and transported to Collada, a smooth beach south of Vera Cruz, in the largest amphibious invasion yet attempted in history. The bulk of the American army—some twelve thousand men—were ashore by nightfall; the Mexicans offered no resistance to the landing. On March 10, General Scott, Johnston, and the rest of the staff came ashore and orders were issued to invest the city and commence a siege. A semi-circle of trenches with artillery emplacements some 7 miles in length surrounded the city. Before opening fire, Scott drafted a flowery invitation to the Mexican governor, Juan Morales, to surrender in order to save the city from destruction. Scott stated he was "anxious to spare the beautiful city of Vera Cruz from the imminent hazard of demolition [and] the inevitable horrors of a triumphant assault."[1] Joseph Johnston was chosen by General Scott to deliver the message to the Mexican governor. On March 22, at 2.00 p.m., Johnston, bearing a white flag and accompanied by a bugler, rode out from the American lines to the southern gate to the city, Puerto de la Merced, and presented the ultimatum. He was courteously asked to wait for a response. Johnston brought back a polite but defiant rejection.

That evening, Scott commenced bombardment with his mortars and howitzers. By March 25, ten 10-inch mortars, four 24-pounders, two 8-inch siege howitzers, three 32-pounders, and three long 8-inch Paixhans were hammering Vera Cruz. The situation in Vera Cruz became untenable. Governor Morales feigned sickness and turned over command to his deputy, General J. J. Landero, then Morales escaped by boat on the night of the 25th. On the following morning, Landero had a white flag hung over the demolished walls of the city and sent Scott a message asking for both sides to appoint commissioners to arrange a convention. The first meeting was on the afternoon of March 26, when the Mexicans made a few demands which were refused. Scott lost patience, threatening to recommence the bombardment, whereupon the Mexicans capitulated and signed the agreement at 9.00 p.m. on March 27. "Commissioners were appointed to arrange terms of surrender, and General Scott selected Captains Joseph E. Johnston and Robert E. Lee to represent us, and nobly they did so," Second Lieutenant Dabney Maury, the pair's friend and a fellow Virginian, recalled. "This selection gave great satisfaction throughout the army. In rich uniforms, superbly mounted, they were most soldierly, as they were the ablest, men in the army."[2] Scott was criticized by some of his officers for laying siege to Vera Cruz rather than assaulting it, but his decision saved countless American lives. Though the weaponry had not changed since Napoleon's time, each side using smooth-bore muskets and cannon, these weapons could still cause many casualties. Scott conducted the rest of the campaign in similar fashion by turning strong Mexican positions, avoiding direct assault when possible, thus keeping casualties low. Joseph Johnston must have learned much from Scott's tactics.

The Mexican dictator, Antonio Lopez de Santa Anna, returned to Mexico City after being badly defeated by Zachary Taylor in the battle of Buena Vista. He learned that Vera Cruz had fallen on March 30, 1847. Santa Anna, surmising that Scott's next move would be to approach Mexico City along the National Highway, scraped together an army of twelve thousand along with 43 pieces of artillery, a force larger than Scott's. He chose a strong position at a pass near the small town of Cerro Fordo to make his stand. Here, the highway was dominated by hills, the most outstanding of which was Cerro Gordo (fat mountain), also known as El Telegrafo, which dominated the landscape with a broad elevation of about one thousand feet. Santa Anna's right flank was protected by a substantial stream, Rio Del Pan. On his extreme left was a deep ravine, and closer to his position was a flat-topped hill named La Atalaya, where he placed only an outpost. Other than that, the terrain was solid chaparral, cut up by gullies and hills, making it seem impassible. His guns were placed atop three separate bluffs on his right, which completely commanded the highway. Santa Anna made his headquarters at his hacienda, El Encero, and directed his operations from there.

On the morning of April 8, General Scott ordered Brigadier General David E. Twiggs to march his division—consisting of 2,600 infantry, two light field batteries, six 24-pounders, two 8-inch howitzers, four 10-inch mortars, and a squadron of dragoons—up the National Highway to see what opposition was on this road. Acting as a scout, Johnston ascertained from the locals that Santa Anna's army was about 4 miles ahead. Twiggs's force had entered the village of Plan del Rio on April 11, and was joined there by the division of Major General Robert Patterson. Patterson was the ranking general but was ill, and had allowed Twiggs to assume command. Twiggs wanted to launch a frontal assault early on April 14, and ordered Johnston and Lieutenant Zealous Tower to reconnoiter the well-situated Mexican army. They pushed forward towards the Mexican batteries, only to have the enemy gunners open fire, severely wounding Johnston twice with grapeshot. Johnston was carried back to Plan del Rio, where he spent two weeks recovering at a hospital whose interior walls were constructed of reeds. Johnston had just been brevetted to lieutenant colonel, effective April 12. He was joined there by his friend, Dabney Maury, who had also been wounded. Another addition to their recovery rooms was John P. Derby, whom Johnston found offensive. Maury narrated the unpleasant encounter:

> A few days after being placed in the house, Dr. Cuyler said to me: "Maury, there's a young fellow, Derby, across the street, lying wounded among the volunteers, who says he is a classmate of yours and wishes to come over here. I would not agree to it without consulting you, for he is a coarse fellow; but I don't like him to be among the volunteers." In that war the volunteers were not regarded as they were in the great war between the States.
>
> Of course I cheerfully agreed to his being brought over, and his cot was placed in the hall besides mine. The partitions of the rooms were of reeds wattled together, so that conversations could be heard from one room to the other. John Phoenix Derby was an incessant talker, and uttered a stream of coarse wit, to the great disgust of Joe Johnston, who endured it in silence, till one day he heard Derby order his servant to capture a kid out of a flock of goats passing our door, when he broke out, "If you dare to do that, I'll have you court-martialed and cashiered or shot!"[3]

In the meantime, Maj. Gen. Robert Patterson took himself off the sick report and resumed command. Patterson postponed the attack until Scott came up with the rest of the army; any attack prior to that was considered premature by the brigade commanders, who believed it would place the army "in danger of a defeat or a victory purchased by a lavish and useless expenditure of life."[4] At noon on April 14, Scott arrived at Plan del Rio and dispatched Capt. Robert E. Lee to direct scouting of Santa Anna's position. Lee found a pathway around Santa Anna's left leading to the rear of the Mexican main flank. Scott had construction parties create a road, called the Trail, along the route Lee took. Scott's forces turned the Mexican strongpoint, which totally collapsed during the battle of Cerro Gordo on April 18. The Mexicans were completely routed.

The American army marched west towards Mexico City and took possession of the town of Jalapa, "a lovely little town, on the slope of the mountains, looking down towards the sea, some ninety miles distant," as Maury described it.[5] Captain Kirby Smith of the 3rd Infantry announced that the mountain village was the "prettiest town I have seen, surrounded by the finest country with the most delicious climate in the world, the thermometer never rising above eighty degrees or falling below sixty."[6] Ten days later, Johnston and the rest of the wounded were carried up to Jalapa by litter bearers with a strong escort and enjoyed the cool air of the mountain town at 4,680 feet. Dabney Maury visited daily with Johnston, whose nephew, Preston Johnston, a lieutenant serving in the 1st Artillery, affectionately tended on him as well. While Johnston recovered at Jalapa, Scott moved his army on to Puebla, several thousand feet higher in elevation and almost a hundred miles further inland, where he was joined by Nicholas P. Trist, a chief clerk in the State Department, who tried to arrange peace with the Mexicans.

Scott needed the time to obtain reinforcements. The one-year enlistments of the volunteer soldiers had expired, and a thousand soldiers were sick and wounded, leaving him with only 5,820 troops. Reinforcements arrived in June, bringing Scott's army to twelve thousand effectives. Scott organized his army into four divisions under Worth, Twiggs, Gideon Pillow, and John A. Quitman. Joseph Johnston, who had recovered from his wounds, was assigned to a new regiment of *voltigeurs*—comprising men from Maryland, Virginia, Pennsylvania, Georgia, and Kentucky—as second-in-command under Colonel Timothy P. Andrews. The unit was brigaded with the 11th and 14th Infantry regiments, the brigade being commanded by Major General George P. Cadwalader, part of Pillow's command.

Scott remained at Puebla for three months, but when negotiations failed; Scott abandoned his communications with Vera Cruz and started his army toward Mexico City on August 7, 1847. By the second week in August, the American army had filed down from the mountains into the Valley of Mexico and was within sight of Mexico City. The valley was hemmed in by "a circle of stupendous, rugged, and dark mountains, forming a most perfect combination of the sublime and the beautiful."[7]

If Scott followed the National Highway, accessing Mexico City from the west, he would be confronted by the bulk of Santa Anna's army in a strong fortification at El Penon Viejo. He assigned two officers, Capt. Robert E. Lee and Major William Turnball, to reconnoiter for various options of approach. They found a passable road over a causeway between Lakes Chalco and Xochimilco, leading to San Augustin, where Scott's army could move on the capital from the south. On August 18, Worth's division was ordered northward toward Mexico City from San Augustin, but its path was blocked by a strong Mexican force under General Nicolas Bravo at the village of San Antonio. Worth's engineers reported that the position could not be outflanked, because to the east was Lake Xochimilco and to the west was an impassible lava bed called the Pedregal, which looked like "a raging sea that had been turned instantly to stone."[8] When Scott heard that the only option was a frontal assault, he ordered Worth to halt and threaten the position while he looked for an alternate route. Scott sent out Lee, who found a roundabout path, passable for infantry, westward across the Pedregal. Scott delegated Brigadier

General Persifer Smith to lead a work party of five hundred men, all elements of Pillow's division, with picks and shovels to improve the path for artillery. Johnston's *voltigeurs* were part of this contingent.

As the Americans made their way out of the Pedregal, they discovered that General Don Gabriel Valencia with some five thousand Mexican soldiers had occupied an imposing bluff between the town of Contreras and the Indian village of Padierna. As Twiggs's lead units descended from Mount Zacatepec, they came under fire. Twiggs had two batteries of artillery under Captain John Magruder unlimber and commence firing. Meanwhile, General Pillow sent General Bennett Riley's brigade to San Geronimo to close the San Angel road and cut off Valencia's retreat. Pillow, fearing that Riley was isolated and in danger, sent Cadwalader's brigade, followed by the 15th Infantry under Colonel George W. Morgan, to move to the right and reinforce him. Indeed, Santa Anna himself with the main body of the Mexican Army, some twelve thousand men, came down the San Angel road. Magruder's batteries held their own for a while against the 72 heavy guns the Mexicans brought to bear, but eventually, outgunned, they were forced to withdraw. Valencia and his men, believing they had beaten off a large-scale American attack, started celebrating. Meanwhile, General Smith moved all his units, which included Johnston's *voltigeurs*, behind Valencia's position for a daybreak attack. Smith sent Captain Lee to Scott to ask for a diversionary attack on Valencia's front; Scott was more than willing to oblige. Smith's forces then hunkered down for the night. At dawn, Valencia's troops found that Santa Anna, instead of reinforcing them, had withdrawn from San Angel toward Churubusco. Panic spread throughout Valencia's ranks. Just then, Smith's soldiers struck and about the same time, Twiggs opened his attack from the east. Assaulted from the front and rear, the Mexicans were totally routed in about 15 minutes.

Preston Johnston

As the American forces converged on Valencia's abandoned camp, Johnston spotted his friend Robert E. Lee and offered congratulations on the victory. Lee took Johnston's hand and told him that his nephew, Preston Johnston, had been struck by a Mexican artillery shell as he manned his guns of the 1st Artillery commanded by John Bankhead McGruder on August 14, and had died during the night. As Lee told Johnston the devastating news, he observed that Joseph Johnston's "frame was shrunk and shivered with agony." Dabney Maury later related a conversation he had with Joseph Johnston touching on this event: "Only a few weeks before General Johnston died, he spoke to me of the death of this bright young lad, who had been so dear to him. He said, 'When Lee came to tell me of Preston's mortal wound, he wept as he took my hand in his.'" Johnston agonized over the loss of Preston, "who was dear to him as a son, a bright and joyous young fellow, full of hope and courage." In a letter to his brother Beverly five days later, Joseph Johnston poured out his heartache: "I loved him more than my own heart. I have never before known the full bitterness of grief. Nobody else could love him as I have done. He was the pride of my heart—the companion of my manhood—& I looked to him for stay & comfort in declining years. I cannot tell you the bitterness of this event."[9] Preston Johnston had been an orphan and Joseph Johnston took the role as his father figure. The memory of this incident remained with Johnston his whole life. After the War Between the States, he wrote of Lee's compassion shown at this time:

> I saw strong evidence of the sympathy of his nature the morning after the first engagement of our troops in the Valley of Mexico. I had lost a cherished relative in that action, known only to General Lee as my relative. Meeting me, he suddenly saw in my face the effect of that loss, burst into tears and expressed his deep sympathy as tenderly in words as his lovely wife would have done.[10]

Mexico City

General Scott pursued the retreating Mexican forces on the San Angel road as they pulled back over the Rio Churubusco to the walls of Mexico City. About the same time, General Worth sent General Newman S. Clarke's brigade through the Pedregal to turn the Mexican position at San Antonio, causing the garrison to flee, thereby opening the San Antonio road to Churubusco. Santa Anna, knowing he had to keep the bridge over the Churubusco River protected for his troops to cross, posted two strongholds to hold back the Americans. One was a *tete de point* at the bridge itself and the other, about five hundred yards to the southwest, was the massive San Mateo Convent. Worth's and Pillow's divisions stormed the Churubusco bridge and carried it by the bayonet. Twiggs's division, along with Johnston and the *voltigeurs*, charged the fortress-like Sam Mateo Convent through fields of tall corn, accompanied by Worth's division on their right. The defenders were driven from their positions in hand-to-hand fighting and the convent was captured. Meanwhile, Brigadier General James Shield's and Brigadier General Franklin Pierce's divisions crossed the bridge near Coyoacan in a turning movement toward the town of Portales, north of Churubusco.

At this juncture, the Mexican foreign minister, Francisco Pacheco, sent a note to Trist and a truce was negotiated. However, the armistice collapsed and hostilities recommenced. On September 7, the day the truce ended, General Scott received a report that a large Mexican force was located at Molino del Rey and Casa de la Mata. Word was that large deposits of gunpowder were there and church bells were being collected to cast into guns. Scott assigned Worth's division to take Molino and Casa de la Mata, two large stone buildings about six hundred yards apart; he attached Cadwalader's brigade from Pillow's division and 270 dragoons under Major Edwin Vose "Bull" Sumner to enhance the attack. On the morning of September 8, Worth commenced his operations to assault the well-defended positions. Cadwalader's brigade was held in reserve. The Molino building was taken by storm after being pounded by Major Generals James Duncan's and Benjamin Huger's batteries. Worth could now concentrate on the Casa Mata. As the Mexicans repulsed the initial attack, Worth detected a large body of Mexican cavalry threatening his left flank. Worth moved the *voltigeurs* to support Duncan's battery to meet this threat, accompanied by Sumner's cavalry. The Mexican garrison at Casa Mata fled and the Americans occupied the structure, but no evidence of a foundry was found. The battle lasted only two hours, but the cost was high due to frontal assaults against the two strongpoints. There were 116 American battle deaths and 665 wounded; of the 341 *voltigeurs* that went into battle, 98 were lost. In his report to Worth, Cadwalader mentions Johnston as one of several officers who had performed gallantly.

After the capture of Molino del Rey on September 8, Scott could concentrate on taking Mexico City. He called a council of war to assess the best course of action. There were no easy solutions; the capital was built on an island in a lakebed and the approaches were along causeways over marshy land. Scott decided to seize the citadel of Chapultepec, hoping to force the surrender of Mexico City. The citadel, once the palace of the Aztec emperors, was a strong building of masonry whose walls rose between 15 and 20 feet and was situated on a high plateau some 150–200 feet above the plain. At the base of the hill was a stone wall 4 feet thick and 20 feet high, which enclosed the grounds and had only one entrance, a gate on the southern face. In its entirety, Chapultepec was three-quarters of a mile in length running east to west and a quarter-mile wide.

Scott placed four heavy batteries to bash its defenses, including 16-pound siege guns, 8-inch howitzers, a 10-inch mortar, and a 24-pounder. The batteries opened up at 5.00 a.m. on September 12 and rained projectiles on the citadel until 7.30 p.m. The assault was fixed for the next day. Scott picked Pillow's division, assembling at the Molino, to make the main assault, with Pierce's division in the lead. Pillow had the *voltigeurs* divided into two battalions of four companies each; Colonel Andrews would command one battalion and Johnston the other. Johnston's men were assigned as the vanguard in the assault securing the southern wall gate. At dawn on September 13, the cannonade recommenced and lasted until 7.30 a.m., at which time the guns were lowered to sweep the defenders of the lower walls for 30 minutes. The lull was Johnston's signal to attack. Johnston's four companies charged the Mexican redoubt at the main gate and broke through to the road going to the citadel. Here they were joined by *voltigeurs* under Andrews and Pierce's brigade. The advance was halted for 15 minutes halfway up the plateau, as the arrival of the scaling ladders was delayed. The Mexican defenders on the parapet fired down blindly, keeping their heads down so as not to expose themselves to the sharpshooters. Major (later Major General) Pierre Gustave Toutant Beauregard had joined the assault as a volunteer, and it appeared to him that "the top of the parapet was one continued sheet of flame." He noted in his memoirs: "We found the gallant Colonel Johnston and his officers encouraging their no less gallant men forward, on the side of the hill, against as terrible a fire as I had yet seen!" During a lull in the firing, Beauregard shouted to Johnston to inspire the men: "Colonel, what will you bet on this shot?" Johnston retorted: "Drinks in the City of Mexico." Beauregard fired his weapon and, not knowing if he hit his mark, called back to Johnston: "You have lost, you will have to pay it." Beauregard was impressed by Johnston's gray-clad soldiers, stating: "I never saw new troops behave as well as this Voltigeur battalion under such trying circumstances and they did infinite credit to their officers."[11] Finally, the ladders were brought up to storm the citadel.

In his official report, Scott described the assault:

> The broken acclivity was still to be ascended, and a strong redoubt midway to be carried before reaching the castle on the heights. The advance of our brave men, led by brave officers, though necessarily slow, was unwavering, over rocks, chasms, and mines, and under the hottest fire of cannon and musketry. The redoubt now yielded to resistless valor, and the shouts that followed announced to the castle the fate that impended. The enemy were steadily driven from shelter to shelter. The retreat allowed not time to fire a single mine without the certainty of blowing up friend and foe. Those who at a distance attempted to apply matches to the long trains were shot down by our men. There was death below as well as above ground. At length the ditch and wall of the main work was reached; the scaling ladders were brought up and planted by the storming parties; some of the daring spirits first in the assault were cast down, killed or wounded; but a lodgment was soon made; streams of heroes followed; all opposition was overcome, and several regimental colors flung out from the upper works, amid long-continued shouts and cheers; which sent dismay into the capital. No scene could have been [more] animating and glorious.[12]

Pillow, the division commander, mentioned Johnston in his report:

> The voltigeur regiment, which was ordered forward in advance as skirmishers to clear the intrenchments and large trees of the large force of the enemy, who were directing a most galling fire into the command—the right wing under the very gallant and distinguished Lieutenant-Colonel Johnston, and the left under the brave Colonel Andrews himself, assisted by his gallant Major Caldwell—having united, cleared the woods and pursued the enemy so hotly that he was not able to ignite his mines, drove him inside the parapet itself, and occupied the broken ground around the ditch of the fortifications, all in the face of the most heavy fire from the enemy's small arms and heavy guns. The ladders arrived, and several efforts were made by both officers and men to scale the walls. But many of the gallant spirits who first attempted it fell, killed or wounded. Colonel Andrews, whose regiment so distinguished itself and [its] commander by this brilliant charge, as also Lieutenant-Colonel Johnston and Major Caldwell, whose activity enabled them to lead this assault, having greatly distinguished themselves by their gallantry and daring. Lieutenant-Colonel Johnston received three wounds, but they were all slight, and did not at all arrest his daring and onward movements.[13]

Johnston's troops were in the lead and the blue flag of the *voltigeurs*' battalion was the first to fly over the parapet. Scott said of him: "Johnston is a great soldier, but he has an unfortunate knack of getting himself shot in nearly every engagement." Johnston was brevetted colonel on September 13, "for gallant and meritorious conduct in the battle of Chapultepec."[14]

With the fall of Mexico City on September 14, 1847, the Mexican army offered only sporadic resistance. Active operations ceased and hostilities came to an end. Brevet Colonel Johnston was placed in charge of expeditions to bring up supplies and reinforcements from Vera Cruz. In the summer of 1848, his regiment of *voltigeurs* was mustered out of service and Johnston's future was in doubt. However, Congress passed a special act on July 19, reinstating him in his rank as a captain in the Topographical Engineers from September 21, 1846. In the year following his return from the Mexican War in 1848, Johnston was assigned to Texas to survey a possible railroad route between San Antonio and El Paso. Dabney Maury related the following anecdote from this time:

> Johnston and I had traversed in Texas the beautiful Wild Rose Pass of the Guadalupe Mountains, through which for many miles the Lympia Creek finds its way. In places, the bare cliffs of basaltic rock rise twelve or fifteen hundred feet above the stream. In other parts, beautiful wooded slopes stretch away for miles, so that the Lympia Canyon has been for years the beautiful wonder of the route from San Antonio to El Paso. One day I asked him how he explained the power of that little stream to make a way for itself through the great mountain barrier, expecting some profound geological solution. I was answered when he said, "I presume the Power that could make the stream could make a way for the stream to pass, sir."[15]

Johnston also served as chief of topographical engineers in the department of Texas from the fall of 1852 until fall 1853, and was supervisor of navigation improvements on the Arkansas, Illinois, Mississippi, and Ohio Rivers from 1853–1855. In 1855, Congress increased the size of the U.S. Army by two regiments of cavalry. Johnston seized upon this opportunity and asked Major General Cadwalader, now retired to a law practice in Philadelphia, to put in a word for him. Cadwalader wrote to the Adjutant General, Samuel Cooper, praising the "valuable and efficient services rendered by Colonel Johnston" in Mexico.[16] Johnston was commissioned lieutenant colonel of cavalry and appointed second in command of the 1st Cavalry Regiment under the now Colonel "Bull" Sumner in March 1855. From May 3 to August 26, 1858, he served as Acting Inspector General of the Utah expedition commanded by Albert Sidney Johnston (no relation).

In the last week of March 1859, President James Buchanan named Joseph Johnston's brother-in-law, Robert McLane, as Minister to Mexico. McLane was authorized to recognize any government in Mexico that he thought was legitimate. In March, McLane and the American delegation sailed for Vera Cruz from Washington, accompanied by Johnston, who was to aid his brother-in-law in negotiations to conclude an agreement. The party landed at Vera Cruz on April 1, and four days later recognized Benito Juarez's government as the legitimate government of Mexico. Johnston stayed on in Vera Cruz for another three weeks until he and McLane boarded the steamer *Alabama* in May for the return trip to Washington.

CHAPTER 4

Promotion and Resignation

On June 10, 1860, Quartermaster General Thomas S. Jesup died; upon his death, Secretary of War John B. Floyd asked Maj. Gen. Winfield Scott, commanding officer of the U.S. Army, to suggest a successor. Scott recommended four candidates: Albert Sidney Johnston, Joseph E. Johnston, Robert E. Lee, and Charles F. Smith. The choice narrowed to two contenders: Albert Sidney Johnston, backed by Jefferson Davis, chairman of the Senate Military Affairs Committee, and Joseph E. Johnston, endorsed by Secretary of War Floyd. The appointment was settled on Joseph E. Johnston and was confirmed in the Senate by a vote of 31 to three on June 20, 1860. The new position carried the rank of brigadier general, making Joseph E. Johnston the first West Point graduate to be promoted to that rank. Floyd was kin to Joseph Eggleston Johnston and some, including Robert E. Lee, accused Floyd of nepotism. It is

Jefferson Davis (1808–89) was a Southern planter, Democratic politician, and hero of the Mexican–American War who represented Mississippi in the U.S. House of Representatives and Senate. He also served as U.S. Secretary of War (1853–57). Davis was chosen to serve as president of the Confederacy in 1861 and held the post until the American Civil War ended in 1865. (Library of Congress)

possible that his selection for this post started bad feelings between Jefferson Davis and Joseph E. Johnston which carried over into the Confederate struggle for independence.

Johnston held his office for only a short time as the political and sectional controversy over States' rights and chattel slavery came to a head. The election of Abraham Lincoln, a member of the Republican Party which upheld an abolitionist platform, as President of the United States on November 6, 1860, induced many Southern States—South Carolina being the first on December 20—to secede from the Union prior to his inauguration on March 4, 1861. Johnston was in much anguish over the crisis; he was not an advocate of secession but his deepest loyalty was with his home state of Virginia.

Letter of Resignation

After Fort Sumter in Charleston harbor was bombarded on April 12 and surrendered the next day, President Lincoln issued a proclamation on April 15 calling for some seventy-five thousand militia to suppress the insurrection. In response, the Virginia convention passed an ordinance of secession by 88 votes to 55 on April 17. Hearing this news, Johnston decided to hand in his letter of resignation to Lincoln's Secretary of War, Simon Cameron, on April 22:

> Sir: With feelings of deep regret I respectfully tender the resignation of my commission in the army of the United States. The feelings which impel me to this act are, I believe understood by the Honorable Secretary of War. I hope that long service, with some labor, hardship, danger, and loss of blood, may give me some claim to ask the early consideration of this communication.[1]

He was the only general in the United States Army who went with the South. Upon arriving in Richmond on the morning of April 25, he reported to Governor Letcher, who appointed him major general in the State service. Johnston served for two weeks in this capacity until the Southern Confederacy took over the conduct of military operations. Johnston accepted a commission of brigadier general, then the highest grade in the Confederate Army, offered by telegraph by President Davis. Davis sent another telegraphic request calling Johnston to Montgomery, Alabama, which was then the Confederate seat of government. After discussions with President Davis and military authorities, Johnston was assigned command of the troops near Harpers Ferry, where the U.S. Armory was located, containing a factory for the manufacture of small arms, especially the .54-caliber rifled musket.

Harpers Ferry

Upon arriving at Harpers Ferry, Johnston conducted a personal reconnaissance of the area and concluded the geography made it a trap for a defending army which could be turned, bottled up, and captured. He wrote a number of letters to Richmond asking to pull back to Winchester before enemy forces seized the railroad leading there, isolating his command. Events soon forced Johnston to evacuate Harpers Ferry. On June 13, it was reported that two thousand Federal troops under the command of Major General George McClellan, with whom Johnston had formed a close personal friendship after McClellan resigned from the Army in the fall of 1856, raided the town of Romney, Virginia, 43 miles west of Winchester, while eighteen thousand troops under Brigadier General Robert Patterson threatened to cross the Potomac below Williamsport, bringing him as close to the railroad at Winchester as Johnston. Johnston decided to pull out of Harpers Ferry and had the machinery and baggage (almost every private soldier had a trunk) removed by railroad to Winchester, and ordered the railroad bridges over the Potomac from the Point of Rocks to Shepardstown destroyed, as well as the Armory. Patterson crossed the Potomac on June 15 and was marching on Martinsburg. Johnston had the Confederate troops march to Bunker's Hill to block Patterson. Just as he was preparing to march, a letter arrived by courier from General Cooper, dated June 13, authorizing him to abandon Harpers Ferry. However, Patterson did not advance further, being deprived of his best troops, Regular infantry and cavalry plus the Regular and Rhode Island artillery, by Lieutenant General Winfield Scott, General in Chief, to defend Washington.

CHAPTER 5

First Manassas

Meanwhile, the Federal government pressed Major General Irwin McDowell to march with thirty-five thousand men against Brigadier General Gustave Beauregard's twenty-three thousand at Manassas, and on July 18 fought with a portion of Beauregard's forces at Blackburn's Ford. Johnston received a telegraph from General Cooper in the Confederate War Department about 1.00 a.m. on July 18: "General Beauregard is attacked; to strike the enemy a decisive blow, a junction of all your effective force will be needed. If practicable, make the movement, sending your sick and baggage to Culpepper Court-House either by railroad or by Warrenton. In all arrangements exercise your discretion."[1] Johnston telegraphed Richmond on July 18 that Patterson was at Charlestown, stating: "Unless he prevents it, we shall move toward General Beauregard to-day."[2] Johnston did not have enough transportation to move the sick—some seventeen hundred—and accommodate a shift to Beauregard, so he left the sick at Winchester under a guard of militia. Johnston covered his movement with a cavalry screen under General Jeb Stuart. Patterson was stymied as the enlistments of his army of some sixteen thousand three-months soldiers began to expire on the 24th, after which they announced they would perform no duty when their term ended; furthermore, his artillery was taken away, compelling him to pull back to the Potomac. General Scott wanted Patterson to occupy and distract Johnston while McDowell gathered a strong force at Washington to strike at Beauregard. Johnston started moving from Winchester about noon on July 18, eluding Patterson. He had his soldiers march through Ashby's Gap to pass the Blue Ridge Mountains, heading for the nearest station of the Manassas Gap Railroad at Piedmont. Major Whiting was sent ahead to secure the necessary railroad transportation to haul the troops the 34 miles to Manassas Junction. The infantry boarded the trains when they became available, while the artillery and cavalry used the wagon road, altogether roughly 8,500 effectives. General Thomas Jonathan

"Stonewall" Jackson's brigade was the first to arrive at Piedmont on Friday, July 19, and found transport; it was followed at 3.00 p.m. by the 7th and 8th Georgia regiments. Johnston embarked for Manassas at 8.00 a.m. on Saturday, July 20, with two regiments under General Bee. Johnston ordered General Edmund Kirby Smith to expedite the departure of the rest of the troops at the Piedmont station. Beauregard had suggested that Johnston advance to Aldie on McDowell's flank and rear at Centreville, but Johnston dismissed the plan as unrealistic and preferred to combine forces, moving directly to Manassas utilizing the railroad with its rapid capacity.

Upon arrival, Johnston went directly to Beauregard's headquarters at the McLean house near Manassas. Johnston, unsure as to his relative rank with

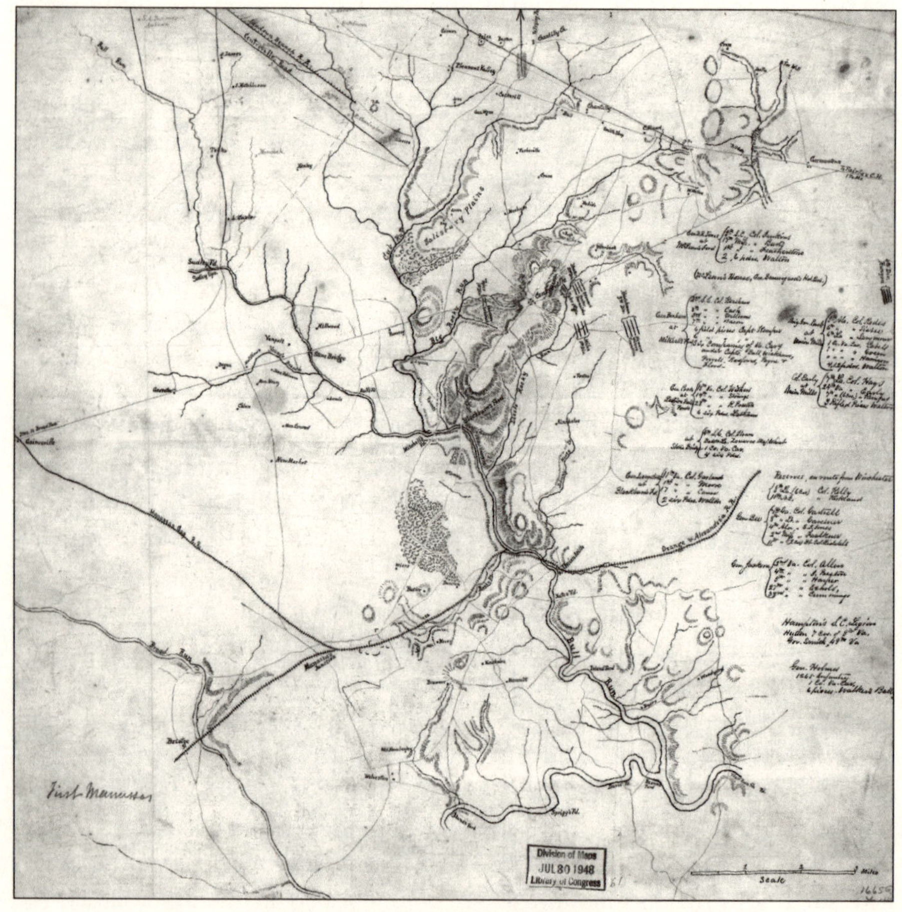

First Manassas. (Library of Congress)
First Manassas map reveals the topography and troop deployment.

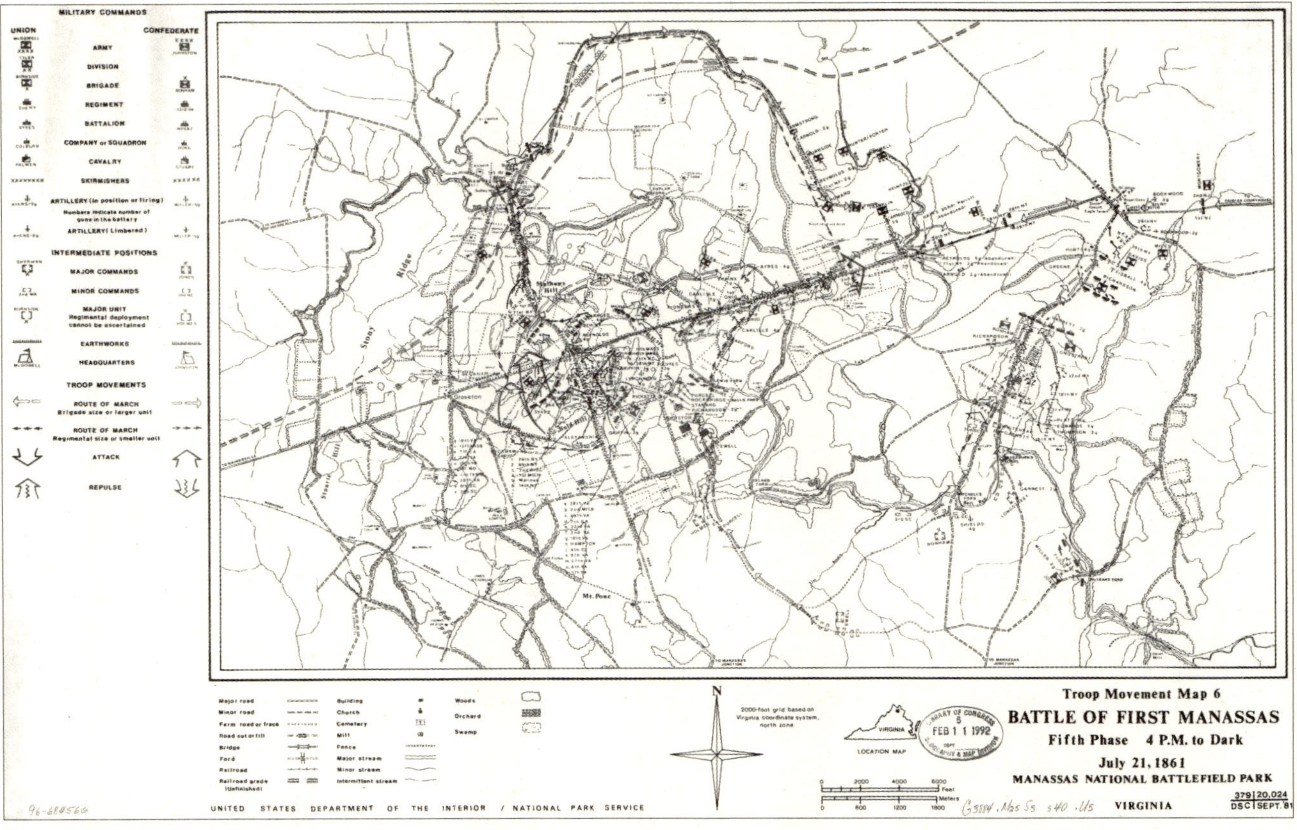

Battle of First Manassas, Troop Movements for Fifth Phase, 4 p.m. to Dark. (National Park Service, Library of Congress) The troop movement shows the dynamics of the battle.

Beauregard, sent President Davis a telegram asking for clarification. President Davis sent a telegram in reply to clear up any misunderstanding: "You are a general in the Confederate army, possessed of the power attaching to that rank. You will know how to make the exact knowledge of Brigadier-General Beauregard, as well of the ground as of the troops and preparations, avail for the success of the object in which you co-operate. The zeal of both assures me of harmonious action."[3] Johnston expressed his opinion to General Beauregard that they attack McDowell's army before General Patterson could connect with it. Beauregard agreed and wanted to converge on Centreville, where McDowell had made his camp.

Lieutenant General Scott had instructed McDowell to turn the Confederate right and seize its communication with Richmond. But McDowell, after examining the situation for three days, found the ground unfavorable for offensive operations, deciding to advance on his right where the country was open, hills gentle, and the Bull Run was fordable at many spots. McDowell's plan was to advance his army in a turning movement around the Confederate left with the hope of destroying the railroad near Gainesville, breaking up communication between Manassas and the Shenandoah Valley of Virginia. He made a demonstration against Stone Bridge while sending a column to Sudley Springs Ford, which was not guarded. Colonel Nathan G. Evans, a West Pointer, perceived that the Federal movement along Warrenton Turnpike was a feint to conceal the real attack at another point. This was verified by a picket at Sudley Springs Ford, who reported a large body of Federal troops crossing there. Simultaneously, Captain Edward Porter Alexander, chief signal officer, sent a signal flag message to Evans informing him of their advance. Evans moved the bulk of his troops to a small ridge in his left rear commanding the road the Federals were using.

"Stonewall" Jackson

Johnston had little time at his disposal to study the disposition of the troops or the topography, so he left arrangements in Beauregard's hands. Johnston and Beauregard had made their field headquarters on Lookout Hill when the sounds of battle on the left began to increase in volume. Johnston grew restless as the fire of musketry and artillery increased in intensity. "All paused for a moment and listened," wrote Alexander. "Then Johnston said, 'The battle is there! I am going.' Walking rapidly to his horse, he mounted and set off at a gallop, followed by his own staff, as fast as they could get their horses. Beauregard only paused to give a few brief orders. Holmes's and Early's brigades, and two regiments of Bonham's with Walker's and Kemper's batteries, were to march to the firing. Jones's brigade was to be recalled to our side of Bull Run."[4]

Johnston recounted: "Passing on the way Colonel Pendleton with two batteries, I directed him to follow with them as fast as possible."[5] The Confederate lines on the left had been driven back to the Henry & Robinson house hill, where Jackson's brigade was making a stand. Jackson received his sobriquet "Stonewall" when Brigadier General Barnard Bee shouted: "There is Jackson standing like a stone wall!"[6] As Johnston rode up, he noticed a large group of soldiers out of position: "The Fourth Alabama Regiment, of Bee's brigade, had lost all its field officers and was without a commander. Colonel S. R. Gist, a volunteer on General Bee's staff, was requested to take command of it."[7]

Johnston approached the color bearer and placed his hand on the staff, saying: "Sergeant, hand me your staff! I will lead you. Follow me."

The sergeant, Robert Sinclair responded as he held onto the staff: "General, don't take my colors from me. Tell me where to carry them & I will place them there."

Johnston relinquished the staff and led the regiment onto the field on Jackson's right. General Bee rode up to Johnston and said in an anguished voice: "General, my command is scattered and I am alone."

Johnston consoled Bee: "I know it was not your fault, Genl. Bee. But don't despair, the day is not yet lost."

Johnston called Bee's attention to another group of soldiers resting along a fence and asked who they were. "They are So. Carolinians," Bee answered.

"Rally them," Johnston commanded, "and lead them back into the fight."[8]

Beauregard

Beauregard suggested that direct tactical command at the point of contact belonged to the second in rank, not to the senior officer of the whole army; Johnston assented and established his headquarters a mile to the rear at Portici, the home of Francis W. Lewis. "After the troops were in good battle order I turned to the supervision of the whole field," Johnston recalled. He went on, stating:

> The enemy's great numerical superiority was discouraging. Yet, from strong faith in Beauregard's capacity and courage, and the high soldierly qualities of Bee and Jackson, I hoped that the fight would be maintained until I could bring adequate reenforcements to their aid. For this Holmes and Early were urged to hasten their march, and Ewell was ordered to follow them with his brigade with all speed. Broken troops were reorganized and led back into the fight with the help of my own and part of General Beauregard's staff. Cocke's

> brigade was held in rear of the right to observe a large body of Federal troops in a position from which Bee's right flank could have been struck in a few minutes.[9]

Alexander noted that for more than two hours, the battle lines fired away at each other, across the front ridge of the plateau, neither side's fire being particularly accurate as they mostly fired at the opponent's smoke:

> That, indeed, is the case in nearly all battles since long-range guns have come into use. It is rare that hostile lines get so near together, and are so exposed to each other's view, that men can select their targets. When this does occur, some decisive result is apt to be reached quickly. Fighting rarely consists now in marching directly upon one's enemy and shooting him down at close range. The idea is now a different one. It rather consists in making it rain projectiles all over the enemy's position. As far as possible, while so engaged, one seeks cover from the enemy's fire in return. But the party taking the offensive must necessarily make some advances. The best advance is around the enemy's flanks, where one meets less fire and becomes opposed by smaller numbers. But here, McDowell, encouraged by early success, endeavored to push straight forward.[10]

At about 3.30 p.m., Gen. Edmund Kirby Smith, Johnston's chief of staff, arrived with three regiments of Colonel Arnold Elzey's brigade, which Johnston personally directed at Smith's request to the left for a flank attack. Smith was wounded as the troops deployed and Elzey took command. At the same time, the brigade of Colonel Jubal Early came upon the field and Johnston instructed him to move to the left, extending the Confederate line to overlap the Federal right. Accompanied by Stuart's cavalry and Beckham's battery, Early launched his attack on the exposed Federal flank, while General Beauregard charged in front, breaking the Federal ranks. "The right of the Federal army fled in wild confusion from the field toward the Sudley Ford, while the centre and left marched off hastily by the turnpike toward Centreville," Johnston reported.[11] President Davis arrived on the field and inquired anxiously as to the outcome, Johnston replying "that we had won the battle."[12] Davis issued no orders to the army, but Johnston chose not to make an effort to take Washington: "All the military conditions, we knew, forbade an attempt on Washington. The Confederate army was more disorganized by victory than that of the United States by defeat. There were strong fortifications, well manned, to cover the approaches to Washington and prevent the establishment of our guns on the south bank of the river."[13]

Robert M. Hughes, in his 1893 biography of Johnston, gives an account of the losses in the battle:

> The aggregate loss of the Confederates in the battle was eighteen hundred and ninety-seven, of which twelve hundred and sixty-seven fell upon Johnston's army. Of his brigade commanders two were killed, and the other two wounded. The total force of Johnston's army engaged was about eighty-three hundred and thirty-four.

> The loss of the Federal army, according to their returns, was twenty-eight hundred and ninety-six. In addition, they abandoned in their retreat twenty-eight pieces of artillery, five thousand muskets, and immense quantities of ammunition and army supplies—acquisitions which were invaluable to the poorly armed and equipped forces of the South, and worth far more than long lines of prisoners. The captured artillery, from its quantity and yet more from its quality, was a specially valuable prize. Not less so were the captured muskets, for every one meant an additional soldier to the armies of the South, whose strength at that period of the war was only limited by the number of arms to put into their hands.[14]

Lack of rifles caused the loss of service of two hundred thousand of the initial three hundred and fifty thousand volunteers in the Confederate cause, Secretary of War Leroy P. Walker reported in July 1861. This shortage plagued the Confederate Army throughout the war, more so in the West than the East.

After First Manassas, Johnston assisted Gustave Beauregard and leading Southern politician William Porcher Miles in the design and production of the Confederate battle flag, it being Johnston's idea to make the flag square.

CHAPTER 6

Technological Changes and Northern Advantages

Beauregard recognized the preeminence of the Federal army facing them and what a vital link was provided by the railroad for mutual support between the two Confederate armies. He stated:

> I was anxiously aware that the sole military advantage at the moment to the Confederates was that of holding the interior lines. On the Federal or hostile side were all material advantages, including superior numbers, largely drawn from the old militia organizations of the great cities of the North, decidedly better armed and equipped than the troops under me, and strengthened by a small but incomparable body of regular infantry as well as a number of batteries of regular field artillery of the highest class, and a very large and thoroughly organized staff corps, besides a numerous body of professionally educated officers in command of volunteer regiments.[1]

The North had many advantages over the South, which is starkly spelled out in Edward Porter Alexander's narrative. Alexander was stationed in San Francisco, California, where he reported to Lt. Gen. McPherson for duty. When he told McPherson that he wished to resign and go with his state and join the Confederacy, McPherson appealed to him not to go because he believed the South was doomed to failure:

> God only knows what may happen to you individually, but for your cause there can be but one result. It must be lost. Your whole population is only about eight millions, while the North has twenty millions. Of your eight millions, three million are slaves who may be an element of danger. You have no army, no navy, no treasury, and practically none of the manufactures and machine shops necessary for support of armies, and for war on a large scale. You are but scattered agricultural communities, and you will be cut off from the rest of the world by blockade. Your cause must end in defeat.[2]

Alexander started on his journey to Richmond, Virginia, and made observations contrasting the preparations for war in the North and in the South:

> The camps near the principal Northern towns were all regiments. Those in the South were mostly of a company each. The arms of the Northern troops were generally the long-range

> rifled muskets. Those of the Southern troops were almost universally the old-fashioned smooth-bore muskets. The Northern troops were always neatly uniformed in blue, their camps seemed well equipped, and there was generally some visible show of military discipline about them. The Confederate uniforms were blue, gray, or brown, and sometimes uniforms were lacking.[3]

Rifled Musket

At the time of the Civil War, the long-range rifled musket replaced the smooth-bore musket as the standard infantry weapon. Rifled muskets (with spiral grooves scored into the bore) improved accuracy and range but had been unwieldy on the battlefield due to the difficult and time-consuming effort to force a round ball down the ridges (also known as lands) and grooves, slowing the firepower of infantry. This all changed in 1849 when a French army captain, Claude E. Minie, devised a bullet made of soft lead, which was elongated with a hollow, cone-shaped base. The diameter of the bullet was slightly smaller than the rifle bore, allowing it to slide down easily. When the weapon was discharged, the ignition of the gunpowder caused the soft lead to expand into the ridges and grooves of the barrel, imparting a spin to the bullet that increased its accuracy and range without diminishing the rate of fire.

While the smoothbore musket had an extreme range of 250–300 yards and had very little accuracy at any range; the rifled musket had an extreme range of half a mile or more, an effective range of 200–250 yards, and was lethal within 100 yards. This new technology in weaponry gave a decided three-to-one advantage to sheltered defenders over exposed attackers, completely changing battlefield conditions.

The United States reigned as the leading firearms producer in the world at the time of the Civil War, especially in mass production and standardization of parts. Moreover, the industrialized North had the majority of the modern arms-manufacturing equipment and most of the mines for raw materials. The North's economic potential to sustain the war effort was far superior to that of the South; 81 percent of the nation's factories were in the North, while the South was struggling to create an industrial base.

In his memoirs, Alexander, appointed by Joseph Johnston as Chief of Ordnance of The Army of Northern Virginia, compared the armaments of the Southern and Northern armies:

> In its early stages we had great trouble with the endless variety of arms and calibers in use, scarcely ten per cent of them being muzzle-loading rifled musket, caliber 58, which was then the regulation arm for the United States infantry. There were several breech-loading small-arms manufactured at the North, but none secured the approval of the United States Ordnance

> Department, although many of them would have made more formidable weapons than any muzzle-loaders. There is reason to believe that had the Federal infantry been armed from the first with even the breech-loaders available in 1861, the war would have been terminated within a year.
>
> The old smooth-bore musket, caliber 69, made up the bulk of the Confederate armament at the beginning, some of the guns, even all through 1862, being old flint-locks. But every effort was made to replace them by rifled muskets captured in battle, brought through the blockade from Europe, or manufactured at a few small [armories] which we gradually fitted up. Not until after the battle of Gettysburg was the whole army in Virginia equipped with the rifled musket. In 1864 we captured some Spencer breech-loaders, but we could never use them for lack of proper cartridges.
>
> Our artillery equipment at the beginning was even more inadequate than our small-arms. Our guns were principally smooth-bore 6 Prs. and 12 Pr. Howitzers, and their ammunition was afflicted with very unreliable fuses. Our arsenals soon began to manufacture rifled guns, but they always lacked the copper and brass, and the mechanical skill necessary to turn out first-class ammunition. Gradually, we captured Federal guns to supply most of our needs, but we were handicapped by our own ammunition until the close of the war.[4]

An excerpt from an English visitor around 1862 published in "Ten Days in Richmond" describes how the Confederate army was armed:

> Entire batteries pass down the road, with "U.S." in prominent white letters on the caissons. It is no exaggeration to say that a great part of the Confederate army has been equipped at the expense of the United States. Flint-locks and fowling pieces have been exchanged for good Minie rifles. There was, however, still so great a want of small-arms that a considerable part of the army were armed with smoothbore of home manufacture, loaded with a ball and three buckshot. This deficiency has, perhaps, not been altogether, a disadvantage, inasmuch as the necessity of getting to close quarters, in order to put themselves on an equity with their opponents, has in no small degree produced among the Confederates that habit of closing with the enemy which has proved so inconvenient to the Northern troops. Men who could not obtain arms have been known to fall in with the rear rank, and go into action on the chance of picking up a musket on the first opportunity.[5]

Another new technology, the railroad, saw its growth explode during the 1840s, revolutionizing transportation. The railroad's rapid heavy-lift capacity changed the dynamics of warfare by allowing large armies to be deployed and provided the logistics to supply them. Every major battle east of the Mississippi was fought within 20 miles of a railroad or a navigable river. By 1860, the North had 22,085 miles of railroad track built by large companies that had continuous connections between distant stations. The South, meanwhile, had but 8,541 miles, which was constructed by small business concerns. There were gaps in many Southern cities where the railroads terminated because the firms refused to connect their tracks with other railroads, which delayed troop movements.

The innovation of the telegraph, meanwhile, allowed communication across vast distances and facilitated the coordination of troop concentration by rail.

CHAPTER 7

Feud Over the General's Rank

After the Battle of First Manassas, the Confederate army advanced to Fairfax Courthouse, with strong outpost at Mason's and Munson's Hills. The Confederate Senate passed a resolution of thanks to Generals Joseph Johnston and Gustave Beauregard and the officers and troops under their command for the victory at Manassas. President Jefferson Davis offered Johnston command of Confederate troops in West Virginia, which Johnston declined because he felt the main Federal thrust would be against the army he now commanded. Johnston complained to Richmond that Colonel Northrop, as head of the Commissary General's department, was not supplying subsistence in a consistent manner, and asked for remedy. Davis backed Northrop, of whom he was a staunch supporter.

On August 31, 1861, President Davis sent to Congress a request for confirmation of his nominations for the rank of five generals under the act of May 16: first, Samuel Cooper, to rank from May 16; second, Albert Sidney Johnston, to rank from May 28; third, Robert E. Lee, to rank from June 14; fourth, Joseph Eggleston Johnston, to rank from July 4; and fifth, Gustave T. Beauregard, to rank from July 21. Johnston had not received the news until the second week in September and was shocked to hear he was not first on the list.

Johnston wrote a long, acrimonious letter of protest to President Davis:

> Sir: I have had the honor to receive through the War Department a copy of the proceedings of Congress on the 31st of August, 1861, confirming the nominations made by the President of the Confederate States of five generals of the Confederate Army, and fixing their relative rank. I will not affect to disguise the surprise and mortification produced in my mind by the action taken in this matter by the President and by Congress. I beg to state further, with the most profound respect for both branches of the Government, that I am deeply impressed with the conviction that these proceedings are in violation of my rights as an officer, of the plighted faith of the Confederacy, and of the Constitution and laws of the land. Such being my views, lest my silence be deemed significant of acquiescence, it is a duty as well as a right on my part at once to enter my earnest protest against the wrong which I conceive had

> been done to me. I now and here declare my claim that, notwithstanding these nominations made by the President, and their confirmation by Congress, I still rightfully hold the rank of first general in the Armies of the Southern Confederacy. I will proceed briefly to state the grounds upon which I rest this claim.

Johnston then delineated the laws enacted and felt that the President had wronged him:

> This action was altogether illegal, and contrary to all laws enacted to regulate the rank of the class of officers concerned. Those laws were:
>
> 1. The act of March 6th, section 8, fixing the military establishment of the Confederacy, and providing for four brigadier-generals, that being the highest grade created.
> 2. The act of March 14th, section 2, adding a fifth brigadier-general, and authorizing the President to assign one of the five to the duties of adjutant and inspector-general.
> 3. Enacting further, "that in all cases of officers who have resigned, or who may, within six months tender their resignations from the Army of the United States, and who have been, or may be appointed to original vacancies in the Army of the Confederate States, the commissions issued shall bear one and the same date, so that the relative rank of officers of each grade shall be determined by their former commissions in the United States army, held anterior to the secession of these Confederate States from the United States."
> 4. The act of May 16th: "That the five general officers, provided by existing laws for the Confederate States, shall have the rank and denomination of general, instead of brigadier-general, which shall be the highest military grade known to the Confederate States. Appointments to the rank of general, after the army is organized, shall be made by selection from the army."
>
> Under the first act, S. Cooper, R. E. Lee, and myself, were brigadier-generals on the 16th of May when the fourth was approved; and under the third ranked relatively, as we had done in the United States army before secession, when I was a brigadier-general, General Cooper colonel, and General Lee lieutenant-colonel in that army. The passage of the fourth act made us generals, and, according to military rule, without affecting this relative rank. It also abolished the grade of brigadier-general in the army to which we belonged. General Cooper, General Lee, and myself, had no commissions if we were not generals. If we were generals, executive action could not give our commissions new dates. The order of rank established by law was—first, J. E. Johnston (brigadier-general U.S.A.); second, S. Cooper (colonel U.S.A.); third, A. S. Johnston (colonel U.S.A.); fourth, R. E. Lee (lieutenant-colonel U.S.A.); G. T. Beauregard (captain U.S.A.). The change in the legal arrangements was made by my removal from the first place on the list to the fourth.

Johnston continued that it was impossible to alter the past; while Congress could vacate his commission and reduce him to the ranks, it could not be denied that he was a general before July 4, 1861. He said that while he had been transferred from being the first-ranking general of the Confederacy to the fourth, the relative rank of others was unchanged. This, he said, had only ever been done before by court-martial, as a "punishment and a disgrace" for a military offense:

> It seems to tarnish my fair fame as a soldier and as a man, earned by more than thirty years of laborious and perilous service. I had but this—the scar of many wounds, all honestly taken in my front and in front of battle, and my father's Revolutionary sword. It was delivered to me from his venerated hand without a stain of dishonor. Its blade is still unblemished as when it passed from his hand to mine. I drew it in war not for rank or fame, but to defend the sacred soil, the homes and hearths, the women and children, aye, and the men of my mother Virginia, my native South. It may hereafter be the sword of a general, leading armies, or of a private volunteer, but while I live and have an arm to wield it it shall never be sheathed until the freedom, independence, and full rights of the South are achieved. When that is done, it may well be a matter of small concern to the Government, to Congress, or to the country, what my rank or lot may be. I shall be satisfied if my country stands among the powers of the world free, powerful, and victorious, and that I, a general, a lieutenant or a volunteer soldier, have borne my part in the glorious strife and contributed to the final blessed consummation. What has the aspect of a studied indignity offered me? My noble associate in the battle has his preferment connected with the victory won by our common toils and dangers. His commission bears the date of the 21st of July, but care seems to be taken to exclude the idea that I had any part in winning our triumph. My commission is made to bear such a date that my once inferiors in the service of the United States and the Confederate States shall be above me; but it must not be dated as of the 21st of July, nor be suggestive of the victory of Manassas. I return to my first position. I repeat, my right to my rank as general is established by the act of Congress of the 14th of March, 1861, and the 16th of August, 1861. To deprive me of that rank it was necessary of Congress to repeal those laws. That could be done by express legislative act alone. It was not done, it could not be done by a mere vote in secret session upon a list of nominations. If the action against which I have protested be legal, it is not for me to question the expediency of degrading one who has served laboriously from the commencement of the war on this frontier and borne a prominent part in the one great event of that war, for the benefit of persons neither of whom has yet struck a blow for the Confederacy. These views and the freedom with which they are presented may be unusual; so likewise is the occasion which calls them forth. I have the honor to be, most respectfully, your obedient servant, "J. E. Johnston, General."[1]

Joseph Johnston, who was the highest-ranking U.S. Army officer to resign and serve the Confederacy, was greatly offended by this action of President Davis, which he viewed as a grave personal insult, feeling so strongly that he composed the above lengthy letter of protest to the president. After writing the letter, he laid it in a bottom drawer for two days, in order to review it calmly and dispassionately. Upon rereading it on September 12, he decided it accurately expressed his feelings and he mailed it. While Johnston did not intend insult or disrespect, Jefferson Davis was irritated and resented it as a personal insult, sending a terse reply on September 14 without answering his assertions:

> Sir: I have received and read your letter of the 12th instant. Its language is, as you say, unusual; its arguments and statements utterly one-sided, and its insinuations as unfounded as they are unbecoming.[2]

Davis gave a number of excuses for his illegal action. However, it is believed that his real motive was to advance Albert Sidney Johnston, who was one of his favorites and for whom he had advocated for the position of quartermaster general in the old army of the United States. Against Davis's wishes, Joseph E. Johnston had been selected to fill the post. Officially, the dispute was over and Johnston did not resign, as many would have. He stoically accepted the outcome, but it remained a point of contention for the rest of his life.

On the last day in September, President Davis came to Fairfax Court House for a meeting with Generals Johnston, Beauregard, and G. W. Smith. About 8.00 p.m. the next day, a formal conference of several hours was called in which the three generals put forward a proposal for a fall offensive to cross the Potomac at the fords above Washington and take a position in the rear of the capital, thus forcing McClellan and the Army of the Potomac out of their entrenchments to attack. Davis wanted to know what force would be considered necessary for such an undertaking. Smith thought fifty thousand would suffice, while Beauregard and Johnston considered sixty thousand more realistic. Davis wanted to know where the extra men would come from to augment the army in Virginia, whose effective strength numbered less than forty thousand. Johnston suggested that an addition of twenty thousand men could be furnished by stripping the seacoast of the Carolinas and Georgia and transferring them to Virginia. The president rejected the idea on political and military grounds, saying it was politically impossible and militarily unsound. The Confederate States of America was a nascent entity, with some of its citizens being of unsure loyalty, and could easily fracture if not safeguarded. Davis said: "The whole country was demanding protection." Besides, weapons shipments had not arrived from Europe in sufficient quantities to arm even raw recruits as reinforcements. All thoughts of aggressive operations had to be abandoned. On October 19, since the council of war precluded offensive operations, the army was pulled back to Centreville from Fairfax Court House, which had only been held as a jump-off point for an advance but was in danger of being turned.

Department of Northern Virginia

Under General Orders No. 15, the Department of Northern Virginia was established on October 22. It was composed of three districts: the Valley district lying between the Alleghany and Blue Ridge Mountains, commanded by Major General Jackson; the Potomac district, commanded by General Beauregard, from the Blue Ridge Mountains to Quantico, on the Potomac River; and the Aquia district, from Quantico to the Chesapeake, commanded by Major General Theophilus H. Holmes. Major General E. Kirby Smith was in command of the reserve. Johnston was in command of the department overall.

In mid-September, Secretary of War Leroy Pope Walker resigned when it became apparent to him that his employment was beyond his capabilities. Davis appointed Judah P. Benjamin to the post, but he had no experience or familiarity with military procedure or planning, which proved a point of contention for Johnston. Benjamin was meddlesome and provoked Stonewall Jackson to submit a letter of resignation when he ordered Jackson to bring Brigadier General William W. Loring and his three Confederate brigades back from Romney to Winchester after Loring complained that the position was precarious. Benjamin had not consulted Johnston or Jackson; Jackson was insulted and sent a formal letter to Benjamin via Johnston, who received it on February 3. Johnston held the letter and wrote to Jackson noting his concern about its contents:

> My Dear Friend: I have just read, and with profound regret, your letter to the Secretary of war asking to be relieved from your present command, either by an order to the Virginia Military Institute or the acceptance of your resignation. Let me beg you to reconsider this matter. Under ordinary circumstances a due sense of one's own dignity, as well as care for professional character and official rights, would demand such a course as yours; but the character of this war, the great energy exhibited by the Government of the United States, the danger in which our very existence as an independent people lies, requires sacrifices from us all who have been educated as soldiers. I receive my information of the order of which you have cause to complain from your letter. Is not that as great an official wrong to me as the order itself to you? Let us dispassionately reason with the Government on this subject of command, and if we fail to influence its practice, then ask to be relieved from positions the authority of which is exercised by the War Department while the responsibilities are left to us. I have taken the liberty to detain your letter to make this appeal to our patriotism, not merely from warm feelings of personal regard, but from official opinion which makes me regard you as necessary to the service of the country in your present position.

The result of this letter, reinforced by the entreaties of Governor Letcher, was that the services of Jackson were saved to the Confederacy.

While the army was in winter quarters, Johnston found it frequently necessary to remonstrate with the War Department on the subject of interference in its internal administration. Secretary Benjamin did not scruple to grant furloughs direct from Richmond on the most lavish scale; the first information which the commander would receive of such action would be their arrival in the mail. In addition, authority was granted to almost any applicant to raise companies of other arms out of the infantry, usually with the result of turning veteran infantry into raw artillerymen. The effect of such meddling on the discipline and numbers of the army may well be imagined. Johnston protested repeatedly against these practices and pointed out their inevitable result.[3]

Judah P. Benjamin (1811–84) was a lawyer who served as Attorney General, Secretary of War, and Secretary of State in the cabinet of Jefferson Davis, making him the first Jewish person to hold a cabinet-level office in an American government. He also became a planter who at one point was the owner of 140 enslaved people. (Library of Congress)

Johnston was summoned to Richmond for a conference after Jefferson Davis took the oath of office as permanent president of the Confederacy on February 18, 1862. Johnston arrived by train on February 20 and was called into the room to join Davis and his cabinet at 10.00 a.m. The meeting was called to discuss pulling the army back closer to Richmond. It lasted until near sunset, Johnston wrote in his *Narrative of Military Operations*: "It terminated without the giving of orders, but with the understanding on my part that the army was to fall back as soon as practicable." Upon leaving the meeting, he was shocked to find out the confidentiality of the deliberations had been breached:

> The discussion was understood to be strictly confidential; yet, on reaching the hotel, going directly from the President's office, I was asked by Colonel Pender, Sixth North Carolina regiment, just arrived in the city on his way to the army, after leave of absence, if I had heard a report that he had found in that house, that the cabinet had been discussing that day the question of withdrawing the army from the line then occupied. On my way back to Centreville next day, I met an acquaintance from the county of Fauquier, too deaf to hear conversation not intended for his ear, who gave me the same information that he had heard, he said, the evening before.
>
> This extraordinary proof of the indiscretion of the members of the cabinet, or of some one of them, might have taught the danger of intrusting to that body any design the success of which depended upon secrecy.[4]

From this point on, Johnston was reticent to share sensitive information with the Davis administration.

"Johnston is their Best Strategist"

Johnston became a focal point for antagonism in Congress to Benjamin's confirmation as war minister. One of the leaders of the opposition was Representative Henry S. Foote of Tennessee, who had attended a dinner party given after Johnston's visit with Davis on February 20. Included among the guests were some 20 other members of the houses of Congress and Johnston. Foote claims Johnston had an important role in blocking Benjamin's reappointment as War Secretary. During the evening, one guest asked Johnston "whether he thought it even possible that the Confederate cause could succeed with Mr. Benjamin as war minister." After some consideration, Johnston answered emphatically "no." His reply was cited in both houses of Congress and "was the end to Benjamin's hopes of remaining in the Department of War."[5] While Congress was debating a resolution of no confidence in Benjamin on March 4, Davis withdrew Benjamin's name and nominated George W. Randolph as Secretary of War, to Johnston's delight. Johnston was considered the best military mind in the Confederate Army; British journalist William Howard Russell remarked in his journal in the fall of 1861: "Johnston is their best strategist."[6]

CHAPTER 8

Johnston Falls Back Behind the Rapidan and Rappahannock Rivers

On July 21, 1861, General Joseph Johnston had been placed in command of the Department of the Potomac and the Confederate Army of the Potomac, followed by the Department of Northern Virginia on October 22, 1861. Johnston made his headquarters at the Connor House in Manassas from July to November 1861.

As spring 1862 was arriving, the Federal Army of the Potomac had been organized into an effective fighting force under General McClellan numbering over one hundred thousand troops. Fearing that McClellan would soon start offensive operations, Johnston accelerated plans to withdraw before McClellan got wind of Confederate intentions to do so. Johnston's forces in the Department of Northern Virginia totaled 47,617 at the end of February, of whom 5,400 were in the Valley District under Jackson and another 6,000 in the Aquia District under Holmes. Reports of increased Federal activity across the Potomac were brought in by Jeb Stuart's cavalry patrols on March 5. On March 7, Johnston directed that the retirement should begin. The army was across the Rappahannock River by March 11, concentrating on the south bank and at Fredericksburg. Johnston informed Davis of the withdrawal in a report on March 13 from his headquarters at Rappahannock Station. Johnston stated further:

> A reserve of ammunition and subsistence kept at Culpeper Court-House is to be removed before the army marches farther. The management of this railroad is so wretched that is it impossible to guess when the removal of these stores will be completed. When it has been I shall cross the Rapidan and take such position as you may think best in connection with those of other troops. By proper management of the railroad it seems to me that from the neighborhood of Gordonsville 20,000 or even 30,000 men might be thrown into Richmond on a single day.

On March 18, Johnston had the left wing of his army move to the south bank of the Rapidan River. Johnston made his headquarters at the house of

Mr. Sidney Jones, about a mile east of the Orange Rail Road Bridge over the Rapidan, on the south side, a few hundred yards back from the river. He had found an ideal strategic position behind two rivers, with interior lines of communication utilizing the Virginia Central Rail Road to quickly shuttle troops to counter Federal offensive operations along a wide front while protecting his base at Richmond from enemy incursions and maintaining railroad connection to the Shenandoah Valley. From analysis of the geography, Johnston expected McClellan to come by one of four routes: one was through Manassas, as McDowell had chosen in July; another by crossing the Potomac near Potomac Creek and then to Fredericksburg; two more by water, either down the Potomac to the lower Rappahannock, landing at or near Urbana, or by Chesapeake Bay with embarkation at Fort Monroe, thence by the Peninsula, between the James and York Rivers. From his new location, he covered all these possibilities, wisely utilizing the new technology of the railroad to shunt troops to counter enemy incursions.

Precipitate Retreat

Davis was surprised and displeased by the disclosure, saying it was "indicating precipitate retreat" and he "was at a loss to believe it." The president continued: "I was as much in the dark as to your purposes, condition, and necessities as at the time of our conversation on the subject about a month since." Davis wanted Johnston to hold his ground and go over to the offensive, stating in a message to him on March 10, which was much too late since the withdrawal had already begun: "Further assurance given to me this day that you shall be promptly and adequately re-enforced, so as to enable you to maintain your position and resume first policy when the roads will permit."[1]

In the weeks following the withdrawal, there were complaints that Johnston had abandoned military ordinance and supplies. Johnston had General French detail demolition crews to spike the heavy guns or throw them in the Potomac as they would be impossible to move with alacrity since the heavy rain had turned the roads to mud. At Thoroughfare Gap, a very extensive meat-curing establishment had been set up by the Government without consulting Johnston and against his wishes. Johnston felt that it should have been located in the interior of the country rather than on the frontier near enemy lines. The plant had to be burned, but of the 2,706,733 pounds of meat in the plant in February, 86.3 percent was evacuated, another 200,000 pounds was given to local farmers to haul away, and only 169,819 pounds was left to be incinerated. Some officers felt the grumbling was unjustified. General Richard Taylor, son of the former president, remarked: "The movement was executed with the quiet precision characteristic of Johnston, unrivaled as a master of logistics." E. P. Alexander commented: "When all is considered the movement was eminently successful as it was judicious."[2] Davis and Lee visited Johnston's headquarters on March 22 to discuss the general strategic situation in Virginia. Upon seeing the new locale, Davis remarked that it was "a position possessing great natural advantages." A Federal army under Major General Ambrose Burnside appeared off the coast of North Carolina, threatening Roanoke Island and New Bern. Davis asked Johnston to dispatch Longstreet's division to North Carolina; Johnston resisted, arguing that G. W. Smith was ill and he needed Longstreet. Ultimately, it was decided that General Holmes, a native of the state, would be dispatched with two brigades of his division.

CHAPTER 9

The Peninsula

Johnston's move to the Rapidan was timely, since McClellan had finally received the consent of President Lincoln on March 8 to put into operation his Urbana plan on March 22. McClellan's intention was "to move by water to Urbana, on the lower Rappahannock, and thence by rapid march to West Point, at the head of the York River, whence he could operate against Richmond, his hope being to throw himself in this manner between Richmond and the Southern army at Centreville." Philippe, Comte de Paris, aide-de-camp to General McClellan, commented:

> At the very moment when all seemed ready for the realization of his grand design, two unforeseen circumstances arose to thwart the calculations of McClellan. The first was the sudden evacuation of Manassas by the Confederates. I do not believe this could be attributed to indiscretions following the councils of war at Washington. I prefer, rather, to ascribe it to the military sagacity of the great soldier [Joseph Johnston] who then commanded the Army of Northern Virginia. His positions at Manassas were protected only by the snow and ice which paralyzed the Federals. With the opening of the season he would be obliged to withdraw behind the Rappahannock. This movement brought the Southern army nearer to Richmond, at the same time placing it on the Urbana route, thus making a landing there impossible for us, and permitting Lee to anticipate McClellan on the Virginia peninsula.[1]

With the Urbana expedition now defunct, McClellan changed to an alternative scheme of landing his forces at the secure base of Fort Monroe, then advancing up the Peninsula to Richmond. President Lincoln and Secretary of War Stanton hesitantly approved, provided Washington was adequately protected. It was agreed that seventy-three thousand troops would be kept for its defense.

Alexander noted: "During the winter the Federal engineers had completely surrounded Washington with a cordon of fortifications consisting

Map of Peninsula between York and James Rivers. (Library of Congress)
This map, discovered in the office of the quartermaster of the Confederate army at Williamsburg, indicates the location of the Peninsula in relation to Richmond (the capital of the Confederacy), explaining why it had to be defended. Williamsburg is the settlement visible top left.

of detached forts impregnable to assault, with heavy guns and permanent garrisons connected by infantry parapets, and batteries for field guns. Within these lines a small movable force could defy any adversary not able to sit down and resort to siege operations."[2] Transports were assembled at Alexandria—some 113 steamers, 188 schooners, and 88 barges—which during the following three weeks shuttled back and forth along the 200-mile route to Fort Monroe. The fleet transported 121,500 troops, 14,592 animals, 1,150 wagons, 240 fieldpieces in 44 batteries of artillery, and 74 ambulances, along with tents, pontoon bridges, ammunition, telegraph wire, and all the impedimenta to feed, clothe, and arm the men. Between March 25 and 29, Confederate scouts, observing the Potomac, brought word that steam transports loaded with Federal troops and military materiel were passing down the river.

"Prince John"

Reports from Major General John B. Magruder, known in the old U.S. Army as "Prince John," convinced President Davis that McClellan was bringing his army to the Peninsula. The Peninsula was about 50 miles long and not more than 15 miles at the widest point, bordered by the York River to the north and James River to the south. It was a low, flat, sandy country, heavily wooded and sparsely populated, and dissected by innumerable streams. At the time, General Magruder opposed the Federals with only about thirteen thousand men, occupying a line some 12 miles in length behind the Warwick River and some slight earthworks. McClellan could have rushed these meager defenses in simultaneous attacks and broken through, but contented himself with cannonading and sharp-shooting. McClellan's intelligence service, the Pinkertons, had created a delusion of exaggerated enemy strength. Magruder reinforced this misconception by displaying and parading the same troops repeatedly at different points. Johnston went to the Peninsula to make a thorough examination of Magruder's works and the means of defense.

Johnston hurried back to Richmond after his inspection with some observations as to the state of affairs on the Peninsula:

> His [Magruder's] defensive line was Warwick River, a tide-water branch of the James; a system of inundations along Warwick Creek, the stream of which the river is the estuary, extending to the bend in its course opposite to Yorktown, and a line of field-works just begun, to connect the inundations with the intrenchments of the village. Gloucester Point, on the north bank of the York River, and directly opposite Yorktown, was also intrenched. Water-batteries had been established at both places, to command the channel between them. General Magruder had placed his left there, because it is the only point where the river could be commanded by such guns as ours. Everywhere else it is about two miles wide, there less than one. The works had been constructed under the direction of engineers without experience in war or engineering. They were then held by about thirty-five thousand men; but the Federal army threatening them amounted to a hundred and thirty-three thousand. This army was provided with an artillery proportionally formidable, including a hundred Parrott guns of the largest calibre, and at least thirty siege-mortars, besides a full proportion of field-batteries.

After surveying the situation, Johnston was convinced that all they could do on the Peninsula was to delay McClellan's progress toward Richmond. He believed that if the Federal forces found the defenses too strong to be taken, they could simply pass around them by crossing the York River. He continued:

> It seemed to me the more probable, however, that he would open the York River to his vessels by demolishing our water-batteries, and passing us by water, unless tempted by discovering the weakness of our unfinished works between Yorktown and the head of the inundations, to force his way through our line there. For these reasons I thought it of great importance

> that a different plan of operations should be adopted without delay; and, leaving General Magruder's headquarters at nightfall, I hastened back to Richmond to suggest such a one, and arrived next morning early enough to see the President in his office as soon as he entered it.

Rifled Cannon

After describing to Davis the position of Magruder's troops and the state of his defensive arrangements, Johnston endeavored to show the president that, although they were the best that could have adopted when devised by Magruder, they were highly unlikely to result in the defeat of McClellan:

> [I] called his attention to the great length of the line compared to the number of troops occupying it; the still unfortified space between Yorktown and the head of the inundations; the fact that these inundations protected the Federal troops as well as the Confederate; the certainty that the Federal rifled cannon mounted out of range of our obsolete "smooth-bore" guns, could destroy the batteries of Yorktown and Gloucester Point; and the very strong probability that General McClellan's plan was to open York River to his fleet by demolishing those batteries with his powerful artillery. That being done, we could not prevent him from turning our position, by transporting his army up the river and landing in our rear, or going on to Richmond and taking possession there.
>
> Instead of only delaying the Federal army in its approach, I proposed that it should be encountered in front of Richmond by one quite as numerous, formed by uniting there all available forces of the Confederacy in North Carolina, South Carolina, and Georgia, with those at Norfolk, on the Peninsula, and then near Richmond, including Smith's and Longstreet's divisions, which had arrived. The great army thus formed, surprising that of the United States by an attack when it was expecting to besiege Richmond, would be almost certain to win; and the enemy, defeated a hundred miles from Fort Monroe, their place of refuge, could scarcely escape destruction. Such a victory would not only decide the campaign, but the war, while the present plan could produce no decisive result.

Conference

President Davis, after listening keenly to what Johnston proposed, said the seriousness of the situation was such that it should be discussed in more detail before any decision was made. Davis suggested that a further meeting be held in his office, attended by Secretary of War Randolph and Robert E. Lee. At Johnston's suggestion, Major Generals Smith and Longstreet were also invited to the conference. Johnston recalled:

> I was confident of the support of the former, for at Fairfax Court-House and Centreville we had discussed the general question, and agreed that the Confederate Government ought to meet McClellan's invasion with all its available forces. In giving the invitation to General Smith, I explained to him the object of the conference, after which we agreed perfectly upon the course to be advocated.

The conference began more than an hour before noon, by my describing, at the President's request, General Magruder's defensive arrangements, as I had done to him, and representing General McClellan's probable design of molesting our batteries at Gloucester Point and Yorktown, and turning our position by transporting his army up the river, could not be prevented, so that the adoption of a new plan was necessary.

Major-General Smith was then asked by the President to give his opinion, and suggested the course we had agreed upon: the assembling all the Confederate forces available for the purpose, near Richmond—Magruder's troops, and Huger's from Norfolk, to arrive among the last—and assail the Federal army when, following Magruder, it came within reach.

In the discussion that followed, General Randolph, who had been a naval officer, objected to the plan proposed, because it included at least the temporary abandonment of Norfolk, which would involve the probable loss of the materials for many vessels-of-war, contained in the navy-yard there. General Lee opposed it, because he thought that the withdrawal from South Carolina and Georgia of any considerable number of troops would expose the important seaports of Charleston and Savannah to the danger of capture. He thought too, that the Peninsula had excellent fields of battle for a small army contending with a great one, and that we should for that reason make the contest with McClellan's army there. General Longstreet took little part, which I attributed to his deafness. I maintained that all to be accomplished, by any success attainable on the Peninsula, would be to delay the enemy two or three weeks in his march to Richmond, for the reasons already given; and that success would soon give us back everything temporarily abandoned to achieve it, and would be decisive of the war, as well as of the campaign.

At six o'clock the conference was adjourned by the President, to meet in his house at seven. The discussion was continued there, although languidly, until 1 a.m., when it ceased, and the President, who previously had expressed no opinion on the question, announced his decision in favor of General Lee's opinion, and directed that Smith's and Longstreet's divisions should join the Army of the Peninsula, and ordered me to go there and take command, the Departments of Norfolk and the Peninsula being added to that of Northern Virginia.

The belief that events on the Peninsula would soon compel the Confederate Government to adopt my method of opposing the Federal army, reconciled me somewhat to the necessity of obeying the President's order.[3]

General Longstreet was reluctant to voice his opinion due to the derision he received from President Davis. Longstreet said that this was the first time that he had been invited to take part in such a high-ranking conference to discuss such momentous matters, so had nothing to say until asked his opinion:

The views intended to be offered were prefaced by saying that I knew General McClellan; that he was a military engineer, and would move his army by careful measurement and preparation; that he would not be ready to advance before the 1st of May. The President interrupted, and spoke of McClellan's high attainments and capacity in a style indicating that he did not care to hear any one talk who did not have the same appreciation of our great adversary. McClellan had been a special favorite of Mr. Davis when he was Secretary of War in the Pierce administration, and he seemed to take such reflections upon his favorites as somewhat personal. From the hasty interruption I concluded that my opinion had only been asked through polite recognition of my presence, not that it was wanted, and said no more. My intention was to suggest that we leave Magruder to look after McClellan, and march, as proposed to Jackson a few days before, through the Valley of Virginia, cross the Potomac, threaten Washington, and call McClellan to his own capital.[4]

One of Joseph Johnston's biographers, Bradley Tyler Johnson, indicated in his works that there was an irreconcilable conflict between the strategic thinking of President Jefferson Davis and that of General Johnston:

> When, therefore, President Davis first met Gen. Johnston in discussion about the conduct of the war at Montgomery, Alabama, early in 1861, Johnston, I doubt not, received his mature suggestion without cordiality, and heard his opinion as to the strategy of the war with expressed dissent.
>
> Mr. Davis had been studying the problem for years. He was a widely-read, vigorous thinker, and he was, as a matter of fact, quite as well equipped on matters of the theory of war as any man living. But right here he and Johnston collided. Johnston disagreed with him absolutely and without qualification. Mr. Davis knew, for he had read history, that a slave population was utterly unreliable in war. He believed, as turned out the fact, that the Southern slaves would be obedient, faithful, and tractable; but he also knew that the superior force of the Master once removed from them, they would become worthless as a producing machine. The experience of the War of the Revolution proved this, as shown in Johnston's Life of Greene; and Mr. Davis was convinced that the protection of Southern territory from contact with the enemy was the only way to preserve social institutions, as well as the industrial organization of the South.

Johnson wrote that Davis had given great thought to his plan for the defense of the Confederacy, working out many details for its protection. The president, Johnson claimed, proposed to hold the coast with garrisons at major ports, and to "protect a line from the Chesapeake along the Potomac, through the mountains of Western Virginia, and make the Ohio and the Missouri the frontiers," covered by various armies deployed within supporting distance of each other. However, Johnson said Joseph Johnston opposed the whole plan, claiming that by trying to protect a three-thousand-mile-long frontier, an enemy could select a point for attack, concentrate his forces on it, and "break it when he pleased":

> The proper policy, he said, was to have no fortified positions and no lines of defence—to concentrate armies at points best adapted for subsistence, and prompt communication, and when the enemy advanced into your country, having the interior lines, to concentrate on him an overwhelming force, and crush him. Then, said he, you will recover all you have lost. "But," replied the President, "wherever a Federal army marches through the South, it will leave destruction and disorganization in its wake. You may drive it back, but you cannot restore the destruction it has caused—not the destruction of property, but the destruction of social order. The negroes, who do not go off, will remain utterly useless."
>
> This discussion, between the statesman and the soldier, could have no end, because there was no maxim common to both, no axiom on which they agreed. And the difference was ineradicable.[5]

In essence, Joseph Johnston was citing to President Davis the well-known maxim of Frederick the Great that "He who defends everything defends nothing."

Assuming command of the Peninsula forces on April 17, Johnston went to his post at Yorktown. His army was augmented by the accession of Longstreet's and Smith's divisions, bringing it to about fifty-three thousand men. Major General Daniel Harvey "D. H." Hill's division occupied Yorktown on the left, Longstreet's division held the center, while Magruder's division made up the Confederate right wing and Smith's division the reserve. Eight thousand men occupied the fieldworks at Gloucester Point and Yorktown on the left flank and Mulberry Point on the right flank.

Siege

McClellan, slowly bringing up his rifled cannon due to the poor condition of the roads, settled down for a siege with some long-range skirmishing and artillery fire. Edward Porter Alexander remarked: "The Federals had an entire regiment armed with rifles with telescopic sights which were wonderfully accurate. We had no guns equal to those at all, but we had many good shots with ordinary guns & from accounts in Northern papers we made it nearly as hot for them as they did for us."[6] It was apparent to Johnston that his position would be untenable as soon as McClellan mounted his long-range, accurate rifled cannon, which would demolish Johnston's batteries with impunity since they were beyond the range of his old-fashioned ship-guns. "The fight for Yorktown," Johnston wrote to Lee, "as I said in Richmond, must be one of artillery, in which we cannot win."[7] On April 30, the first shells of McClellan's siege guns, fired to get the range of the Confederate works; fell about the village of Yorktown. McClellan's batteries had about one hundred of the coastal Parrott guns, which weighed more than 10 tons each, firing 200-pound shells, plus 30 mortars in addition to more than three hundred pieces of smaller field artillery. Johnston announced to his staff on May 1 that evacuation of Yorktown must begin:

> It was evident that the enemy was pursuing the course predicted, and preparing to demolish our batteries on the York River. The greater range of his guns would have enabled him to do it without exposure, and at the same time to inflict great loss upon our garrisons. I could see no other object in holding the position than that of delaying the enemy's progress, to gain time in which arms might be received and troops organized. But, as the additional day or two to be gained by enduring a cannonade would have been dearly bought in blood, I determined to remain in the position only as long as it could be done without exposing our troops to the powerful artillery, which I doubted not, would soon be brought to bear upon them.[8]

While General Joseph Johnston clearly realized the impact that the new technology of the rifled cannon had on the battlefield, President Jefferson Davis and Gen. Robert E. Lee had not grasped the full significance of this development. Not only that, but Davis and Lee failed to comprehend the precarious position Johnston's army was in on the Peninsula. His position could be turned by the superior Federal fleet on either the York or James Rivers, and by means of transports land troops far in the rear of the defending army, cutting it off from Richmond.

CHAPTER 10

Williamsburg

On Saturday, May 3, Johnston ordered his army to fall back through Williamsburg toward Richmond. Masked by an artillery barrage, the Confederate troops pulled out of the trenches after dark, the Confederate cavalry keeping the fires burning in the rebel camps to deceive the Federals. Confederate officer and historian E. P. Alexander noted that the withdrawal was not discovered by the enemy until after daylight on May 4 Federal cavalry immediately started in pursuit, followed during the day by five divisions of infantry commanded by Smith, Hooker, Kearney, Couch, and Casey, with Sumner in overall command. Alexander continued:

> Besides these, Franklin's division was loaded upon transports during the day, and early on the 6th sailed up the York to intercept us near West Point. Two other divisions, Sedgwick's and Richardson's were also to have been sent by water, and McClellan remained in Yorktown to see them loaded and dispatched. But the fighting next day at Williamsburg proved so severe that he rode to the front and had both divisions to follow him. Near Williamsburg, Magruder had, some months before, selected a line of battle across the Peninsula four or five miles long, on which he had at a few places some slight intrenchments with slashings of timber in front, and, about the centre, an enclosed fort of some size, called Fort Magruder.[1]

Fort Magruder

The roads here were mired, which greatly slowed the progress of the supply, ammunition, and artillery trains. The Confederates lacked sufficient wheeled vehicles to transport the sick and wounded; Johnston appealed to the Confederate navy to send a gunboat to carry them off. A large quantity of materiel had been transported to West Point by water, then forwarded by rail to Richmond. Fifty-six naval guns had to be abandoned because there were not enough horses to haul them away. The divisions of G. W. Smith and D. H. Hill marched from Yorktown along the Yorktown and Williamsburg road;

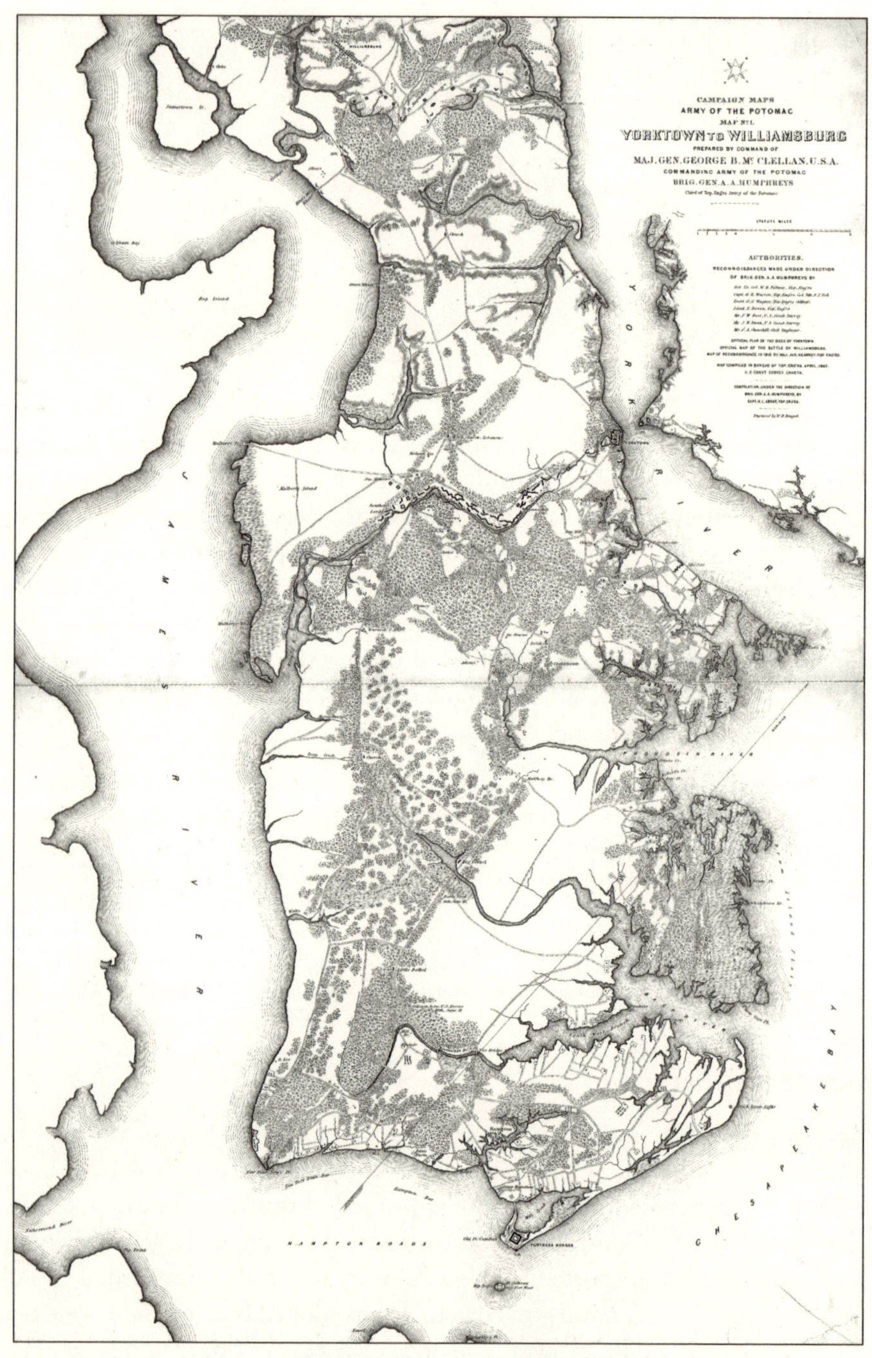

Williamsburg. (Library of Congress)
General McClellan moved his army against Longstreet at Williamsburg.

Williamsburg, May 5, 1862. (Library of Congress)
Map showing the disposition of the forces involved.

Magruder's and Longstreet's by the Hampton and Lee's Mill road, Jeb Stuart's cavalry masking the retrograde movement. The Confederate army assembled at Williamsburg about noon on May 4 along a line of light fieldworks consisting of 13 redoubts about 2 miles in front of Williamsburg, where the Peninsula was about 8 miles wide. The largest redoubt was Fort Magruder, a bastion 600 yards wide, a mile east of Williamsburg. It was flanked on the right by College Creek, which flowed into the James River, and on the left by Queen's Creek, which emptied into the York River. The field batteries at the fort had the range to fire where the two roads up the Peninsula converged and came together, the firm land at this crossroads being constricted by swamps and marshy ravines. The stop at Williamsburg was a temporary one to allow the troops time to rest and eat, and they had to press on. Moxley Sorrel, then serving as a captain with the Confederate forces, explained the circumstances: "The capital must be covered; besides, both our flanks were endangered by the enemy's immense superiority on the water."[2] Johnston rode along the road to check on the progress of the march; he came upon a gun crew with a 12-pounder Napoleon stuck in a deep hole. Lieutenant F. Y. Dabney told the following anecdote of General Johnston coming to the rescue of the gun crew:

> Every effort was made by the drivers to dislodge the gun, but without avail; and I found when I got to the wheels, with as many as could be utilized, that the horses could not be made to work in concert. The whole line to the rear was at a dead stand-still, when I observed a party of mounted officers coming down the road from the front, and in a few moments more I recognized General Johnston at the head. We all were covered in mud and straining every muscle to extricate the gun, when the general, resplendent in uniform, white gauntlets, and polished cavalry boots, rode up and halted by our side. I gave the military salute and stood like a criminal awaiting sentence. To my surprise he remarked in a very kindly tone: "Well, Lieutenant, you seem to be in trouble." "Yes sir," I replied; "and I am afraid we shall have to abandon this gun." "Oh no; I reckon not! Let me see what I can do." Whereupon he leaped from his horse, waded out in the mire, seized one of the wheel-spokes, covered as it was with mud, and called out "Now, boys, altogether!" The effect was magical, and the next moment the gun jumped clear of the mud-hole. After that our battery used to swear by "Old Joe."[3]

When McClellan found the entrenchments at Yorktown empty on the morning of May 4, he ordered his Chief of Cavalry, General Stoneman, to pursue with his division, comprising a little over four regiments of cavalry, and four batteries of regular horse artillery, supported by Brigadier General Joseph Hooker's division on the Yorktown road followed by Kearny's division. At the same time, W. F. Smith's division was brought up on the Hampton road and those of Couch and Casey in the rear of Smith.

Riding to the rear of his army, Johnston received dispatches from his cavalry commander, Gen. Jeb Stuart. About 4.00 p.m., Stuart reported that his cavalry rearguard was driven in and followed by the Federal cavalry. Johnston sent Brigadier General Lafayette McLaws with Semmes's and Kershaw's brigades, plus the batteries of Manly and McCarthy, to reoccupy the fort and redoubts to support the rearguard. McLaws drove back the Federals and took a piece of artillery stuck in the mud which 10 horses could not extricate. At sunset, Kershaw and Semmes were relieved by Anderson's and Pryor's brigades of Longstreet's division. Eventually, Longstreet countermanded the march of his whole division of six brigades and brought it back to hold the Federals in check. Johnston rode forward to join the main body, pushing forward his leading divisions to meet the forces he expected McClellan to send by water to West Point.

"Longstreet's Clear Head and Brave Heart"

Torrential rain drenched the battlefield all night and into the morning of May 5. At 7.30 a.m., Brig. Gen. Joseph Hooker sent forward skirmishers and called on artillery—Battery H of the 1st U.S. Artillery and the 6th New York Battery—to soften up Longstreet's line. Hooker attacked and was repulsed, then Longstreet counterattacked at 12 noon and drove Hooker back. The 9th Alabama and 19th Mississippi regiments captured both Federal batteries, which were left upon the ground, all their horses having been killed, but of the 12 rifled cannons seized, only four could be extracted, so deeply were they bogged down in the mud. Longstreet's troops were running low on ammunition and the reserve ammunition was in wagons that were pulling away, so some of the regiments were sent back to fill their cartridge boxes from the fallen of the enemy and their comrades. Longstreet requested Maj. Gen. D. H. Hill to bring his entire division, which was directed to Longstreet's left, where Hancock's brigade was threatening. Johnston and his staff returned to the field at Williamsburg around 3.30 p.m.; Longstreet offered him command, but Johnston refused. In his official report, Johnston stated: "Upon this I rode upon the field, but found myself compelled to be a mere spectator, for General Longstreet's clear head and brave heart left me no apology for interference."[4] E. P. Alexander recorded this incident:

> During the day Gen. Johnston spent two or three hours with Gen. Longstreet on the field & all of us accompanied him. I remember seeing a man with a severe scalp wound coming back from the firing line & Gen. Johnston spoke to him saying, "My man, I hope you are not badly hurt." The man, wiping the blood from his eyes (the wound was just at the top of his forehead), answered, "No, General, damn 'em. They all shoot too high."[5]

"Superfluous Aggressiveness"

Brigadier General Jubal A. Early held the line facing Brigadier General Winfield Scott Hancock's position and believed he could take the Yankee battery in his front on the edge of the woods. According to Alexander, D. H. Hill and Early both went with this left column but got into trouble due to "superfluous aggressiveness." Alexander asserted:

> On the extreme right of the Federals, Gen. Hancock had discovered some vacant intrenchments—part of Magruder's old line, before mentioned. With five regiments, parts of two brigades, and 10 guns, he occupied a commanding ridge, and opened artillery toward the Confederate lines. Early, on the lower ground and in the woods, could not see Hancock's position, but suggested an attack to Hill. Hill approved, but referred the question to Johnston. Johnston, who had left the battle entirely to Longstreet's direction, referred it to the latter.

> Longstreet very properly refused to give permission, as we fought only to cover our retreat up the Peninsula, and it was assured. But this message taken to Hill did not satisfy him. He was a brother-in-law of Stonewall Jackson and was a soldier of the same type.[6]

In his memoirs, Johnston recalled the matter a little differently:

> About five o'clock General Early sent an officer to report that a battery, that had been firing upon Fort Magruder and the troops near it, was near in his front, and asked permission to attack it. The message was delivered to General Longstreet in my presence, and he referred it to me. I authorized the attempt, but enjoined caution in it.[7]

Longstreet later said he had voiced his objections to attack but was overruled by Johnston's acquiescence:

> I ordered that the move should not be made, explaining that we were only fighting for time to draw off our trains, that aggressive battle was necessary on our right in order to keep the enemy back in the woodland from the open, where, by his superior artillery and numbers, he might deploy beyond our limits, and turn us out of position; that on our left there was no cause for apprehension of such action, and we could not risk being drawn into serious delay by starting new work so late in the day.[8]

Alexander wrote that Hill's men had to advance more than half a mile, through woodland and swamp. He said Hill deployed the four regiments in line of battle through a wood, Early commanding the two regiments on the left, while Hill led the two on the right. Alexander said there was then confusion over orders to the attacking Confederate regiments, which became disorganized:

> Early mistook one of Hill's commands to his own wing, for the order to charge, and he led off at once with his left regiment, the 24th Va., which had open ground before it. Hill's extreme right regiment, the 5th N.C., also had open ground in front, and, soon becoming aware that a charge had been begun, it also advanced without orders. Hill, tangled in wood and swamp with the two centre regiments, could do nothing. After passing the wood between them, the two outside regiments could see each other and the Federal guns, now scarcely 500 yards distant in front. These guns immediately opened a severe fire of shell and canister. The 5th N.C. obliqued to its left to close the wide gap between them and both advanced to the charge, reserving their fire generally until within 150 yards of the enemy. A large portion of Hancock's infantry lay concealed behind the crest of the ridge until the two regiments, now with ranks disorganized by their advance, were within 30 yards, when the Federals raised and fired, advancing over the crest and continuing the fire for 15 or 20 rounds.[9]

Hancock's official report on the action included the following:

> The plunging fire from the redoubt, the direct fire from the right and the oblique fire from the left, were so destructive that, after it had been ordered to cease and the smoke arose, it seemed that no man had left the ground unhurt who had advanced within 500 yards of our line. The enemy was completely routed and dispersed. The enemy's assault was of the most determined character. No troops could have made a more resolute charge. The 5th North

Carolina was annihilated. Nearly all of its superior officers were left dead or wounded on the field. The 24th Virginia suffered greatly in superior officers and men.[10]

Early was wounded in the shoulder. "That was not war," Alexander asserted.

We were on defensive, merely fighting to delay the enemy for the day, to let our trains get ahead. It was our role to make the enemy take the offensive, which is generally the hot & bloody end of the battle. For it is better to lie down shoot at them coming a half mile than to have them lie down & shoot so at you. Now the day was practically already gained, & we had no business to do any unnecessary fighting, & Hancock's occupying those old works did us no harm whatever.[11]

The Battle of Williamsburg cost the Confederates 1,603 in killed, wounded and missing, while the Federals suffered 456 killed, 1,410 wounded, and 373 missing, a total of 2,239 casualties.

The greater part of the Confederate army resumed their march soon after dark, halting and resting at Barhamsville on May 6. The day after the action, Longstreet's and D. H. Hill's divisions, with Stuart's cavalry, forming the rearguard, marched at daybreak, covered some 12 miles, and encamped at the "Burnt Ordinary," with no indication of active pursuit. All the wounded unable to walk had to be left at Williamsburg, amounting to about four hundred.

In the evening, Major General Smith sent intelligence to Johnston at Burnt Ordinary that a large body of Federal troops had landed at Eltham's Landing, just across the river at West Point. General William B. Franklin's division had been taken by transports to the mouth of the Pamunkey River on the southern shore of the York River to intercept the Confederate pullback, arriving at 5.00 p.m. on the 6th. It was joined by a brigade of Brigadier General John Sedgwick's division on the 7th and supported by the navy. During the night, it disembarked and the next morning took a defensive position, sending Newton's and Slocum's brigades through a large wood to reconnoiter the surrounding country. General Johnston had to deal with this latest development and entrusted General Smith with this service. Smith assigned the task to Wade Hampton's and John Bell Hood's brigades under Whiting. An officer with the initials J. H. L. related the following anecdote—Hood "Felling The Enemy"—as to what transpired:

Immediately after the battle of Williamsburg, as the Confederates under Johnston were moving back toward Richmond, neither by land nor water, but by a half-and-half mixture of both, General Johnston ordered me to go at once to General Hood. "Tell him," he said, "that a force of the enemy, estimated from three to five thousand, have landed on the York River, and are ravaging the country. His brigade must immediately check the advance of this force. He is to feel the enemy gently and fall back, avoiding an engagement and drawing them from under the protection of their gun-boats, as an ample force will be sent in their rear, and if he can draw them a few miles from the river, their capture is certain."

J. H. L. continued that the order was given and General Hood repeated it to his brigade's colonel, "and the Texas boys, who were 'spilling for a fight,' charged upon the enemy, who outnumbered them greatly, drove them back to the shelter of their gun-boats, killing and capturing several hundred." Returning to headquarters, J. H. L. gave a report of this engagement, which was not in accordance with the expectations or orders of General Johnston, who

> seemed greatly annoyed, and sternly ordered me to repeat the exact verbal orders given Hood. Just as I did so, General Hood rode up. He was asked by General Johnston to repeat the orders received from me. When he did so, "Old Joe," with the soldierly and game-cock air which characterized him, said: "General Hood, have you given an illustration of the Texas idea of feeling an enemy gently and falling back? What would your Texans have done, sir, if I had ordered them to charge and drive back the enemy?" Hood replied: "I suppose, General, they would have driven them into the river and tried to swim out and capture the gun-boats." With a smile, General Johnston replied: "Teach your Texans that the first duty of a soldier is literally to obey orders."[12]

During the action, the Federals reported 48 killed, 110 wounded, and 28 missing, totaling 186; the Confederates loss was just eight killed and 40 wounded, and they captured 46 prisoners.

Alexander witnessed an outburst from General Johnston, who was frustrated and under great stress due to previous events on the York River:

> The general seemed for some cause to be in a terrible temper—the only occasion I ever saw him exhibit it. He was splendidly mounted & without saying a word to his staff he set out, at the first, at full speed or as near it as could possibly be made through the mud & around all the wagons, guns, ambulances, &c. which encumbered the road. Evidently he was trying his best to leave every one of his staff & couriers out of sight.

Alexander, however, and a group of some 15 others started after the general. Threading between wagons and guns, Alexander gradually got ahead of the others, closing up to about 20 yards behind Johnston.

> At one place we got into a long sort of lane—with [a] fence on each side—& just ahead of us went an ambulance. As Gen. J. neared it, at a full gallop, he took the left side of the road to pass it. But the ambulance driver could hear the approaching splashing without being able to see, as the ambulance curtains were all down & wishing to give more room for the rapid riders to pass, he also at the same moment swerved out to the left, heading the general off & pocketing him in a fence corner where he had to rein up his horse so suddenly that he almost went over its head. There he stood penned, unable to get out forward or back, for the driver had also stopped the ambulance, & I drew up just behind looking on. I don't think I ever saw any one fly into such a fury in my life. I had never heard the general use an oath, but now his face was red as blood, "God damn you!" he shouted, "what do you mean? Give me a pistol & let me kill this infernal blankety-blank," at the same time reaching over the fence corner to me. I had my revolver in my belt, but I pretended not to, & held back & looked around, while the poor ambulance driver, scared almost to a jabbering idiot,

> whipped at his team, & presently got the ambulance along & let the general out of his corner. Then he started on as before & soon after dark we got to the little hotel in a little country village where we spent the night. The staff & couriers were arriving for an hour afterward.[13]

One of Johnston's staff officers, however, remarked that the general's "passion, which was sometimes of unseemly violence, was always as quickly followed by regret and acknowledgement so hearty and full that one could never harbor resentment against as true and right-minded a gentleman as ever lived."[14]

CHAPTER II

Guarding Richmond

On May 10, 1862, General Johnston wrote once again to Lee advocating a concentration of force at Richmond, with all troops of North Carolina and eastern Virginia.

Concentration

The next day, Johnston received a letter from President Davis, the first since the campaign had begun. Rather than addressing the issue of concentration to meet the threat imposed by McClellan, the president revisited an old matter, the reorganization of the army by states. Johnston, astounded, poured out his annoyance in a letter to his wife, Lydia: "I got yesterday one of the President's letters such as are written to gentlemen only by persons who can not be held to personal accountability. I can not understand the heart or principles of a man who can find leisure in times like these to write four pages of scolding to one whom he ought, for the public interest, to be on good terms with."[1] Davis, it seemed, was completely disassociated from the military crisis facing the Confederacy.

Ironclad *Virginia*

On May 14, Johnston received intelligence that the ironclad *Virginia* (known in the North as the *Merrimack*) had been destroyed on May 11. After Major General Huger abandoned Norfolk and had the Gosport Navy Yard destroyed, General Wool occupied the city with five thousand Federal troops. This left the *Virginia* in a precarious situation; it had no base from which to obtain fuel and ammunition, and the ship's draught was too great to ascend the James River to Richmond. Captain Josiah Tattnall took the vessel to Craney

Island, a few miles northwest of Norfolk. He lit a long fuse that ignited the 16-ton powder magazine and scuttled the "iron diadem" of the Confederate navy. With the *Virginia* no longer a threat, a Federal flotilla of five gunboats steamed into the James River. They encountered Fort Darling, about 6 miles below Richmond, perched upon the summit of Drewry's Bluff, rising some 200 feet, which was manned by three heavy naval guns plus two 8-inch and one 10-inch columbiads supported by Confederate sharpshooters. These forces commanded a sharp bend in the James. A double line of obstructions, made of scuttled old schooners and sunken piles of huge stone-filled cribs, blocked the 120-yard-wide river. The flotilla was repulsed, suffering 25 killed and wounded. This occurrence induced Johnston to order the Confederate forces to cross the Chickahominy River on May 15 to meet the Northern army approaching from either the York River or along the James. He had to draw back to the outskirts of Richmond on the 17th due to a scarcity of water.

General Johnston was visited by President Davis and General Lee, who inquired what plans he had. Johnston elucidated his strategy: "I explained that I had fallen back that far to clear my left flank of the navigable water, and so avoid having it turned; that we were too weak to assume the offensive, and as the position I then held was an excellent one, I intended to await the Federal attack there."[2]

McClellan too had some strategic decisions to make regarding the line of operations to be followed—either along the James River or from White House, crossing the upper Chickahominy:

> The army was admirably placed for adopting either, and my decision was to take that of the James, operating on either bank as might prove advisable, but always preferring the southern. I had urgently asked for reenforcements to come by water, as they would thus be equally available for either line of operations. The destruction of the Merrimac on the 11th of May had opened the James River to us, and it was only after that date that it became available. My plan, however, was changed by orders from Washington. A telegram of the 18th from the Secretary of War informed me that McDowell would advance from Fredericksburg, and directed me to extend the right of the Army of the Potomac to the north of Richmond, in order to establish communication with him. The same order required me to supply his troops from our depots at White House. Herein lay the failure of the campaign, as it necessitated the division of the army by the Chickahominy, and caused a great delay in constructing practicable bridges across that stream; while if I had been able to cross the James, reenforcements would have reached me by water rapidly and safely, the army would have been united and in no danger of having its flank turned, or its line of supply interrupted, and the attack could have been much more rapidly pushed.[3]

McDowell was near Fredericksburg with thirty-one thousand men, and upon the arrival of eleven thousand more under Shields—who had been detached from General Banks in the Valley—was ordered by Washington on May 17 to cooperate with McClellan in his campaign against Richmond. President Davis had placed General J. R. Anderson with about nine thousand men at Hanover Junction to observe McDowell. President Lincoln insisted that McDowell move overland rather by water to save time and to keep his army between Washington and Johnston's Confederate army. McClellan reorganized his army into five corps of two divisions each, and deployed three corps—Gen. Edwin V. Sumner's II Corps, Gen. William B. Franklin's VI Corps, and General Fitz-John Porter's V Corps, about eighty thousand troops in all—along the north bank of the Chickahominy to cover his base at White House and link up with McDowell's corps. He deployed two corps—Major General Erasmus D. Keyes's IV Corps and Major General Samuel P. Heintzelman's III Corps, totaling some thirty-seven thousand troops—to cross at Bottom's Bridge, to the south side of the river, on May 22, constituting his left wing. McClellan extended his right flank even farther. Longstreet stated in his memoirs:

> On the 26th, General McClellan ordered General Fitz-John Porter to organize a force to march against a Confederate outpost near Hanover Court-House. Porter took of Morell's division three brigades—Martindale's, Butterfield's, and McQuade's—Berdan's Sharp-shooters and three batteries, two regiments of cavalry under General Emory, and Benson's horse battery; Warren's brigade to march up the right bank of the Pamunkey in connection with operations projected for the fighting column.
>
> The Confederate outpost was commanded by Brigadier-General Lawrence O'Bryan Branch, six regiments of infantry, one battery under Captain Latham, and a cavalry regiment, under Colonel Robertson. The result of the affair was the discomfiture of General Branch, with the loss of one gun and about seven hundred prisoners. Losses in action, not including prisoners: Confederate, 265; Federals, 285.[4]

Johnston decided to attack McClellan's extreme right wing, where Porter's corps was posted, before McDowell could join him. Johnston entrusted his second-in-command, Major General Gustavus W. Smith—designated as "wing commander"—to lead the assault at dawn on May 29. He was to utilize three of his seven divisions: Smith's own division (temporarily under Brigadier General Whiting), a new division created by combining Anderson's and Branch's brigades to be commanded by A. P. Hill, newly promoted to major general, and two brigades of Magruder's division with Brigadier General David R. Jones as acting commander. Huger's division, reduced to three brigades as one of his brigades had been transferred to Drewry's Bluff by the government, was called up to Johnston's army from Petersburg. Johnston's plan of battle was as follows:

> I was intended that Major-General Smith, with his own division and that of A. P. Hill, should move against the extreme right of the Federal army, and that Magruder's and Huger's, crossing by the New Bridge, should form between the left wing and the Chickahominy,

> while Longstreet's and D. H. Hill's divisions, their left thrown forward, assailed the right flank of the two corps on the Williamsburg road, and on the Richmond side of the stream. I supposed that the bridges and fords of the little river would furnish means of sufficient communication between the two parts of the Confederate army.[5]

However, when Johnston called a council of a number of his major generals to receive instructions for the expected battle on the night of 28 May, General Stuart brought news that his cavalry patrol observing McDowell's corps reported that McDowell was heading back north to Fredericksburg. It turned out that Stonewall Jackson had routed General Nathaniel Banks (an abysmally inept commander) at Strasburg on May 23 and at Winchester two days later, and was moving up the Valley on the Potomac. Alexander commented that the Valley was the only route by which a Confederate army could invade Maryland and threaten Washington form the rear:

> Cool judgment at the head of affairs, after Washington had once been fortified against an attack by open assault, might have laughed at any idea of real danger from such an invasion. It should have been clear to all that no invasion could maintain itself long enough to carry on a siege, or to do more than to fight one great battle. The trouble was the lack of railroad transportation. Wagons alone would have to be relied upon to bring all supplies from Staunton, Va., a distance via the Valley roads of nearly 200 miles to Washington. But fear, approaching panic, took possession of Washington whenever a Confederate force appeared in the Valley, and every other operation would be suspended to concentrate all efforts upon driving it out.
>
> This oversensitiveness of the Federals cut its greatest figure in 1862, and was, more than once, the only salvation of Richmond. For the Confederate generals understood it, and as the situation in front of Richmond became more threatening, they sought more earnestly to reenforce the Valley.[6]

CHAPTER 12

Seven Pines

News of McDowell's withdrawal induced Johnston to revert to an earlier plan of assailing the Union left flank. On May 23, Hatton's Tennessee brigade, placed in observation at Savage's Station to establish if the enemy had crossed the Chickahominy, encountered a detachment of Keyes's IV Corps and drove it back. Johnston pulled his troops back to let the enemy advance and increase the interval between their left and right wings. Longstreet wanted to follow through with the present plan. He wrote that at nightfall the troops marched to their assigned positions. Johnston had earlier told Smith, Magruder, Stuart, and Longstreet that McDowell's line of march had been changed and he was now heading north, whereupon Smith proposed that their plans be changed in view of the "very strong ground at Beaver Dam Creek." Longstreet continued:

> I urged that the plan laid against the concentrating columns was made stronger by the change of direction of McDowell's column, and should suggest more prompt and vigorous prosecution. In this Magruder and Stuart joined me. The pros and cons were talked over till a late hour, when at last General Johnston, weary of it, walked aside to a separate seat. I took the opportunity to draw near him, and suggested the Federal position behind Beaver Dam Creek, so seriously objected to by General Smith, could be turned by marching to and along the high ground between the Chickahominy and Pamunkey Rivers; that the position of the enemy when turned would be abandoned without a severe struggle, and give a fair field for battle; that we should not lose the opportunity to await another possible one. General Johnston replied that he was aware of all that, but found that he had selected the wrong officer for the work.[1]

This turning movement would have threatened the Union base at White House and possibly forced McClellan to attack. Yet Johnston had lost confidence in Smith and did not think he could properly complete the task without uselessly sacrificing his troops in an assault by main force. Smith wrote of the situation:

> About sunset, May 28th, I reported to General Johnston that A. P. Hill's division would be close in front of Mechanicsville, on the north side of the Chickahominy, before midnight,

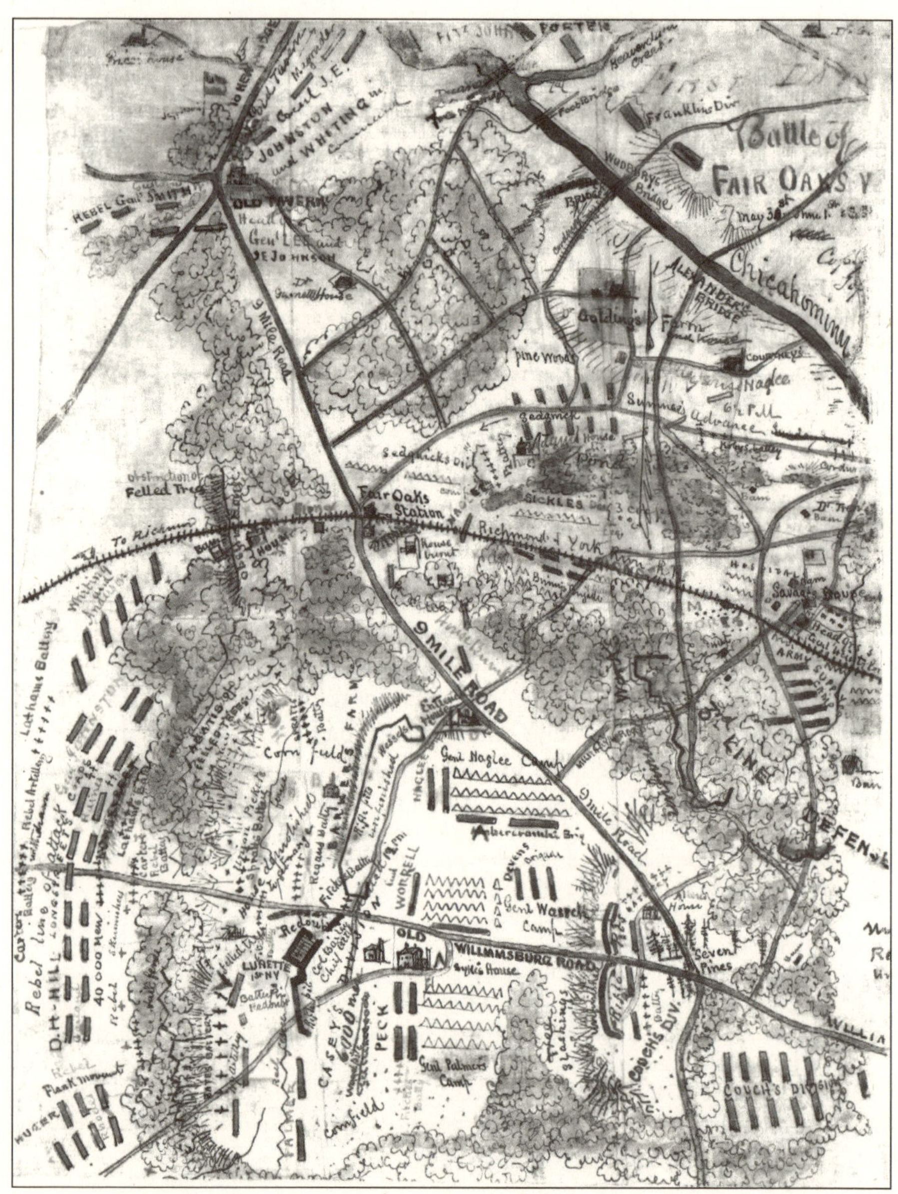

Seven Pines, May 31, 1862. (Library of Congress)
This map of the battle of the battle shows the layout of the roads at Seven Pines.

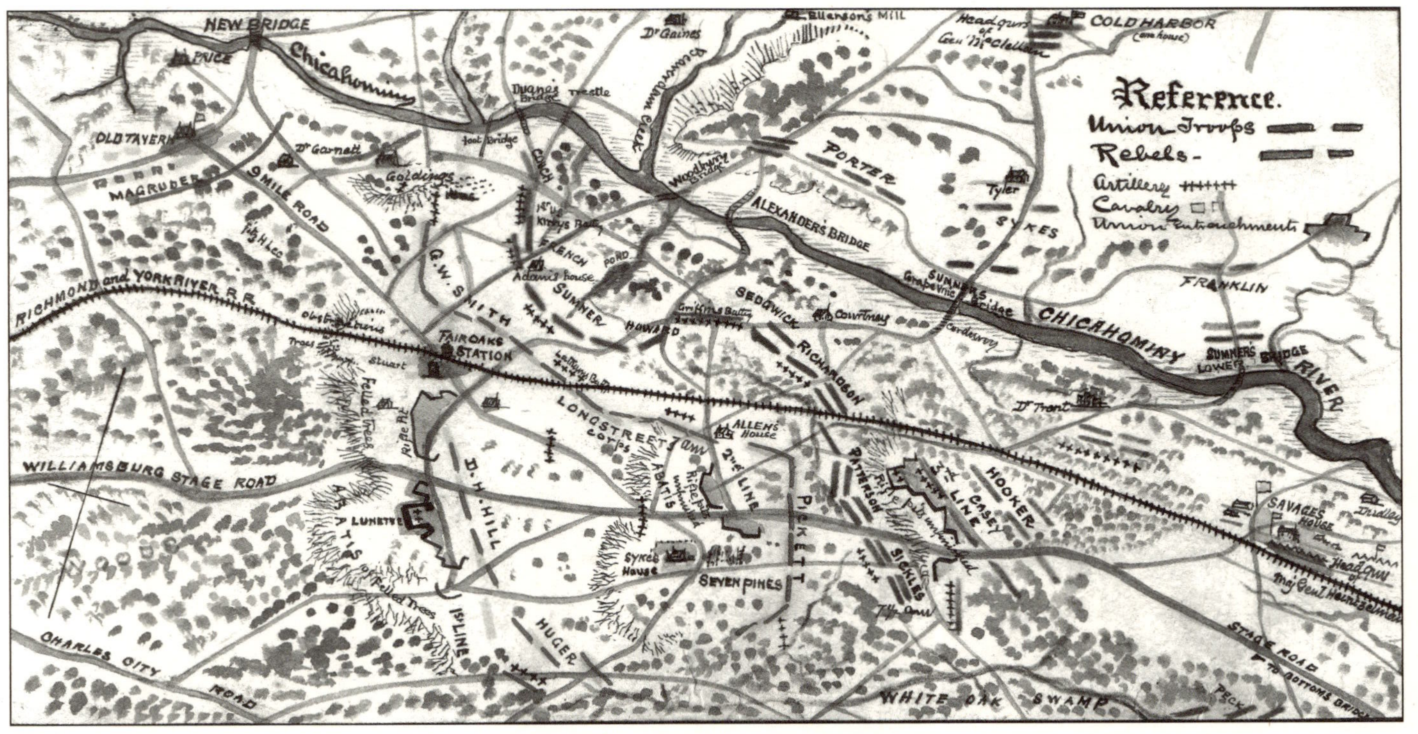

Seven Pines, June 1, 1862. (Library of Congress)
How the troops were disposed on the second day of the battle of Seven Pines.

> with orders to attack that place at dawn on the 29th. As soon as A. P. Hill's attack commenced, my division and D. R. Jones's division would cross the Meadow and Mechanicsville bridges, and the three divisions, constituting the new left wing of Johnston's army under my command, would make a prompt and combined attack on the right of the Federals, strongly posted at Beaver Dam Creek. I was satisfied that the three divisions could carry the works at that place by open assault, but it would be a bloody business—called for, however, by the necessity for prompt action before McDowell could join McClellan. I did not know, in any detail, what General Johnston intended to do with the rest of his forces during the contest I was ordered to initiate, but I was perfectly satisfied that he would use the whole strength of his army against McClellan, and, if possible, defeat him before McDowell could arrive.[2]

On May 30, General D. H. Hill directed that armed reconnaissance be made on the Charles City road by Brigadier General Robert Rodes's brigade and on the Williamsburg road by Brigadier General Samuel Garland's brigade to check McClellan's dispositions on his left flank. General Rodes did not find any enemy in his path, but General Garland found a strong picket line 2 miles west of Seven Pines, indicating the presence of a large force. Hill reported this to Johnston soon after noon; Johnston informed Hill that he would lead an attack the next morning. Johnston set up his battle plan as follows:

> Longstreet, as ranking officer of the troops on the Williamsburg road, was instructed verbally to form D. H. Hill's division as first line, and his own as second, across the road at right angles, and to advance in that order to attack the enemy; while Huger's division should march by the right flank along the Charles City road, to fall upon the enemy's flank when our troops were engaged with him in front. Federal earth-works and abatis that might be found were to be turned. G. W. Smith was to protect the troops under Longstreet from attack by those of the Federal right wing across the Chickahominy; and, if such transfer should not be threatened, he was to fall upon the enemy on the Williamsburg road. Those troops were formed in four lines, each being a division. Casey's was a mile west of Seven Pines, with a line of skirmishers a half mile in advance; Couch's was at Seven Pines and Fair Oaks—the two forming Keyes's corps. Kearney's division was near Savage's Station, and Hooker's two miles west of Bottom's Bridge-the two forming Heintzelman's corps.[3]

General Silas Casey's main line of defense was a quarter-mile-long line of earthworks with rifle pits covered by abatis, in the center of which was an unfinished five-sided earthen redoubt defended by six pieces of artillery. Casey had an advanced picket line supported by the 103rd Pennsylvania Regiment, but failed to send out scouts or patrols.

Violent Storm

Johnston had a conference with Longstreet during the afternoon of May 30 and gave him verbal instructions as to the battle the next day. Alexander recounted the result of this conference:

The conference was prolonged by the coming up of a violent rainstorm, scarcely second to any in violence, according to my recollection, that I saw during the war. Over three inches of rain must have fallen in the first two hours, and it kept up, more or less, until late at night. It was hoped that this rain would make our task easier by rendering the Chickahominy impassable for reenforcements to the enemy. Indeed, it did have this effect, but not until the night of the day after the rain. The immediate effect was only to make all of our marchings and manoeuvres slower and more difficult, and the flat, swampy country of much of the battle-field was entirely inundated … Johnston's only chance, therefore, lay in taking the offensive. He had no such works to rely upon as the Federals had around Washington. There were, indeed, a few small enclosed forts, erected during the first year of the war, each armed with a few of the smooth-bore guns of that day, but they were located too near the city limits to have any value.[4]

Johnston had decided to attack and was optimistic that such a rainstorm would cause the Chickahominy to swell over its banks, passable only by bridges, further isolating McClellan's left wing—about two-fifths of his army, consisting of Heintzelman's and Keyes's corps, against which he was concentrating 23 of his 27 brigades.

Johnston gave Maj. Gen. Gustavus W. Smith the following written orders on the evening of May 30:

General: If nothing prevents, we will fall upon the enemy in front of Major-General Hill (who occupies the position on the Williamsburg road from which your troops moved to the neighborhood of Meadow Bridge) early in the morning—as early as practicable. The Chickahominy will be high, passable only by the bridges—a great advantage to us.

Please be ready to move by the Gaines road, coming as early as possible to the point at which the road to New Bridge turns off. Should there be cause of haste, General McLaws, on your approach, will be ordered to leave his ground for you, that he may re-enforce General Longstreet. A copy of this has been sent to General Whiting, who is directed to act upon the order in your absence.[5]

Johnston also wrote orders to Maj. Gen. Benjamin Huger that evening:

General: The reports of Maj. Gen. D. H. Hill give me the impression that the enemy is in considerable strength in his front. It seems to me necessary that we should increase our force also. For that object I wish to concentrate the troops of your division on the Charles City road and concentrate the troops of Major-General Hill on that to Williamsburg. To do this it will be necessary for you to move as early in the morning as possible to relieve the brigade of General Hill's division now on the Charles City road. I have desired General Hill to send you a guide. The road is the second large one diverging to the right from the Williamsburg road; the first turns off near the toll-gate. On reaching your position on the Charles City road learn at once the routes to the main roads to Richmond on your right and left, especially those to the left, and try to find guides. Be ready, if an action should be begun on your left, to fall upon the enemy's left flank.

P. S.—It is important to move very early.[6]

Unfortunately, General Huger was not informed that Longstreet had direction of operations on the right, nor did he know the plan of attack or that his arrival on the Charles City road to relieve Rodes, who was to join D. H. Hill, would be the trigger for the general assault.

Johnston dispatched another written message to Huger on the next day, but it was still vague and failed to clarify the plan of battle:

> General: I fear that in my note of last evening of which there is no copy, I was too positive on the subject of your attacking the enemy's left flank. It will, of course, be necessary for you to know what force is before you first. I hope to be able to have that ascertained for you by cavalry. As our main force will be on your left, it will be necessary for your progress to the front to conform at first to that of General Hill. If you find no strong body in your front, it will be well to aid General Hill; but then a strong reserve should be retained to cover our right.[7]

Longstreet's troops bivouacked for the night near the Fairfield Race Course on the Nine Miles road. He recalled that Huger's division was to march via the Charles City road to the head of the White Oak Swamp, file across it and move down its northern margin, while Hill maneuvered by the Williamsburg road to the enemy's front. Longstreet's division, meanwhile, would march along the Nine Miles road and a lateral road across the rear of Hill on the Williamsburg road, and Smith via the Gaines road to Old Tavern on the Nine Miles road. Longstreet elaborated:

> The tactical handling of the battle on the Williamsburg road was left to my care, as well as the general conduct of affairs south of the York River Railroad, the latter line being the left of the field to which I had been assigned, the right wing.
>
> While yet affairs were under consideration, a terrific storm of vivid lightening, thunderbolts, and rain, as severe as ever known to any climate, burst upon us, and continued through the night more or less severe. In the first lull I rode from General Johnston's to my head-quarters, and sent orders for early march.[8]

General Johnston's headquarters was located at the Stubb House, where he could oversee the left wing and keep a watch on General Smith:

> Being confident that Longstreet and Hill, with their forces united, would be successful in the earlier part of the action against an enemy formed in several lines, with wide intervals between them, I left the immediate control, on the Williamsburg road, to them, under general instructions, and placed myself on the left, where I could soonest learn the approach of Federal reenforcements from beyond the Chickahominy. From this point scouts and reconnoitering parties were sent forward to detect such movements, should they be made.[9]

At 6.00 a.m., the lead brigade of Whiting's division reached the Fairfield Race Course on the Nine Miles road, where they encountered Longstreet's troops, who had cooked rations, packed the wagons, and were ready to move. Whiting grew testy because he was under orders to move as early as possible, though he was not on the prescribed road, and McLaws's division (whom he might have to relieve) was north of the Nine Miles road. Whiting sent a message to Johnston's headquarters asking if the impasse could be cleared, to which Johnston replied via his Assistant Adjutant-General P. Mason:

> General: General Johnston directs me to say, in answer to yours of this date, that Longstreet will precede you. What he said about McLaws was merely in case of emergency. He has given no orders to Magruder.[10]

"This quieted Whiting for a time," General G. W. Smith asserted, "but, as the delay continued, he became impatient, and having heard that I was at General Johnston's headquarters, he came there to see if I could have his line of march cleared of Longstreet's troops." At about 8.00 a.m. Smith sent his aide-de-camp, Captain Beckham, to consult with Longstreet, whose division, Johnston informed him, "was on the Nine-mile road and he was probably with it; but, if not, he might be found on the Williamsburg road with that part of his command."[11] Beckham sent an orderly back at 9.00 a.m. reporting that neither Longstreet nor his division were on the Nine Mile road, and that Beckham was riding across to the Williamsburg road to see if he could locate Longstreet there. Meanwhile, Smith, instead of directing his forces as ordered on the left wing, cajoled Johnston to have Longstreet recall three of his brigades to go down the Nine Mile road. Johnston sent one of his aides, Lieutenant J. B. Washington, to find Longstreet with orders "to send three brigades by the Nine-mile road."

An aggrieved Longstreet later denounced:

> Subsequent events seem to call mention just here that General Smith, instead of moving the troops by the route assigned them, marched back to the Nine Miles road near the city, rode to Johnston's head-quarters about six in the morning, and reported that he was with the division, but not for the purpose of taking command from General Whiting. As General Johnston did not care to order him back to his position as commander of the left wing, he set himself to work to make trouble, complained that my troops were on the Nine Miles road in the way of his march, and presently complained that they had left that road and were over on the Williamsburg road, and induced General Johnston to so far modify the plans as to order three of my brigades down the Nine Miles road to the New Bridge fork.
>
> The order was sent by Lieutenant Washington, of Johnston's staff, who, unused to campaigning, failed to notice that he was not riding on my line of march, and rode into the enemy's lines. This accident gave the enemy the first warning of approaching danger; it was misleading, however, as it caused General Keyes to look for attack by the Nine Mile road.[12]

The order thus never reached Longstreet.

The progress of Longstreet's men by lateral roads leading to the Williamsburg road was arrested about a mile from that road by the swelled current of Gillis Creek. The lead regiment decided to build an improvised bridge over the creek by placing a wagon mid-stream as a trestle, with planks leading from it to each bank, but it was so narrow that the division had to pass in single file, delaying the march by an hour. Concurrently, Huger's division arrived to cross the creek at the same location. As Longstreet's troops had precedence, they crossed first, but then realizing Huger's men had to precede them, they turned off the road, letting Huger's division file past to go to the Charles City road. Meanwhile, Longstreet and Huger met at a farmhouse on the Williamsburg road, where D. H. Hill had made his headquarters to discuss the battle arrangements. Longstreet recounted:

> Upon meeting General Huger in the morning, I gave him a succinct account of General Johnston's plans and wishes; after which he inquired as to the dates of our commissions, which revealed that he was the ranking officer, when I suggested that it was only necessary for him to take command and execute the orders. This he declined. Then it was proposed that he should send two of his brigades across to join on the right of the column of attack, while he could remain with his other brigade, which was to relieve that of General Hill on the Charles City road. Though he expressed himself satisfied with this, his manner was eloquent of discontent. The better to harmonize, I proposed to reinforce his column by three of my brigades, to be sent under General Wilcox, to lead or follow his division, as he might order. I gave especial orders to General Wilcox to have care that the head of his column was abreast the battle when it opened, and rode forward to join General Hill, my other three brigades advancing along the Williamsburg road.[13]

Beckham found Longstreet with his division resting on the Williamsburg road opposite the Charles City road, and reported back to Smith, who relayed the report to Johnston after 10.00 a.m.

Huger's column did not arrive on the Charles City road until after 10.30 a.m. Having advanced within 1,000 yards of the Federal picket line, Hill, impatient to attack, appealed to open the signal gun. Longstreet held him back to wait for Rodes's brigade to join him and Huger to get in position for a flank attack before going in. According to Johnston, the condition of the ground and several minor streams delayed the troops, although "those of Smith, Longstreet, and Hill were in position quite early enough. But the soldiers of Norfolk, who had seen garrison services only, were unnecessarily stopped in their march by a swollen rivulet. This unexpected delay led to interchange of messages for several hours between General Longstreet and myself, I urging Longstreet to begin the fight, he replying."[14] Finally, the leading elements of Rodes's brigade approached, Longstreet authorized an advance, and the signal guns were fired at 1.00 p.m. Longstreet had waited five hours for Huger, but he was still not ready in time to attack the enemy's left flank and rear. Longstreet cited offensive operations in his official report:

> Agreeably to verbal instructions from the commanding general, the division of Maj. Gen. D. H. Hill was on the morning of the 31st ultimo formed at early hour on the Williamsburg

> road as the column of attack upon the enemy's front on the road. A brigade was placed on each side of the road to advance to the attack, and each was supported by one of the other brigades of the same division. In advance of each of the columns of attack a regiment as skirmishers were deployed. The plan for the forward movement was that fields should be passed by flank movement of the regiment of skirmishers, and the woods in front, once in our possession, the brigades were to advance rapidly, occupy them, and move rapidly forward. Abatis and intrenched positions were ordered to be taken by flank movement of the brigades or brigade in front of them, the skirmishers engaging the sharpshooters and the supporting brigade occupying the position of the brigades during the flank movement.[15]

General Hill launched his attack—with 8,500 men in four brigades—against the first line of defense, consisting General Silas Casey's division stretching across the Williamsburg road about a mile west of Seven Pines. General Smith explained in detail:

> In moving to attack, Rodes's brigade was on the south side of the road, supported by Rains; Garland's brigade, on the north side of the road, was supported by G. B. Anderson. All were in the dense and marshy woods, wading through water occasionally from two to three feet deep, the whole way was obstructed by undergrowth, which often prevented commanders from seeing more than one company of their men at a time. General Hill had taken the precaution to order every man to wear in action a white strip of cloth around his hat as a battle-badge. Garland moved a few minutes before Rodes was ready. His skirmishers soon struck the Federal picket-line, and the shock of Garland's brigade fell upon the small regiment of raw troops that had been ordered into the woods to support the Federal pickets. That regiment fell back to the abatis just in time to prevent being enveloped and destroyed. And it was soon driven through the abatis in great disorder. It lost about one-fourth its numbers in a few minutes, and was broken to pieces in crossing the abatis under close and deadly fire. This regiment could not again be rallied.[16]

Longstreet had two of his brigades, those of Kemper and R. H. Anderson, behind Hill to support the main assault. Pickett's brigade was ordered north to cover the York River railroad, repel any attack from that direction, and be ready to join Hill's onslaught. As the ground was heavily wooded and soggy, and thus not conducive to the use of artillery, the Confederates had only the batteries of Bondurant and Carter on hand.

The Federals had Palmer's brigade on the left, Wessell's in the center, and Naglee's on the right supporting Spratt's battery placed four hundred yards in advance of the earthworks on the north side of the road. General Garland pushed his troops under galling fire through the abatis directly at Spratt's battery. G. B. Anderson arrived on the field, putting in three regiments to assist Garland, and moved the 27th Georgia to the left to turn the Federal right, captured the two-gun battery, and took that end of the line. Meanwhile, Brig. Gen. Robert Rodes led his troops against the front of the redoubt and was hotly engaged on the south side of the road. General Hill ordered Bondurant's battery into action and personally led Captain Thomas H. Carter's battery of five guns to a position within four hundred yards of the redoubt, from which they could rake the defenders. Hill detached General Rains to make a wide flank movement around Casey's left and into the rear of the redoubt. Confederate sharpshooters placed in the woods at the fringe of White Oak Swamp picked off the artillery horses at the battery, as well as the officers and gunners trying to spike the guns. Suffering nearly 40 per cent casualties and threatened with encirclement, Casey's men evacuated the position. Rodes took advantage of the commotion, rushing in and gaining the redoubt, battery, and rifle pits; some artillerists acting as infantry manned the guns and turned them on the retreating Federals. General Couch sent as many reinforcements to Casey as he could spare, making efforts to recapture the redoubt and the lost artillery, but they were repulsed. Hill had taken the first line of defense and was quickly advancing on the second line. Longstreet left the tactical handling of the main assault to General D. H. Hill, ordering more back-up to sustain the momentum. Longstreet later recorded:

> When General Hill reported that he must use Rains's brigade to march around the redoubt, other orders were sent General Wilcox to leave General Huger's column and march to his position on the right of General Hill's battle, directing, in case there were serious obstacles to his march by the Charles City road, to march over to and down the Williamsburg road. A slip of paper was sent General Johnston reporting progress and asking co-operation on the left.[17]

Longstreet also sent R. H. Anderson's brigade. General D. H. Hill's official report stated that his division had beaten Casey's reinforced division, driving the Federal troops into the woods and swamps:

> It was desirable, however, to press the Yankees as closely as possible. I therefore sent back to General Longstreet and asked for another brigade. In a few minutes the magnificent brigade of R. H. Anderson came to my support. A portion of this force, under Colonel Jenkins, consisting of the Palmetto Sharpshooters and the Sixth South Carolina, was sent on the extreme left to scour along the railroad and Nine-mile road, and thus get in rear of the enemy, while a portion, under General Anderson in person, was sent on the immediate left of the redoubt, into the woods, where the Yankees hid after being repulsed by the fire of Carter's battery and the captured guns, under the direction of General Rodes.[18]

General Keyes prepared to defend the second line at Seven Pines held by Couch's division, placing Peck's brigade on the left, Devens in the center, and those regiments not detached from Brigadier General John Abercrombie's brigade on the right. Casey's troops tried to make a stand in front of the abatis of Couch's line, assisted by a regiment of Deven's brigade sent forward by General Keyes, but were driven through the abatis and could not be rallied until they had retreated beyond the earthworks. Hill carried the second line of defense at 2.00 p.m. Micah Jenkins's flanking move with his two South Carolina regiments and the 27th Georgia had cut off Couch near the Adam's house at Fair Oaks Station with four regiments and two companies of infantry and Brady's six-gun battery; the Federal forces were on the run. Hill continued to press the Federals, writing in his official report:

> I now resolved to drive the Yankees out of the woods on the right of the road, where they were still in strong force. General Rains was near them, and a written order was carried to him by my adjutant to move farther to the right. I regret that that gallant and meritorious officer did not advance farther in that direction. He would have taken the Yankees in the flank, and the direct attack of Rodes in front would have been less bloody. The magnificent brigade of Rodes moved over the open ground to assault the Yankees, posted strongly in the woods. He met a galling fire, and his advance was checked. A portion of his command met with a disastrous repulse. Kemper's brigade was now sent me by General Longstreet, and directed by me to move directly to the support of Rodes. This brigade, however, did not engage the Yankees, and Rodes' men were badly cut up.[19]

Kemper's brigade had been caught in a horrendous crossfire from Kearney's brigades of Heintzelman's corps on their right flank and artillery from the second line, and had to dive into the empty Federal earthworks for cover.

At this juncture, General Wilcox had still not made his appearance on the Williamsburg road as ordered. General Longstreet sent a courier and a guide with orders to remain with General Wilcox until he reported to Longstreet's headquarters. Wilcox filed his three brigades into the Williamsburg road, followed by two brigades of Huger's division; unfortunately, the guide brought him back to the Charles City road, effectively removing these troops from the engagement. Only two of Wilcox's regiments managed to join Hill's men. Longstreet noted: "Again I reported the cramped condition of our work, owing to the artillery practice from beyond the railroad, and asked General Johnston to have the division that was with him drive the force away and loose our left. This note was ordered to be put into General Johnston's hands."[20]

General Smith had been kept inactive until Johnston could ascertain the battle had started by listening for the sound of musketry. However, an acoustic shadow muffled the noise of battle, preventing Johnston from hearing. It is believed that this phenomena was produced during the battle by a temperature inversion caused by low cloud cover, where air temperature is warmer than near the surface, causing the sound waves to refract up away from the ground and then down, producing rings of audibility. Citizens in Richmond some 10 miles from the battlefield heard the fighting sounds, but General Johnston, only 2 miles away, could not. At 2.30 p.m., General Smith offered to dispatch a staff officer to make certain what was happening. Johnston acquiesced, Major Jasper Whiting leaving to seek information. Within a half hour, Gen. Robert E. Lee rode into Johnston's headquarters to get a handle on the situation. Sounds of battle started to filter in from the south; Lee thought he had heard the sound of musketry, but Johnston dismissed it as only an artillery duel. At 4.00 p.m., Major Whiting came back with news of Longstreet's engagement at the same time as a courier arrived with a note from Longstreet asking for support on his left. Longstreet declared in the note that although the enemy was in retreat, reinforcements were required "to keep the drive going." He mentioned flanking fire from the enemy in front of G. W. Smith, which was particularly annoying, especially on green troops, who were always "as sensitive about the flanks as a virgin."

Wasting no time, Johnston mounted his horse and rode from his headquarters to take charge of operations. Just as he departed, President Davis, Cabinet members, and some officials of the government arrived from a different direction. Since there was no activity discovered of the Federal troops from the other side of the Chickahominy, Johnston directed General Whiting's three brigades—those of John Bell Hood, Evander M. Law (in temporary command of Whiting's brigade as Whiting was in immediate command of Smith's division), and James J. Pettigrew—to move against the Federal right flank down the Nine Mile road, which curved south to Fair Oaks Station, then crossing the Richmond and York River Railroad. Magruder's division was left in reserve. As General Johnston rode with Hood's brigade past the railroad, he noticed Federal soldiers (consisting of three regiments under Abercrombie and a four-gun battery) marching quick-time toward the Chickahominy by the road to the Grapevine Bridge. Johnston pushed Hood's brigade on to make contact with Longstreet's left, but Hood was moving into a vacuum since Colonel Jenkins previously had struck far into the rear of the enemy down Nine Mile road. Hood's troops floundered around for an hour before making their way back to the Nine Mile road. Johnston stated: "In that position my intercourse with Longstreet was maintained through staff-officers, who were assisted by General Stuart of the cavalry, which was then unemployed; their reports were all of steady progress. It was then about 5 o'clock."[21]

Meanwhile, Johnston and Whiting met to discuss the situation. Johnston urged Whiting to move across the railroad toward Fair Oaks to help Longstreet, but Whiting was not comfortable with an enemy force in his flank and rear. Colonel B. W. Frobel of the Confederate States Engineer Corps, then a major on Whiting's staff, wrote an account in 1868 of what transpired, stating that Johnston and Whiting were following immediately after Whiting's brigade:

> As Whiting's brigade reached the road near the railroad crossing, I was sent to halt it. On returning after doing this, I joined Generals Whiting and Johnston, who were riding toward the crossing. General Whiting was expostulating with General Johnston about taking the division across the railroad—insisting that the enemy were in force on our left flank and rear. General Johnston replied: "Oh! General Whiting, you are too cautious." At this time we reached the crossing, and nearly at the same moment the enemy opened an artillery fire from the direction pointed out by General Whiting. We moved back up the road near the small white house. Whiting's brigade [a portion of it] was gone; it had been ordered forward to charge the batteries [two separate sections of one battery] which were firing on us. The brigade was repulsed, and in a few minutes came streaming back through the little skirt of woods to the left of the Nine-Mile road near the crossing. There was only part of the brigade in this charge. Pender [commanding a regiment] soon rallied and re-formed those on the edge of the woods. General Whiting sent an order to him to reconnoiter the batteries, and if he thought they could be taken to try again. Before he could do so some one galloped up, shouting, "Charge that battery!" The men moved forward at double-quick, but were repulsed as before, and driven back to the woods.[22]

The Confederates had brought no artillery to counter the battery fire due to the impractical condition of the ground. General Gustavus Smith arrived and assumed command, bringing Hampton's, Pettigrew's, and Hatton's brigades to bolster the attack of Whiting's brigade under Colonel Law. Believing Smith was only contending with a brigade, Johnston felt Smith was quite strong enough to cope with them.

However, Smith was not only combating an isolated brigade of Couch's division but also Brigadier General Sedgwick's division of Sumner's II Corps. General McClellan, who had heard the din of battle Johnston could not distinguish, ordered Sumner to cross the river and go to the aid of the two corps on the other side. Sumner had two temporary bridges constructed, made of unhewn timber planks held together by ropes, floated and tossed in the flow. The rushing current had buckled and torn them from their pilings, with water knee-deep in the center. Sumner started his men across, despite the warnings of an engineer officer that the condition of the bridges made a crossing not only unsafe but impossible. "Impossible?" Sumner roared. "Sir, I tell you I can cross! I am ordered!"[23] The weight of the columns of troops and their horse-drawn artillery settled the bridges to their moorings and they crossed in time to aid Couch. Sedgwick, commander of Sumner's lead division, recounted: "Upon debouching into the open field near Adam's house, we found Abercrombie's brigade of Couch's division sustaining a severe attack and hard pushed by the enemy."[24] The infantry of Sedgwick's division fanned out right and left of Couch's defensive line, and the five 12-pounder Napoleons of Battery I, 1st U.S. Artillery—commanded by 22-year-old First Lieutenant Edmund Kirby—dominated the field. The Federal cannon-fire prevailed; repeated Confederate assaults were repelled and General Smith was fought to a standstill. Smith sent for Hood's brigade from his right and posted it, about dark, near Fair Oaks Station. At their parting, Hood said: "Our people over yonder are whipped."[25]

The battle drew to an indeterminate close as darkness began to fall. Johnston related events towards the end of the day's fighting:

> The contest on the left was continued with equal determination by the two parties, each holding the ground on which it had begun the fight. This condition of affairs existed on the left at half-past six o'clock, and the firing on the right seemed then to be about Seven Pines. It was evident, therefore, that the battle would not be terminated that day. So I announced to my staff-officers that each regiment must sleep where it might be standing when the contest ceased for the night, to be ready to renew it at dawn next morning.[26]

Johnston Wounded

At about 7.00 p.m., Joseph Johnston rode to a small rise about 200 yards north of Fair Oaks with his young orderly and a staff colonel to view the battle. The armies were still engaged and shots were flying thick and fast. The young colonel was weaving and bobbing as the enemy bullets whizzed by, which drew Johnston's attention. Jocularly, Johnston spoke to him: "Colonel, there is no use dodging; when hear them they have passed." Right after saying this, a bullet struck the general's right shoulder, but the wound was so minor he did not even dismount. Moments later, a shell burst nearby; pieces struck his chest and thigh, breaking some ribs and knocking him from his horse. The severity of the blow rendered him unconsciousness. His consciousness did not return until he was placed upon a stretcher. One of Johnston's young couriers, Drury L. Armistead, raised him from the ground and carried him back a quarter-mile, where his staff secured a litter to convey him to an ambulance. As Johnston was being borne to the rear, President Davis, who was with General Lee, rode up, dismounted, and rushed to Johnston's side, manifesting great concern. He asked if there was anything he could do. Johnston opened his eyes and shook his head, saying he did not know the seriousness of his wound but "feared a fragment of shell had injured his spine." Johnston became aware that he had left behind his pistols and sword, saying aloud: "That sword was the one worn by my father in the Revolutionary war, and I would not lose it for ten thousand dollars; will not someone please go back and get it and the pistols for me." Armistead went back, found the items, and returned them to the general. Johnston was so grateful he gave Armistead one of his pistols.[27]

Firing ceased, halted by darkness, before Johnston was carried a mile from the field. Being incapacitated, command devolved temporarily to Maj. Gen. Gustavus W. Smith, the next in rank. However, Smith became sick, suffering from an affliction of the central nervous system. The strain of responsibility left him prostrated with paralysis, and within two days he would leave the army. General Lee was called on by President Davis to relieve Smith of command.

According to the Official War Records, Confederate casualties in the battle of Seven Pines amounted to 6,134, including 980 dead, while Northern losses totaled 5,031, of whom 790 died. Johnston listed spoils hauled in by the Confederates: "Three hundred and fifty prisoners, ten pieces of artillery, six thousand and seven hundred muskets and rifles in excellent condition, a garrison-flag, and four regimental colors, medical, commissary, quartermaster's and ordnance stores, tents, and sutlers' property, were captured and secured."[28]

Longstreet, feeling strong affection and respect for Johnston, said of him:

> General Johnston was skilled in the art and science of war, gifted in his quick, penetrating mind and soldierly bearing, genial and affectionate in nature, honorable and winning in person, and confiding in his love. He drew the hearts of those about him so close that his comrades felt that they could die for him. Until his recovery the Confederacy experienced a serious deprivation.[29]

Johnston had kind words for Longstreet too: "The skill, vigor, and decision with which these operations were conducted by General Longstreet are worthy of the highest praise."[30]

General Johnston always felt that he could have won the battle on the second day had he not been disabled. He had no confidence in Smith either and felt President Davis should have replaced him immediately. Johnston later stated: "The only thing he [President Davis] ought to have done, or had time to do, was postpone almost twenty hours—the putting General Lee, who was near, in command of the army."[31] However, on June 10, D. H. Hill wrote privately to his wife that he believed the Confederates had the advantage and General Lee should have pressed the battle more vigorously: "Genl. Johnston was wounded & Genl. Lee did not order a pursuit. We will never have such another opportunity."[32]

The day after his injury, Johnston was borne to the residence of his friend, Mr. Crenshaw, on Church Hill, in Richmond, where he could be attended by the physicians. The rifle ball had pierced near his right shoulder blade but missed the bone. Johnston's shrapnel wounds were more serious, with a frightful bruise involving the fracture of three ribs. This produced an obstinate adhesion of the lungs to the side and a constant tendency to pleurisy.

The doctors bound him up and prescribed a most active treatment with bleeding, blistering, and depletions of the system, in accordance with the medical practices of the day. His confinement was tedious and full of suffering, only mitigated by the presence of his wife, Lydia, who moved into the house and added her ministrations for his recovery. He was unable to ride on horseback until November. Johnston took nearly six months to recuperate and reported for duty at the War Office about November 12, though still not completely healed. Johnston received high praise from the *Richmond Examiner* in an editorial on June 4:

> He is the only commander on either side in this contest that has yet proven, beyond all question, a capacity to manoeuvre a large army in the presence of one yet larger; to march it, fight it, or not fight it, at will, and while doing so, to baffle the plans of the ablest opponents in every instance. Time may yet produce another, but no living man in America is yet ascertained to possess a military knowledge so profound, or a decision of character so remarkable. He is one of those who can take responsibility; who is never a nose of wax; and who can hold out with the solidity of a rock against all foolish projects formed for him by others.[33]

Generals, politicians, friends and admirers stopped by to pay their respects, while sent solicitations by mail. One such letter to Lydia from General Lee, sent from near Richmond on June 2, was especially gratifying:

> My Dear Mrs. Johnston: I am so grieved at the general's wound, on his account, yours, and the country's. I heard of it on the field, but he was carried from it before I could get to him. I called at his quarters on my way back to the city at night, afterward sent to the Spottswood, but I could hear nothing of him. I was very glad yesterday to hear Dr. Gibson's report of him, and trust he may only suffer temporary inconvenience. You must soon cure him. In the meantime the President has thought it necessary that I should take his place. I wish I was able, or that his mantle had fallen on an abler man. Remember me kindly to him, and tell him he has my sincere sympathy. Please, when you can, let me know how he recovers.[34]

Lack of Confidence

An elderly gentleman of Richmond called to pay his respects and express sympathy for Johnston: "General, I not only deplore this because of the suffering it entails upon you, but I consider it a great national calamity." To his great amazement, Johnston suddenly raised himself upon his elbow, and with his peculiar energy of expression said:

> No, sir. The shot that struck me down is the very best that has been fired for the Southern Confederacy yet. For I possess in no degree the confidence of our government, and now they have in my place one who does possess it, and who can accomplish what I never could have done,—the concentration of our armies for the defence of the capital of the Confederacy.

This conversation was related by Dr. Fauntleroy, his medical attendant and the Chief Surgeon of the army, who was present.[35]

Indeed, the concentration that Johnston had implored President Davis to bring to Richmond was put in motion, and the army Johnston had commanded was augmented between June 1 and 26, when Lee attacked McClellan. General Holmes brought fifteen thousand men from North Carolina (who were in Richmond awaiting Davis's approval to join Johnston's army), another twenty-two thousand men transferred from South Carolina and Georgia, and sixteen thousand men came from the Valley in the divisions of Jackson and Ewell.

Surprisingly, President Davis expressed a very favorable opinion of Joseph Johnston in a private letter to his wife, Varina, written on June 23: "General J. E. Johnston is steadily and rapidly improving. I wish he were able to take the field. Despite the critics, who know military affairs by instinct, he is a good soldier, never brags of what he did do, and could at this time render most valuable service."[36]

General Huger

By June 12, Johnston had access to Longstreet's official report, which had not a good word to say about the conduct of General Huger at Seven Pines. Longstreet wrote that Huger's division was supposed to make a strong flank move around the left of the Federal position before attacking their rear:

> The division did not get into position, however, in time for any such attack, and I was obliged to send three of my small brigades on the Charles City road to support one of General Huger's which had been ordered to protect my right flank. I have reason to believe that the affair would have been a complete success had the troops upon the right been put in position within eight hours of the proper time. The want of promptness on that part of the field and the consequent severe struggle in my front so greatly reduced my supply of ammunition, that at the late hour of the move on the left I was unable to make the rush necessary to relieve that attack.[37]

On June 24, Johnston submitted his official report, which reiterated Longstreet's evaluation of General Huger's performance:

> Major-General Longstreet, unwilling to make a partial attack, instead of the combined movement which had been planned, waited from hour to hour for General Huger's division. At length, at 2 p.m., he determined to attack without those troops. He accordingly commenced his advance at that hour, opening the engagement with artillery and skirmishers. Had Major-General Huger's division been in position and ready for action when those of Smith, Longstreet, and Hill moved, I am satisfied that Keyes' corps would have been destroyed instead of being merely defeated. Had it gone into action even at 4 o'clock the victory would have been much more complete.[38]

Huger, disputing the criticisms that Longstreet and Johnston lodged against him, asked Johnston to prefer charges against him to be litigated in a court-martial. If this could not be done, Huger requested a court of inquiry to examine the facts. On October 4, Johnston wrote to the Secretary of War, George W. Randolph, that he had no disposition to prefer charges against Major General Huger. President Davis never ordered a court of inquiry.

A few days after issuing his official report, Johnston received a copy of General G. W. Smith's report. Smith made reflections about Longstreet's movement and references to Longstreet's note complaining of Johnston's delay in supporting his left. Johnston sent a letter to Smith dated June 28:

> I inclose herewith the first three sheets of your report, to ask a modification—or omission, rather. They contain two subjects which I never intended to make generally known, and which I have mentioned to no one but yourself, and mentioned to you as I have been in the habit of doing everything of interest in a military way. I refer to the mention of the misunderstanding between Longstreet and myself in regard to the direction of his division, and that of his note to me, received about 4 o'clock, complaining of my slowness, which note I showed you. As it seems to me that both of these matters concern Longstreet and myself alone, I have no hesitation in asking you to strike them out of your report, as they in no manner concern your operations. I received information of L.'s misunderstanding (which may be my fault, as I told you at the time) while his troops were moving on the Williamsburg road, and sent to L. to send three brigades by the Nine mile-road, if they had not marched so far as to make the change involve a serious loss of time; this, after telling you of the misunderstanding. Your march from General Semmes's headquarters [the advance made by the division under Whiting, from the point where it was halted, near Old Tavern] was not in consequence of the letter from [Major] L. Whiting had gone at my request, with your permission, to ascertain the state of things with Longstreet. Just before 4 o'clock we heard the musketry for the first time, and [General] Whiting was ordered to advance. Just then, Major W. rode up and reported from L., and a moment after the note was brought me-which, after reading it, I showed to you.[39]

William Swinton outlined the topography of the Chickahominy River, which played such a part in the movements of the Confederate and Federal forces in the prelude to and during the battle of Seven Pines, in his book *Campaigns of the Army of the Potomac*:

> The Chickahominy rises in the highlands northwest of Richmond, and enveloping it on the north and east, empties into the James many miles below the city, and after describing around it almost the quadrant of a circle. In itself this river does not form any considerable barrier to the advance of an army; but with its accessories it constitutes one of the most formidable military obstacles imaginable. The stream flows through a belt of heavily timbered swamp. The tops of the trees rise just about to the level of the crests of the highlands bordering the bottom, thus perfectly screening from view the bottom-lands and slopes of the highlands on the enemy's side. Through this belt of swamp the stream flows sometimes in a single channel, more frequently divided into several, and when but a foot or two above its summer level,

overspreads the whole swamp. The bottom-lands between the swamp and the highlands, in width from three-quarters of a mile to a mile and a quarter, are little elevated at their margin above the swamp, so that a rise of the stream by a few feet, overflows large areas of these bottoms, and even when not overflowed they are spongy and impracticable for cavalry and artillery.

It is commonly supposed that it was the freshet in the Chickahominy, caused by the storm of the night of the 30th, that prompted General Johnston to attack; but he had fully resolved to strike before the storm came on, on the mere chances of the situation of the Union army.

The Confederate commander was not a man to let slip such an opportunity; and, so soon as reconnaissances had fully developed the position of that portion of the Union army which lay on the Richmond side of the Chickahominy, he determined to act. It was a situation in which, by bringing two-thirds of his own force to bear against one-third of the Union force, he might hope not merely to defeat but to destroy the exposed wing.[40]

CHAPTER 13

Geographical Command

When Johnston reported to the War Department for duty, he found that he was to be assigned to the West under Special Orders No. 225 and 275, dated November 24, 1862.

Johnston was appointed to the command of the departments of General Braxton Bragg located in Tennessee after his retreat from Kentucky, outnumbered by Federal forces at Nashville commanded by Major General William Rosecrans; Lieutenant General E. Kirby Smith commanding a small independent force in eastern Tennessee; and Lieutenant General John C. Pemberton, recently appointed to command a small army of twenty-three thousand men in the Department of Mississippi and East Louisiana, with garrisons at Port Hudson and the bastion at Vicksburg, observing the Federal army of forty-five thousand under Major General Ulysses S. Grant near Holly Springs. West of the Mississippi River, Maj. Gen. Theophilus H. Holmes commanded about fifty-five thousand troops in Arkansas without serious opposition, but was not under Johnston's authority.

> General J. E. Johnston, C. S. Army, is hereby assigned to the following geographical command, to wit: Commencing with the Blue Ridge range of mountains running through the western portion of North Carolina, and following the line of said mountains through the northern part of Georgia to the railroad south from Chattanooga; thence by that road to West Point, and down the west or right bank of the Choctawhatchee River, and down that river to Choctawhatchee Bay (including the waters of that bay) to the Gulf of Mexico.
>
> General Johnston will, for the purpose of correspondence and reports, establish his headquarters at Chattanooga, or such other place as in his judgment will best secure facilities for ready communication with the troops within the limits of his command, and will repair in person to any part of said command whenever his presence may for the time be necessary or desirable.[1]

Prior to the actual issue of the orders, Johnston was informed of his proposed assignment. He was invited to a conference with the Secretary of War, General George W. Randolph, where he expressed his views:

> Without actual assignment, I was told, on reporting, that the Government intended to place the Departments of Tennessee and Mississippi under my direction. This intimation justified me, I thought in suggesting to the Secretary of War, General Randolph, that, as the Federal troops invading the Valley of the Mississippi were united under one commander, our armies for its defense should also be united, east of the Mississippi. By this junction, we should bring about seventy thousand men against forty-five thousand, and secure all the chances of victory, and even the destruction of the Federal army; which, defeated so far from its base, could have little chance of escape. That success would enable us to overwhelm Rosecrans, by joining General Bragg with the victorious army, and transfer the war to the Ohio River, and to the State of Missouri, in which the best part of the population was friendly to us. I visited him in his office for this purpose, and began to explain myself. Before I had finished, he asked me, with a smile, to listen to a few lines on the subject; and, opening a large letter-book, he read me a letter to Lieutenant-General Holmes, in which he directed that officer to cross the Mississippi with his forces, and unite them with those of Lieutenant-General Pemberton. He then read me a note from the President, directing him to countermand his instructions to Lieutenant-General Holmes.

A couple of days later, continued Johnston, Randolph retired from the War Department, "to the great injury of the Confederacy." Johnston made the same recommendation to the new Secretary of War, James A. Seddon: "This suggestion was not adopted, nor noticed."

George Wythe Randolph (1818–67) was a Virginia lawyer, planter, politician, and Confederate general. After representing the city of Richmond during the Virginia Secession Convention in 1861, for eight months in 1862 he was the Confederate States Secretary of War during the Civil War, then served in the Virginia Senate representing Richmond until the war's end. (Library of Congress)

Lieutenant General Theophilus H. Holmes was one of "President Davis's Pets," Confederate commanders who were favorites of the president. Davis wanted Holmes to be kept in command in Arkansas, "despite the prayers of the State and the irrepressible complaints of the army." "If," said a journal of these times, "General Holmes be not in his dotage, the English language possesses no synonym to indicate his stupidity and inertia."[2]

Flamboyant Senator Louis T. Wigfall

Louis T. Wigfall (1816–74) served as a Confederate States senator from Texas from 1862–65. He briefly served as a Confederate brigadier general of the Texas Brigade at the outset of the Civil War. He was also an enslaver. (Library of Congress)

By the fall of 1862, Joseph Johnston and Lydia took residence on Grace Street with the family of Louis T. Wigfall, a senator from Texas and member of the Military Affairs Committee, and his wife, Charlotte. Wigfall was born in Edgefield County, South Carolina, where he studied law. He was a flamboyant personality, frequently brawling, drinking heavily, and gambling extravagantly, which eventually led to bankruptcy. He moved to Texas in 1848, served in the state legislature, and became a United States Senator in 1859 with ardent secessionist sentiment. During the bombardment of Fort Sumter, he had himself rowed out to ask the Federal commander if he struck his flag. He was on Davis's personal staff at Montgomery and continued when the government moved to Richmond but resigned prior to the battle of First Manassas to command a Texas regiment with a commission of colonel. Subsequently, Davis promoted him to brigadier general, leading a brigade. His service in the military was brief, for in February 1862 his constituents in Texas elected him to the Confederate Senate, though he retained the title of general.

Davis and Wigfall had a cordial relationship until the fall of 1862, when Wigfall felt snubbed after he had conversed with Davis about a replacement for Secretary of War George Randolph, who had resigned on November 15, only to find out later that Davis had already decided on James Seddon (one of Wigfall's recommendations) prior to their meeting, though this was never divulged in their discussion. A further point of contention arose after Wigfall introduced a bill to allow army commanders to appoint their own staff officers, each of whom would be given the rank of brigadier general, despite the fact that tradition dictated that the president nominate generals.

Wigfall's bill passed both houses of Congress, but notwithstanding, Davis vetoed it. Johnston and his wife shared a home with the Wigfalls at the time, and in all probability, Wigfall had discussed this legislation with Johnston beforehand. From then on, relations between Wigfall and Davis became more strained as Wigfall openly criticized the president's military policies in the senate as detrimental to the cause, aligning himself with the opposition and "the western concentration bloc." As there were no political parties, opposition to President Davis took on a personal aspect, which Davis considered synonymous with treason. This feud tainted Johnston as well, since Davis branded all who associated with Wigfall as disloyal. R. Barnwell Rhett, editor of the *Charleston Mercury*, commented on Jefferson Davis's character traits: "He regarded him as an accomplished man, but egotistical, arrogant, and vindictive, without depth or statesmanship."[3]

Before General Johnston left Richmond, a breakfast was given in November in his honor and to celebrate the reconciliation between two of his prominent political friends, Senator Henry S. Foote of Tennessee and Senator William L. Yancey of Alabama. The bountiful breakfast lasted two hours, with toasts and jests. Yancey rose and called for fresh glasses of champagne, and with a sign to Johnston that he was to remain seated, proposed a toast: "This toast is to be drunk standing." As the guests rose, Yancey announced: "Gentlemen, let us drink to the health of the only man who can save the Confederacy—General Joseph E. Johnston!" Johnston rose from his seat with a glass in his hand, turned to Yancey, and said in a grave tone: "Mr. Yancey, the man you describe is now in the field, in the person of Robert E. Lee. I will drink to his health." Not to be outdone in courtesy, Yancey countered: "Your modesty is only equaled by your valor!"[4]

Johnston left Richmond on Saturday, November 29, but did not reach Chattanooga, the location of his headquarters chosen by the War Department, until early on the morning of December 4; a tiresome journey of five days due to the poor management of Southern railroads, which led to delays caused by no less than three accidents. Upon reaching his headquarters in Chattanooga, Johnston found a telegram from Adjutant General Samuel Cooper informing him that Lieutenant General Pemberton was under attack by Grant's superior forces and Pemberton was falling back in the direction of Vicksburg. Cooper noted that General Holmes had been "peremptorily ordered" to send reinforcements from Arkansas and urged Johnston to send a sufficient force from General Bragg's command to aid Pemberton. Johnston reacted:

> I replied immediately, by telegraph as well as by mail, that the troops near Little Rock could join General Pemberton sooner than those in Middle Tennessee; and requested General Bragg

> by telegraph, to detach a large body of cavalry to operate in General Grant's rear and cut his communications. On the following day, the 5th, at Murfreesboro', I again wrote to General Cooper by mail and by telegraph, giving him General Bragg's estimates of his own force and that of General Rosecrans, and endeavoring to show that he could not give adequate aid to General Pemberton without giving up Tennessee, adding, that troops from Arkansas could reach the scene of action in Mississippi much sooner than General Bragg's; and saying, besides, that I would not weaken the Army of Tennessee without express orders to do so. He was also informed that two thousand cavalry would be detached to break the Louisville and Nashville Railroad, and four thousand to operate on General Grant's communications.[5]

The day after reaching Chattanooga, Johnston took a train to Murfreesboro to learn first-hand the condition of Bragg's army, which numbered about forty-two thousand. While he was making his inspection, he received a telegram summoning him to Chattanooga to meet with President Davis, who had arrived there on December 10. Johnston found that the object of the meeting was that Davis wanted to confer with him about transferring a strong body of troops from the Army of Tennessee to Pemberton, which Johnston opposed. Davis went on to Murfreesboro to consult with Bragg, who also argued that reinforcements could be more easily obtained from Holmes. Davis was not convinced and returned to Chattanooga, directing Johnston to issue orders for Major General Carter L. Stevenson's division, along with a brigade of Major General McCown's division—amounting to ten thousand infantry and artillery—to move immediately by railroad to Jackson, Mississippi. Johnston learned from Davis that Holmes was not ordered across the Mississippi River; rather, he was to use his discretion to do so only if he felt certain for the safety of Arkansas.

While Davis was at Chattanooga, news came that a battle was fought at Fredericksburg, causing some apprehension. Johnston was amazed and envious of Lee's victory at Fredericksburg, where Burnside launched waves of frontal attacks against Lee's army in an elevated and fortified position. "What luck some people have," he confided to Wigfall. "Nobody will ever attack me in such a place."[6]

Late on the afternoon of December 16, Jefferson Davis left Chattanooga for Vicksburg, desiring Johnston to accompany him. The journey was long and tedious, by way of Atlanta, Montgomery, and Mobile, arriving at Jackson on the morning of December 19. On the 20th, Davis and Johnston went to Vicksburg and spent two days examining its entrenchments. Johnston observed:

> The usual error of Confederate engineering had been committed there. An immense intrenched camp, requiring an army to hold it, had been made instead of a fort requiring only a small garrison. In like manner the water-batteries had been planned to prevent the

> bombardment of the town, instead of to close the navigation of the river to the enemy; consequently the small number of heavy guns had been distributed along a front of two miles, instead of being so placed that their fire might be concentrated on a single vessel. As attack was supposed to be imminent, such errors could not be corrected.[7]

Johnston and the president traveled north to visit Lieutenant General Pemberton's army near Grenada, which was constructing entrenchments to contend the passage of the Yallabusha River by the Federal army. Johnston felt the defenses were far too extensive to be of any value.

Johnston's strategic concept was for Pemberton to assemble an active field army to maintain mobility and meet any Federal incursion against Vicksburg or Port Hudson, utilizing the 18,000 at Vicksburg plus 15,000 at Grenada, 10,000 at Port Hudson, and 3,600 at Jackson and Columbus, a total of 46,600 men. He did not want to place large bodies of troops in static positions at Vicksburg and Port Hudson, where they could be bottled up; rather, he wanted a small force to defend and hold them "until succored by the active army." This consideration was contrary to Pemberton's fixation on holding Vicksburg at all costs with all his troops. In reply to Pemberton's request stating, "I want all the troops I can get," Johnston countered: "It is necessary to send to Vicksburg just the troops you want, not all we have. Can you not estimate the number necessary?"[8]

Concentrating on Interior Lines

Before Davis went back to Richmond, Johnston sent a memo to Davis on December 22:

> No more troops can be taken from General Bragg. Our great object is to hold the Mississippi. The country beyond the river is as much interested in that object as this, and the loss to us of the Mississippi involves that of the country beyond it. The 8,000 or 10,000 men which are essential to safety ought, therefore, I respectfully suggest, to be taken from Arkansas, to return after the crisis in this department. I firmly believe, however, that our true system of warfare would be to concentrate the forces of the two departments on this side of the Mississippi, beat the enemy here, and then reconquer the country beyond it, which he might have been gained in the mean time.[9]

Biographer Bradley Taylor Johnson wrote of "the old difference of opinion" between President Davis and the head of the Confederacy's second army: "One was for holding on to lines, and protecting territory, the other was for abandoning territory, concentrating on interior lines, destroying his enemy, in detail, and thus eventually securing the country, and positions abandoned, to accomplish this result."[10]

It took three weeks for Major General Stevenson's division, without artillery or wagons, to travel by railroad from Tennessee to Mississippi. Two of its brigades participated in the defense of Haynes Bluff to repel Major General William T. Sherman's assault on December 27–28, but all its wagons and artillery were strung out along the roads. However, the crisis in Mississippi had passed, it being reported on December 27 by Major General Loring, commanding at Grenada, that General Grant's army was retiring. Grant had marched on Grenada as a distraction for Sherman's move on Vicksburg. Grant's supply line had been cut by the destruction of the Federal depot at Holly Springs, Mississippi, on December 20 by Major General Van Dorn, with some 3,000 cavalry capturing two thousand prisoners, carrying off what they could, and despoiling large stores of provisions, ammunition, and six thousand muskets. Simultaneously, Brigadier General Nathan Bedford Forrest, with two thousand cavalry, successfully broke up the Louisville and Nashville Railroad near Jackson, Tennessee, destroying large quantities of military stores and paroling 1,200 prisoners.

When Major General Rosecrans was informed that a large detachment of troops had been transferred from Bragg's army in Tennessee to Pemberton in Mississippi, he marched his forces from Nashville to Murfreesboro on December 26. The two armies confronted each other in front of Murfreesboro, and on December 31 both generals decided to attack in similar fashion—General Bragg attacked in echelon by his left, consisting of Lieutenant General Hardee's corps, while Rosecrans had his left lead the attack. The battle lasted until January 3, 1863, the armies facing each other without serious fighting for the remainder of that day. Bragg, believing that Rosecrans was receiving large reinforcements, withdrew across the Duck River to Tullahoma. Bragg had a force of about thirty thousand infantry and artillery, plus five thousand cavalry; he lost 9,865 men, including 1,200 severely wounded and 300 sick left in Murfreesboro. He captured 30 pieces of artillery, six thousand small arms, and large numbers of wagons and other military stores. Rosecrans reported a force of 43,400 infantry and artillery and 3,300 cavalry being involved in the battle, of whom 1,533 were killed, 7,245 wounded, and 3,489 lost as prisoners. In a letter to General Johnston dated January 11, published in the Official War Records,[11] Bragg said:

> The unfortunate withdrawal of my troops when they were not absolutely necessary elsewhere has saved Rosecrans from destruction. Five thousand fresh troops as a reserve on the first day's battle would have finished the glorious work. I told the President, Grant's campaign would be broken up by our cavalry expeditions in his rear before Stevenson's command could meet him in front; but he was inexorable, and reduced me to the defensive, or, as he expressed it, "Fight if you can, and fall back beyond the Tennessee."[12]

Castles in the Air

William J. Hardee (1815–73) was a Confederate general in the American Civil War who wrote a popular infantry manual used by both the North and the South. (Library of Congress)

Johnston was frustrated by his assignment, writing to Wigfall from Chattanooga on December 4, 1862: "Nobody ever assumed a command under more unfavorable circumstances."[13] It was a mission, not a military command. Davis did not want Johnston but was forced to reinstate him by public opinion. Davis's vision of military strategy was not in accord with Johnston's generalship. The president's refusal to unite Holmes with Pemberton went against Johnston's plan for concentration rather than dispersion, which weakened Confederate resistance to Union incursions. Johnston lamented to Wigfall on December 15: "This has blown away some tall castles-in-the-air. I have been dreaming of crushing Grant with Holmes' & Pemberton's troops, & with the latter, Bragg & Kirby Smith marching to the Ohio. Our troops beyond the Mississippi seem to be living in great tranquility." Johnston objected to the structure of his geographical command: "Mississippi and Arkansas should be united to form it. Not this state [Tennessee] & Mississippi—which is divided by an impassable river & impracticable country. The troops in Middle Tennessee could reach Fredericksburg much sooner than Mississippi. Then General Holmes' communications depend upon our possession of the Mississippi. It is certainly his business to at least assist in the maintenance of his communications."[14]

Johnston saw the futility of his status as no more than an inspector general with great responsibility and no powers to conduct a campaign or control the armies within his jurisdiction. All he could do was shuffle detachments from one army to reinforce the other. Generals Bragg and Pemberton reported their actions directly to Richmond, bypassing Johnston. "My own position does not improve on acquaintance," Johnston wrote to Wigfall. "It is little, if any, better than being laid on the shelf."[15] Johnston twice asked Davis to relieve him of command, but Davis declined.

> Being convinced, before he left Jackson, that my command was little more than nominal, I so represented it to him, and asked to be assigned to a different one, on the ground that two armies far apart, like those of Mississippi and Tennessee, having different objects, could not be commanded by the same general. After reflection, he replied that the seat of government was so distant from the two theatres of war, that he thought it necessary to have an officer nearer, with authority to transfer troops from one army to the other in an emergency. If such an officer was needed, I certainly was not the proper selection; for I had already expressed the opinion distinctly that such transfers were impracticable, because each of the two armies was greatly inferior to its antagonist; and they were too far from each other for such mutual dependence.

Davis's reply was: "The difficulty arising from the separation of troops of your command is realized but cannot be avoided."[16]

After the battle of Murfreesboro, General Bragg became aware that the sentiment of his subordinates toward him had soured. He sent a circular letter soliciting a vote of confidence, which elicited replies from Hardee, Polk, Breckinridge, and Cleburne, largely in the negative. These letters were forwarded to Richmond. Polk added a private letter to the president advising him to have Bragg transferred to some other post, concluding:

> I think, too, that the best thing to be done in supplying his place would be to give his command to General Joseph E. Johnston. He will cure all discontent, and inspire the army with new life and confidence. He is here on the spot, and I am sure will be content to take it. If General Lee can command the principal army in his department in person, there is no reason why General Johnston should not. I have therefore, as a general officer of this army speaking in behalf of my associates, to ask respectfully that this appointment be made; and I beg to be permitted to do this urgently. The state of this army demands immediate attention, and its position before the enemy, as well as the mind of its troops and commanders, could find relief in no way so readily as by the appointment of General Joseph E. Johnston.[17]

General Braxton Bragg

While Johnston was inspecting the defenses of Mobile, Alabama, on January 22, he received a telegram from Jefferson Davis directing him to proceed to Bragg's headquarters; a letter of explanation was at Chattanooga. Johnston found the letter from the president, dated January 22, at Chattanooga, informing him of the bad feeling against Bragg but expressing the president's confidence in General Bragg. Johnston, as commander of the Department of the West, was asked to investigate and ascertain whether Bragg had lost the confidence of the army, then advise Davis what action was required. It became apparent to Johnston that he was designated to replace Bragg if he was to be dismissed. This went against Johnston's sense of personal honor and integrity; he believed officers should be advanced on their own merit and not at the expense of their fellows. Under these conditions Johnston felt compelled to sustain Bragg, writing to Davis: "I am glad to find that your confidence is unshaken. My own is confirmed by his recent operations, which in my opinion, evince great vigor and skill. It would be very unfortunate to remove him at this juncture, when he has just earned, if not won, the gratitude of the country." Johnston concluded: "After seeing all the troops I shall write again. I respectfully suggest that, should it then appear to you necessary to remove General Bragg, no one in this army or engaged in this investigation ought to be his successor."[18]

Braxton Bragg (1817–76) is one of the most widely derided commanders of the Civil War, and for good reason. Although personally brave in combat, Bragg was a poor tactician and strategist, and an even worse army commander. (Library of Congress)

On March 9, while Johnston was in Mobile, he received the following telegram from the Secretary of War, James Seddon: "Order General Bragg to report to the War Department here for conference. Assume yourself direct charge of the army in middle Tennessee."[19] Johnston arrived at Tullahoma on March 18 to learn that Mrs. Bragg was critically ill with typhoid fever and General Bragg was attending to her. On April 10, Johnston wrote to President Davis that he was under medical care for a recurrence of illness and lingering problems as a consequence of his Peninsula wounds, and was confined to bed. Johnston telegraphed the Secretary of War asserting that Bragg's departure to Richmond was to be postponed due to the circumstances and he would take command of the army but issue no official statement of the change. Johnston proposed that if a conference was necessitated between the War Department and Bragg, an officer should be sent from the War Department for that purpose. Johnston quickly won the respect, admiration, and affection of the officers and men, which Bragg could not command and which made him jealous. Dr. Charles Todd Quintard, who served the Army of Tennessee as both surgeon and chaplain, reported: "I found General Johnston a charming man. He was of perfectly simple manners, of easy and graceful carriage and a good conversationalist."[20] On March 30, Lieutenant General Leonidas Polk sent another letter to President Davis (marked "Private"), hoping to achieve General Bragg's removal from the Army of Tennessee and putting Johnston in his place, articulating the essence of Johnston's dilemma in his relationship with Bragg:

> My idea is—my conviction rather—that if the presence and offices of General Bragg were entirely acceptable to this army, the highest interests—military interests—of the Confederacy would be consulted by transferring him to another field, where his peculiar talent—that of organization and discipline—could find a more ample scope. For that kind of service he has, undoubtedly, peculiar talent. His tastes and natural inclination fit him for it, and he has the advantage now of large and fresh experience. The application of that talent is not always easy or agreeable where it exists, yet there are few armies which would not be benefited by it, even if the benefit came from without. My opinion is that the general could be of service to all the armies of the Confederacy, if placed in the proper position. Such a position would be that of a place in the Adjutant and Inspector General's Department at Richmond. Assign him the duties of Inspector-General. If the duties are attended to as the imperfectly organized and disciplined condition of our troops require, they will furnish full employment for any single mind; and from my observations while in Richmond, it would be a great relief to General Cooper, whose energy and business capacity, great as they are, seemed well-nigh overtaxed.
>
> The general could not object to the position on the score of rank, as the ranking officer of the army now holds that position. It is as competent to assign General Bragg as any other officer to that duty, and as his specialty is that which the office of Inspector General covers, his resources and capacity would be felt throughout the army.
>
> This done, the way is clear for assigning General Johnston to the command of this army, a measure which would give universal satisfaction to officers and men.
>
> Colonel Johnston informed me he thinks General Johnston desires to keep General Bragg in his present position. I think the case would be more properly stated by saying he does not wish to be, or seem to be, the cause of his removal. I have conversed with him on the subject, and he feels a delicacy, as I understand it, in touching the case of a man to whose command he might succeed in the event of his being removed from it. I do not think I misapprehend his feelings, though, of course, think them morbid, and, in the present relations of the parties, misplaced. I know that General Johnston thinks himself half employed, and that he would be much better satisfied commanding an army in the field than doing the duties of administering a department.
>
> Whether General Johnston is the best man for the place or not is not the question. The army and the West believe so, and both would be satisfied with the appointment, and I believe it is the best that could be made.[21]

Johnston's own health became delicate as his old wound became troubling, and he had to put himself in the care of a surgeon. On April 10, he reported to Davis that he was unable to serve in the field, adding: "General Bragg is therefore necessary here." Fortunately, Bragg's wife had recovered from her illness in the first week of April.

Biographer Robert M. Hughes made this observation of Johnston's orders to assume command in the West:

> A perusal of this order indicates that it was well termed a "geographical command." It did not assign him to the leadership of any specific army, but to an immense domain, containing different armies with different objects, his only power being to detach troops from one to the other—a useless authority, since each was outnumbered by its own foe, and all were too far separated to render it practicable to detach thus in time to afford mutual succor. Nor could he take command of one of these armies without the unpleasantness of superseding its immediate commander—an act which generosity to his subordinate forbade. The two largest of these armies were commanded by Generals Bragg and Pemberton, both well-known proteges of the President, the former always quarreling with his inferior generals, the latter a man who had been raised to the next highest grade in the Confederate service without having participated in any signal achievement, and without having made any impression at any place to which his previous assignments had called him. Johnston's position, in brief, was simply that of a scapegoat, on whom the delinquencies of the President's favorites might be placed in case of disaster.[22]

Hughes's observation is an accurate description of Johnston's situation. Any failure would be placed on his shoulders.

CHAPTER 14

Vicksburg

In the meantime, Union forces consolidated their entire effort in capturing the citadel at Vicksburg, the object being to open and control the Mississippi River and split the Confederacy. General Grant took personal charge of operations on the river. Jefferson Davis viewed Vicksburg as "the nailhead that held the South's two halves together." The Mississippi was under Federal sway except for the portion of the river between Port Hudson, Louisiana, and Vicksburg, Mississippi. Bradley Tyler Johnson described the topography:

> They [Confederates] fortified the positions at Vicksburg and Port Hudson on the east bank of the Mississippi, about four hundred miles apart by the river, and one hundred miles by the roads on the east side. The course of the Mississippi is the most tortuous in the world. Its current flows in every direction—south, east and west.
>
> Where its immense flood has cut away a bank of alluvion until it reaches a rocky bluff, it turns short round on itself, and flows back in the direction from which it comes, thus making loops, miles in extent, but the sides of which are only a few miles apart. Vicksburg is situated on a high bluff at the end of one of those loops.
>
> In the Northeast section of the State of Mississippi rises the Big Black River, which flows in a Southwesterly course until it empties into the Mississippi, just above Grand Gulf, probably seventy miles below Vicksburg by land.
>
> The Yazoo flows from the Northeast, and enters the Mississippi nine miles north of Vicksburg.[1]

Vicksburg stood on a series of formidable bluffs above the river, affording it strong natural defenses. Philippe, Comte De Paris, commented on the state of the Confederate defenses there:

> The Confederate engineers had laid out a vast intrenched camp along these various ridges, whose irregular form was adapted to the character of the ground, and which, by encircling the whole plateau, presented a line of fortifications of nearly eight miles in extent on the land-side and about four miles on the river-side. As far as one may judge by an examination of the map, this sketch gave Vicksburg the appearance of a great intrenched camp. The Confederates, as usual, had yielded to the natural temptation of inexperienced armies,

Defenses of Vicksburg. (Library of Congress)
Operations against Vicksburg blocked and controlled navigation on the Mississippi River.

Vicksburg and the Rebel Batteries, 1862. (Library of Congress)
Location of Rebel batteries dominating the Mississippi River

> believing that they are adding to the strength of a position by multiplying to excess the works defending it. This defect had not escaped the observation of the sagacious Johnston upon his visit to the Army of the Mississippi in December, 1862; but, as we have already remarked in regard to the batteries commanding the river, he had pointed out this defect in vain: his advice was not heeded. Experience has shown how well founded were his criticisms. If these works had been so constructed as to afford shelter only to a garrison of from seven or eight thousand men, they would have been quite sufficient to secure Vicksburg the role belonging to that place by not allowing the batteries intended to block the passage of the river to be taken in the rear; they could have sustained a siege long enough to allow an army of relief time to come to deliver the garrison, and Pemberton would never have thought of shutting himself up in it with all his troops. The extent of the space they occupied, on the contrary, neutralized their value unless defended by an army. It was the fear of disgarnishing them which influenced Pemberton during the whole campaign, not allowing him to quit the place lest it should be left without a sufficient garrison.[2]

General Johnston outlined the military dispositions of the forces on the Mississippi:

> General Grant was then in northern Mississippi, with an army formed by uniting the detachments that had been occupying Corinth and various points in southern West Tennessee. He was preparing for the invasion of Mississippi, with the special object of gaining possession of Vicksburg by the combined action of his army and Admiral Porter's squadron, which was in readiness. To oppose him, Lieutenant-General Pemberton, who commanded the Department of Mississippi and East Louisiana, had an active army of 23,000 infantry and artillery, and above 6,000 cavalry, most of it irregular. There were also intrenched camps at Vicksburg and Port Hudson, each held by about six thousand men, protecting batteries of old smooth-bore guns, which, it was hoped, would prevent the Federal war vessels from occupying the intermediate part of the Mississippi. Lieutenant-General Holmes was then encamped near Little Rock with an army of above fifty thousand men, as General Cooper, adjutant-general, reported to the President in my presence. There were no Federal forces in Arkansas at the time, except one or two garrisons.[3]

General Grant had tried different experiments to circumvent the defenses at Vicksburg. He settled on a plan of moving his army down the west bank of the Mississippi to Hard Times, then having the Federal fleet with transports under Rear Admiral Porter run the gauntlet of Confederate guns at Vicksburg to ferry his troops across the Mississippi and disembark below Vicksburg. Grant chose Bruinsburg Landing, Mississippi, which was pointed out as a good high and dry landing site by an enslaved person who was abducted from the east bank. It also provided access to Grand Gulf, about 10 miles south, a rebel bastion mounting 16 guns, among which was a battery of five heavy guns established by Pemberton about April 28 atop a promontory 50 feet high. Grant wanted Grand Gulf as a supply port. An amphibious invasion was fraught with danger; if it was defeated at the beachhead, there would be no avenue of retreat. On the night of April 30, Grant moved twenty thousand men across the Mississippi

John C. Pemberton (1814–81) was made a lieutenant general in the Confederate Army and assigned to defend Vicksburg and the Mississippi River. Upon Vicksburg's surrender, he voluntarily resigned his commission and served as a lieutenant colonel of artillery for the remainder of the war, a testimonial of his loyalty to the South. (Library of Congress)

and established his beachhead. He had taken no chances of being overwhelmed at his landing spot, having Sherman's corps make a feint at Haynes Bluff near Vicksburg to divert Pemberton's attention. He also had Colonel Benjamin H. Grierson lead a raid of seventeen hundred cavalrymen through Mississippi, starting from LaGrange, Tennessee, on April 17, and ending up at Baton Rouge, Louisiana, on May 2, tearing up rail lines and burning Confederate workshops and warehouses. General Pemberton did not have sufficient cavalry to deal with the raid, and had to detach several brigades of infantry to protect Confederate property. Pemberton wired Johnston of the landing and sent a telegraph to the War Department calling for large reinforcements, to which Johnston added: "They cannot be sent from here without giving up Tennessee." On May 1, Johnston advised Pemberton: "If General Grant's army lands on this side of the river, the safety of Mississippi depends on beating it. For that object you should unite your whole force." The next day, Johnston again telegraphed him: "If Grant's army crosses, unite all your troops to beat him; success will give you back what was abandoned to win it."[4]

According to Johnston's biographer, Robert Hughes, these two telegrams were models of military correspondence, expressing Johnston's entire theory of war, "the theory of concentration for decisive blows, regardless of danger to fixed points. In this case the operation recommended was so palpable that the only wonder is why Pemberton had not adopted it without waiting for suggestions."[5]

Port Hudson and Vicksburg had ceased to be of any value once the Federal fleet had bypassed them and was in possession of the Mississippi River, breaking Confederate communications with the Trans-Mississippi, the region west of the great river.

General Grant's troops were on the low ground at Bruinsburg, 2 miles from the bluff. He moved quickly, sending McClernand's corps on the only route to

Grand Gulf, leading inland along the high ground through the little town of Port Gibson, 12 miles east of Bruinsburg and 6 miles southeast of Grand Gulf.

General John S. Bowen

Commanding the Confederate forces at Grand Gulf was 32-year-old Brigadier General John S. Bowen, a cool and highly regarded officer, who decided to deploy his 5,500 men at Port Gibson, making good use of the rugged terrain in that area to confront Grant's twenty thousand. Bowen had deduced Grant's plan as early as April 20, four days after the boats had passed the batteries, and communicated it to Pemberton. If Pemberton had acted swiftly on Bowen's warning, leaving a small garrison at Vicksburg and moving most of his force to aid Bowen at Port Gibson, he would have outnumbered and likely defeated this portion of Grant's force and thus ended the threat to Vicksburg. But while Grant was dynamic and decisive, Pemberton was static and inert, holding fast to the environs of Vicksburg. Bowen was attacked on May 1, and after a magnificent fight against overwhelming odds was compelled to withdraw. The Confederate losses amounted to 832 men, while the Federals, according to official returns, suffered 875 casualties. Finding his position turned, Bowen spiked his guns, blew up his magazine, and abandoned Grand Gulf, which Grant occupied on May 3. Grant then decided on another plan, cutting loose from his base at Grand Gulf and marching into the interior. His troops were to carry with them little but ammunition and live off the subsistence of the countryside. He gathered an assortment of wagons for transport (farm wagons, fine carriages, surreys, buckboards, buggies, and carts drawn by assorted horses, mules, and oxen) and brought in farm animals from the surrounding area.

General Johnston was in the dark at Tullahoma. He did not receive dispatches from Pemberton until May 5, but they contained no information as to the movement of Grant's army nor the outcome of the battle near Port Gibson. When Johnston asked for clarification on these two points Pemberton replied providing no mention of Grant's forces, but indicated General Bowen was driven from the field at Port Gibson. Although Pemberton transmitted his own positions, cipher difficulties prevented an accurate translation.

On the evening of May 9, the Secretary of War sent the following dispatch to General Johnston at Tullahoma:

> Proceed at once to Mississippi and take chief command of the forces there, giving to those in the field, as far as practicable, the encouragement and benefit of your personal direction. Arrange to take for temporary service with you, or to be followed without delay, three thousand good troops who will be substituted in General Bragg's army by a large number

> of prisoners returned from the Arkansas Post capture, and reorganized, now on their way to General Pemberton. Stop them at the point most convenient to General Bragg.
>
> You will find reenforcements from General Beauregard to General Pemberton, and more may be expected. Acknowledge receipt.

Johnston replied at once: "Your dispatch this morning received. I shall go immediately, although unfit for field-service."[6]

"I Am Too Late"

General Johnston, accompanied by his physician, boarded a train at Tullahoma on the morning of May 10, heading for Jackson, Mississippi, about 300 miles away. He had to take a roundabout route through Atlanta, Montgomery, and Mobile, roughly doubling the distance, to avoid Federal threats on the direct routes, and did not arrive at Jackson until May 13, quite exhausted from the trip. Johnston set up his headquarters at the Bowman House Hotel in Jackson. Brigadier General John Gregg reported to Johnston that he had been ordered by Lieutenant General Pemberton to move from Port Hudson with his brigade of 2,500 men to Raymond, about 15 miles west of Jackson. At Raymond, on May 12, he became engaged with McPherson's ten-thousand-man XVII Corps, and after a spirited battle was driven back to Jackson, accompanied by the brigade of Brigadier General W. H. T. Walker from General Beauregard's department. Gregg had met Walker, who was marching to join him, at Mississippi Springs. On May 13, Johnston sent a dispatch to Secretary of War James Seddon: "I arrived this evening, finding the enemy's force between this place and General Pemberton, cutting off the communication. I am too late."

Regardless of him being too late, the Comte De Paris held General Johnston in high esteem:

> The news of the battle of Raymond decided Grant to modify his plans. In fact, Gregg would not have undertaken such a march to meet McPherson without feeling that he was well supported: the Federal commander had, moreover, just been informed that General Johnston, whose presence was worth a whole army, was expected at Jackson with the reinforcements sent from Tullahoma. He feared that McPherson was not strong enough alone to capture the capital of Mississippi, and he resolved to start eastward with all his forces in order to assist him.
>
> This movement had not been made a moment too soon, for, since the morning of the 13th, Grant had had a dangerous enemy before him; Johnston had arrived in Jackson. This illustrious chieftain, who had given evidence of his prowess at Bull Run and on the Virginia peninsula, had not exercised active command since the serious wound he had received in the preceding year on the battlefield of Fair Oaks. At the close of the year 1862, as we have stated, he had been invested with supreme authority, although purely nominal, over all the armies of the West. Mr. Davis was accused of not liking this general, so deservedly popular, but public opinion had imposed this choice upon him, which reduced Braxton Bragg and

> Pemberton, the supposed favorites of the President, to the rank of subordinates. Johnston, after having commanded ad interim Bragg's army for a few days in February, and inspected Vicksburg shortly after, had taken up his quarters at Chattanooga, where he very soon fell seriously ill, and had not quite recovered when the news of the battle of Port Gibson reached him. He understood at once the danger that Pemberton was incurring, and, judging of the situation from a wider and more correct point of view than the latter, telegraphed to him, "Concentrate all your forces to beat Grant: success will restore you what you have sacrificed to obtain it." If Pemberton had followed this advice, the issue of the campaign would probably have been different. At the same time Johnston received the tardy instructions of Mr. Davis, ordering him to proceed in person and direct the campaign against Grant; but, being still sick, he was not able to reach Jackson until the 13th of May, too late to join Pemberton.[7]

Forsaking Tennessee

General Pemberton was getting desperate and applied to the War Department to send General Bragg to his aid. But the Secretary of War, Seddon, responded that Bragg was under Johnston's command and Johnston must decide what course of action to take. Johnston's retort was that if Bragg came to Mississippi it meant forsaking Tennessee, which was a political question, not a military one, so the responsibility for this decision rested with the government. Johnston urged that Tennessee be retained, declaring it was "the shield of the South."

Johnston was hoping to build up his forces and would soon have eleven or twelve thousand at Jackson. Pemberton's army was at Edwards' Depot, 20 miles from Vicksburg, and his headquarters at Bovina, some 8 miles from Vicksburg. Pemberton's dispatch of May 12 led Johnston to believe that Grant's army was south of Edwards' Depot; a corps had been detached to seize Clinton Station and break Confederate communications, destroying the railroad tracks and telegraph wires. Johnston sent a note to Pemberton:

> I have lately arrived and learn that Major General Sherman is between us with four divisions at Clinton. It is important to re-establish communication, that you may be reinforced. If practicable, come up in his rear at once. To beat such a detachment would be of immense value. The troops here could cooperate. All the strength you can quickly assemble should be brought; time is all-important.

What he believed to be Sherman's corps was in reality two divisions of McPherson's corps. Johnston had his staff prepare his dispatch in triplicate and sent by three different couriers to ensure the message was delivered to Pemberton. One of the messengers was a Union spy who had been expelled from the city of Memphis by General Stephan A. Hurlbut, Grant's commander there. Hurlbut had publicly labeled the man disloyal to the Union and had him exiled. But the whole incident was staged. The spy rode straight to McPherson's lines, delivering Johnston's message to McPherson, who passed it on to Grant; it was then returned to the courier to carry to Pemberton. General Pemberton's answer was carried to Grant, then forwarded to Johnston.

Scouts reported both McPherson's XVII Corps and Sherman's XV Corps, 12 miles southwest of Jackson, were marching on Jackson. General Johnston, realizing he could not defend the city of Jackson with the two brigades available, determined to evacuate via the Canton road to the north. He left General Gregg to post the brigades of Brigadier General W. H. T. Walker and Colonel Peyton H. Colquitt astride the Clinton road, and the 3rd Kentucky Mounted Infantry Regiment and a handful of sharpshooters, to slow Sherman's approach. The resistance impeded the advance of the Federal troops and allowed time to remove military property and the money and archives of the state, sending them northward towards Canton via the Mississippi Central Railroad.

General Grant wanted to seize Jackson to break up the two rail lines passing through the city, preventing reinforcements from reaching Johnston and Pemberton. With Jackson being a manufacturing town, Grant ordered it to be torched, thus depriving the Confederates of vitally needed supplies. Northern journalist Sylvanus Cadwallader reported: "Foundries, machine shops, warehouses, factories, arsenals and public stores were fired as fast as flames could be kindled."[8] Sherman's soldiers tore up the railway tracks and twisted the heated rails around trees.

Pemberton called a council of war, composed of his general officers, at the camp of his army at Edwards' Depot to discuss Johnston's order. The majority of the council favored compliance with Johnston's order, while Generals Loring and Carter Stevenson suggested a movement to cut off Grant's supply line from the river, unaware that Grant was living off the country. Pemberton was in favor of remaining stationary. Pemberton decided to side with the minority and marched south upon Dillon's. Had Pemberton followed orders, he would have found that his only foe at Clinton was Hovey's division of XIII Corps, which he could have crushed or held in check with a small number of troops while he marched northeast to join Johnston.

Grant Feared Johnston

General Johnston's strategy was for a combination of all Confederate forces to oppose and destroy Grant's army. Johnston noted: "I am anxious to see a force assembled that may be able to inflict a heavy blow upon the enemy."[9] He maintained that geographical sites and important military positions had only a relative value in the ultimate objective of operations, which was to vanquish your adversary by a concentration of troops. This entailed the conservation of soldiers, who were irreplaceable and invaluable to the Confederacy, which had a much smaller manpower pool to draw from than the Federals. "General Grant told me," Sherman said, "that Johnston was about the only general on that side whom he feared."[10] Johnston was an excellent tactician and strategist, and Grant respected his abilities.

On May 15, 10 miles north of Jackson on the Canton road, Johnston sent Pemberton another letter: "Our being compelled to leave Jackson makes your plan impracticable. The only mode by which we can unite is by your moving directly to Clinton, informing me, that we may move at that point with about 6,000 troops."[11] This time, Pemberton decided to comply and had his army, which had covered only 6 miles southward, countermarch in response to Johnston's peremptory orders. While Pemberton was sluggish in his movements, Grant pursued a vigorous offensive to keep the two Confederate armies separated. He abandoned Jackson, ordering the destruction of the railroad bridge over the Pearl River, and advanced west towards Pemberton. Grant concentrated his forces against Pemberton, whom he intercepted near Baker's Creek at a hill on the farm of Sid Champion. Pemberton had twenty-three thousand men to oppose thirty-two thousand Federals of McClernand's and McPherson's corps in the battle of Baker's Creek, or Champion's Hill as the Federals named it. Although he put up a gallant contest, Pemberton suffered a devastating defeat, losing 3,839 killed, wounded, and missing, plus three thousand able-bodied prisoners and thirty pieces of artillery. Grant's losses amounted to 426 killed, 1,842 wounded, and 189 missing. Pemberton fell back to the Big Black River, where he was again attacked and hurled back to works around Vicksburg, 12 miles to the west. Grant occupied Snyder's Mill or Haynes Bluff, establishing a base on the Yazoo River, and thus successfully separated the two Confederate armies. Writing to Johnston from Bovina on May 17, Pemberton summarized events, adding: "I respectfully await your orders." He received the following communication from Johnston, written from a camp between Livingston and Brownsville, about noon on May 18:

> Your dispatch of to-day by Captain [Thomas] Henderson was received. If Haynes' Bluff is untenable, Vicksburg is of no value and cannot be held. If, therefore, you are invested in Vicksburg, you must ultimately surrender. Under such circumstances, instead of losing both troops and place, we must, if possible, save the troops. If it is not too late, evacuate Vicksburg and its dependencies, and march to the northeast.

In his official report, Pemberton expressed astonishment when he received these instructions: "The evacuation of Vicksburg! It meant the loss of the valuable stores and munitions of war collected for its defense; the fall of Port Hudson;

the surrender of the Mississippi River, and the severance of the Confederacy." He sent a reply to Johnston on May 18:

> On the receipt of your communication, I immediately assembled a council of war of the general officers of this command, and having laid your instructions before them, asked the free expression of their opinions as to the practicability of carrying them out. The opinion was unanimously expressed that it was impossible to withdraw the army from this position with such morale and material as to be of further service to the Confederacy. I have decided to hold Vicksburg as long as is possible with the firm hope that the Government may yet be able to assist me in keeping this obstruction to the enemy's free navigation of the Mississippi River. I still conceive it to be the most important point in the Confederacy.[12]

Johnston believed that Pemberton's estimate of the military value of Vicksburg may have been reasonable five or six weeks earlier, when the commanders of the Federal squadrons believed that its batteries were too powerful to be passed by their vessels-of-war. However, by now, "those batteries had been proved to be ineffective, for Admiral Porter's squadron had passed them, and in that way had made 'the severance of the Confederacy' before the end of April, that General Pemberton apprehended would be permitted, if he obeyed my order, to save his army by withdrawing it to the northeast, on the 18th of May."

Johnston replied to Pemberton's letter: "I am trying to gather a force which may attempt to relieve you. Hold out."[13] Grant attested that Vicksburg could have been evacuated and Pemberton's troops saved at this juncture:

> We were now assured of our position between Johnston and Pemberton, without the possibility of a junction of their forces. Pemberton might indeed have made a night march to the Big Black, crossed the bridge there, and, by moving north on the west side, have eluded us, and finally returned to Johnston. But this would have given us Vicksburg. It would have been his proper move, however, and the one Johnston would have made had he been in Pemberton's place. In fact, it would have been in conformity with Johnston's orders to Pemberton.[14]

Even as late as May 29, when Pemberton wrote to Johnston that escape from Vicksburg was impossible, two of the eight roads leading out of town were virtually unguarded by Grant's army, which would have allowed the Confederate army to vacate the city.

Secret Dispatch

President Jefferson Davis wanted to micromanage military operations and made decisions in Richmond which hampered his field commanders. At times he sent orders to subordinate commanders without consulting or informing their commanders. A most egregious example of this practice was conspicuous during the Vicksburg campaign. What Johnston did not know was that prior to his arrival at Jackson, Mississippi, Davis had sent private telegrams to General Pemberton without informing Johnston or clearing it with him, so as to diminish and undermine his authority to command and reduce his effectiveness. Edward A. Pollard of Virginia, editor of the *Richmond Examiner* during the war, reported that on May 7, Davis sent a secret dispatch to Pemberton as follows: "Want of transportation of supplies must compel the enemy to seek a junction with their fleet after a few days' absence from it. To hold both Vicksburg and Port Hudson is necessary to a connection with trans-Mississippi. You may expect whatever is in my power to do."

Here was a command superior to that of Johnston, which Pemberton was obliged to obey. He did so, in the spirit and in the letter. Whatever may have been the blunders that his inexperience in the field might have led him to commit, it cannot be said that he failed in fidelity to his trust; or that his disobedience to the orders of his immediate superior was not excused by the order which had come to him from the superior of both.

There was long an unpleasant suspicion in the Confederacy that President Davis had a secret and underhanded correspondence in the governing of military campaigns, writing to subordinate commanders and thus displacing or diminishing the authority of the commander in chief, whom he had nominally appointed. We shall see other remarkable instances of this disreputable interference with the conduct of armies in the field. But in the present case, the proof is in black and white, that Pemberton was the creature of Davis; that he was receiving secret instructions from him when all orders of the latter should have passed through Johnston, and the suggestion occurs that even the violation of this usual and respectful form must have involved a sinister purpose, and a dishonorable confidence, if not a positive conspiracy against the authority of Johnston. The latter was placed in the field to bear responsibility of a campaign which he never ordered, and the secret history of which remained at Richmond, to be disclosed or to be retained, according as the result might make to the credit or discredit of the military genius of the president.

Pollard had this to say of General Pemberton, who was an untried commander with no military experience:

> In all periods of the war there was a parcel of Confederate commanders known as "the President's Pets." The use of such a phrase shows how familiar was public sentiment in the South with the fact that the President was a man of prejudices, and how persistent in asserting them. One of these pets was John C. Pemberton. He was a native of Pennsylvania, and in the old Federal service had been a Captain without distinction. He had yet fought not a single battle in the Confederacy; he had not made one record of meritorious service therein; he had never commanded troops in action, not a regiment, not a company, not a man. By a single

> stroke of the pen Mr. Davis had made this man a Lieutenant-General, giving him one of the seven great commissions authorized by the Confederate Congress, over the heads of such men as Gustavus W. Smith, D. H. Hill, A. P. Hill, the brilliant young Southern Generals who had really done the fighting of the war. He was appointed to an independent post, no less than that of Charleston. Thence a great outcry of public opinion compelled the President to remove him; the story got out that General Pemberton had decided that this important city was untenable; he was accused of incompetency, treachery even was hinted, and Mr. Davis had to recall his favorite from a command barren of any action with the enemy, and fruitful only of disgraceful rumors. But the President had that evil temper which, forced to make some show of compliance to opposition, yet insults and defies it by making at the first opportunity an aggravation of the cause of complaint—actually defying public opinion, showing contempt for it, even taunting it by the very enlargement of the offence of which it dared to complain. This unhappy temper, this mean and spiteful resentment of public opinion will be found running through the whole of Mr. Davis's administration. Pemberton was removed from Charleston, only to receive strident promotion. The country saw with astonishment and dismay this untried commander—a man who had absolutely nothing to support him but the personal affection of Mr. Davis—placed over the Department of Mississippi and Louisiana, and in command at Vicksburg, the critical point of the Mississippi Valley, the Western correspondent to Richmond!
>
> No explanations but that of sheer obstinacy, can be possibly afforded for this choice by Mr. Davis of a commander for a post the second in importance in the Confederacy. But it is almost unaccountable, the degree of tenacity with which he clung to his favorite in the midst of a storm of public indignation. Delegations visited him with protests from the people, and army alike; the Legislature of his own State, Mississippi, passed resolutions complaining of the appointment. Outside the forms of public dissension, other agencies were employed upon the President by those who understood how narrow were his resolutions, and how accessible he was to paltry and irregular influences in conducting the public business. His brother Joseph Davis was induced to travel to Richmond, and to attempt to dissuade him from Pemberton. But all protests were unavailing, and the President had the invariable answer that he had discovered in Pemberton a great military genius; that his choice would be soon approved by brilliant victories; that the country had only to wait for the tests of his judgment. Mr. Davis might possibly have thought that he was acting for the public good; there is no bias which so easily eludes self-inspection, and at the same time is so patent to the world, as favoritism; yet even if the President had discovered a military jewel in this obscure man, even if Pemberton had been a mute Napoleon awaiting occasion, the thought should have occurred to Mr. Davis that the confidence of soldiers is an essential element in the success of a General, and that as long as his favorite lacked this he was not the man to command the second army of the Confederacy. It is a maxim in the science of military command that no matter what the cause of distrust of troops, the distrust itself is sufficient to disqualify the General for his position. And Pemberton's soldiers distrusted him from the moment he took command, to the time he marched them out to the field of surrender.[15]

On the very next day, May 8, Pemberton sent a telegram to Major General Franklin Gardner, in command of the troops at Port Hudson: "Return with 2,000 troops to Port Hudson, and hold it to the last. President says both places must be held."[16] As commander in chief, President Davis's directives superseded General Johnston's orders and frustrated his ability to manage the campaign effectively. On May 19, Johnston sent instructions by telegraph and courier to Major General Gardner to evacuate Port Hudson and move all his troops, field pieces with their ammunition, and means of transport towards Jackson since the investment of Vicksburg rendered his position of no value. Gardner did not comply and appealed for help on May 21. Johnston sent another courier and told Gardner: "You cannot be re-enforced. Do not allow yourself to be invested. At every risk save the troops, and, if practical, move in this direction."[17] But it was too late; the courier could not deliver the message as the Federals had placed Port Hudson under tight siege.

Fremantle

Reinforcements began to arrive at Canton, one of which was the division of Brigadier General States Rights Gist consisting of three weak brigades, in all about 5,500 troops. Accompanying them was a young British officer, Lieutenant Colonel Arthur James Lyon Fremantle of the Coldstream Guards, who was touring the Confederacy. The soldier-writer met General Johnston and made observations in his diary about his character. They had conversations and discussions on a wide range of topics. Fremantle jotted down his impressions of Johnston in his notes on May 20:

> General Gist and I cantered on in front of the column, and reached General Johnston's bivouac at 6 p.m.
>
> General Johnston received me with much kindness, when I presented my letters of introduction, and stated my object in visiting the Confederate armies.
>
> In appearance, General Joseph E. Johnston (commonly called Joe Johnston) is rather below middle height, spare, soldierlike, and well set up; his features are good, and he has lately taken to wear a grayish beard. He is Virginian by birth, and appears to be about fifty-seven years old.
>
> He talks in a calm, deliberate, and confident manner. To me he was extremely affable, but he certainly possesses the power of keeping people at a distance when he chooses, and his officers evidently stand in great awe of him. He lives very plainly, and at present his only cooking utensils consisted of an old coffeepot and frying pan—both very inferior articles. There was only one fork (one prong deficient) between himself and staff, and this was handed to me ceremoniously as the "guest."
>
> He has undoubtedly acquired the entire confidence of all the officers and soldiers under him. Many of the officers told me they did not consider him inferior as a general to Lee or anyone else.
>
> He told me that Vicksburg was certainly in a critical situation, and was now closely invested by Grant. He said that he (Johnston) had 11,000 men with him (which includes Gist's), hardly any cavalry, and only sixteen pieces of cannon; but if he could get adequate reinforcements, he stated his intention of endeavoring to relieve Vicksburg.

Fremantle found Johnston to be very knowledgeable about military history: "General Johnston is a very well-read man, and agreeable to converse with. He told me that he considered Marlborough a greater general than Wellington. All Americans have an intense admiration for Napoleon; they seldom scruple to express their regret that he was beaten at Waterloo."[18]

On May 23, Fremantle accompanied Johnston on a locomotive from Canton to Jackson, Mississippi, and recorded what they conversed about, including Johnston's view of the capabilities of Gen. Thomas Jonathan "Stonewall" Jackson:

> On the way we talked a good deal about "Stonewall" Jackson. General Johnston said that although this extraordinary man did not possess any great qualifications as a strategist, and was perhaps unfit for independent command of a large army, yet he was gifted with wonderful courage and determination, and a perfect faith in Providence that he was destined to destroy the enemy. He was much indebted to General Ewell in the Valley campaigns. "Stonewall" Jackson was also most fortunate in commanding the flower of the Virginian troops, and in being opposed to the most incapable Federal commanders, such as Fremont and Banks.
>
> Before we had proceeded twelve miles we were forced to stop and collect wood from the roadside to feed our engine. The General worked with so much energy as to cause his "Seven Pines" wound to give him pain.
>
> We were put out at a spot where the railroad was destroyed, at about four miles from Jackson. A carriage ought to have been in waiting for us, but by some mistake it had not arrived, so we had to foot it. I was obliged to carry heavy saddlebags. Major Eustis very kindly took my knapsack, and the General carried the cloaks. In this order we reached Jackson, much exhausted, at 9:30 a.m.
>
> General Loring came and reported himself soon after. He is a stout man with one arm. His division had arrived at Jackson from Crystal Springs about 6,000 strong; Evan's brigade, about 3,000, had also arrived from Charleston; and Maxey's brigade was in the act of marching into Jackson, I calculate, therefore, that General Johnston must now have nearly 25,000 men between Jackson and the Yahoo.[19]

General Grant tried assaults against the Vicksburg defenses with all his forces, which ended in bloody and fruitless conflicts. Grant decided on a different plan, conducting a regular siege and thereby incurring fewer losses. Their unsuccessful assaults, Grant said, "convinced officers and men that this was best, and they went to work on the defenses and approaches with a will. With the navy holding the river the investment of Vicksburg was complete. A long as we could hold our position, the enemy was limited in supplies of food, men and munitions of war, to what they had on hand. These could not last always."[20] According to his report, Grant had a force of 2,991 officers and 47,500 enlisted men on May 31, which stretched his army thin to cover the 12-mile investment that enclosed Vicksburg. In addition, he had to protect his rear from Johnston's attack. When an officer suggested that Johnston might enter Vicksburg with thirty thousand men to break the siege, Grant replied that the besieging Federal forces were the only troops who wanted to get into the city: "The rebels who are in now want to get out, and those who are out want to stay out. If Johnston tries to cut his way in we will let him do it, and then see that he don't get out. You say he has 30,000 men with him? That will give us 30,000 more prisoners than we now have."[21] General-in-Chief Henry W. Halleck complied with Grant's requests for reinforcements, sending large numbers to tighten the ring around the river port. Johnston's scouts estimated that the Federal army was receiving additions of approximately twenty thousand men. Indeed, by June 14, Grant's strength was raised to seventy-seven thousand. He divided his army into two, with forty-three thousand men under his personal command in lines of contravallation surrounding the Vicksburg defenses to keep Pemberton trapped and another thirty-four thousand men under Sherman in lines of circumvallation to prevent interference by Johnston. Grant's report listed 4,412 officers and 70,866 enlisted men present for duty as of June 30.

Johnston was trying in every way he could to gather a force at Jackson large enough to threaten Grant and Sherman, allowing Pemberton to evacuate Vicksburg and save his army. But Johnston had numerous obstacles to overcome to make this happen:

> All supplies that had been collected in the department were, of course, with the troops in Vicksburg and Port Hudson.
>
> The troops coming from the East, by railroad, had brought neither artillery nor wagons. Frequent drafts upon the country had so much reduced the number of horses and mules, that it was not until the end of June that artillery and wagons, and draught-animals enough for them, could be procured, generally from long distances—most of the artillery and wagons from Georgia. Some twelve pieces, found without carriages, were mounted on such as could be made in Canton.
>
> There was want of provision and forage in the department, but they were still to be collected; and we had small means of collecting them, and none of transporting them with a moving army.[22]

Johnston appealed to Richmond to draw troops from throughout the Confederacy to augment his army. He wired General Cooper on May 25: "It is important that I should know what troops to expect. Please inform me and have them urged on; they come too slowly." That night he telegraphed again: "Of the 10,000 men promised from Carolina and Georgia, but 6,500 have arrived. Do urge them forward."[23] By the first week in June, Johnston had only twenty-three thousand men under his command to assault Grant. Adding to the predicament, his army lacked the means of operating for more than four days away from the railroads. Johnston told Secretary of War James

Seddon on June 10: "I have not at my [disposal] half the number of troops necessary." On June 15, he again telegrammed Seddon:

> I cannot advise in regard to the points from which troops can best be taken, having no means of knowing, nor is it for me to judge which is best to hold—Mississippi or Tennessee; that is for the Government to determine. Without some great blunder of the enemy we cannot hold both. The odds against me are much greater than those you express. I consider saving Vicksburg hopeless.

This message alarmed Seddon, who replied the next day: "Vicksburg must not be lost without a desperate struggle. The interest and honor of the Confederacy forbid it. I rely on you still to avert the loss. If better resources do not offer, you must hazard attack. It may be made in concert with the garrison, if practicable, but otherwise without, by day or night, as you think best."[24] Grant wrote long afterwards that he thought Johnston did not wish to "sacrifice the lives of his soldiers in a useless gamble": "Johnston evidently took in the situation, and wisely, I think, abstained from making an assault on us because it would simply have inflicted loss on both sides without accomplishing any result."[25]

Longstreet's Plan

In the meantime, as General Longstreet arrived in Richmond on May 6 from his Suffolk campaign, he stopped in at the War Office to see James Seddon and then Robert E. Lee, discussing matters relating to the situation of Pemberton's forces holed up at Vicksburg and how best to go to their aid:

> He informed me that he had in contemplation a plan for concentrating a succoring army at Jackson, Mississippi, under the command of General Johnston, with a view of driving Grant from before Vicksburg by a direct issue-at-arms. He suggested that possibly my corps might be needed to make the army strong enough to handle Grant, and asked me my views. I replied that there was a better plan, in my judgment, for relieving Vicksburg than by a direct assault upon Grant. I proposed that the army then concentrating at Jackson, Mississippi, be moved swiftly to Tullahoma, where General Bragg was then located with a fine army, confronting an army of equal strength under General Rosecrans, and that at the same time the two divisions of my corps be hurried forward to the same point. The simultaneous arrival of these reinforcements would give us a grand army at Tullahoma. With this army General Johnston might speedily crush Rosecrans, and that he should then turn his force toward the north, and with his splendid army march through Tennessee and Kentucky, and threaten the invasion of Ohio. My idea was that, in the march through those States, the army would meet no organized obstruction; would be supplied with provisions and even reinforcements by those friendly to our cause, and would inevitably result in drawing Grant's army from Vicksburg to look after and protect his own territory. Mr. Seddon adhered to his original views; not so much, I think, from his great confidence in them, as from the difficulty of withdrawing the force suggested from General Lee's army. I was very thoroughly impressed with the practicality of the plan, however, and when I reached General Lee I laid it before

> him with the freedom justified by our close personal and official relations. The idea seemed a new one to him, but he was evidently seriously impressed with it. We discussed it over and over, and I discovered that his main objection to it was that it would, if adopted, force him to divide his army. He left no room to doubt, however, that he believed the idea of an offensive campaign was not only important, but necessary.
>
> At length, while we were discussing the idea of a western forward movement, he asked me if I did not think an invasion of Maryland and Pennsylvania by his own army would accomplish the same result, and I replied that I did not see that it would, because this movement would be too hazardous, and the campaign in thoroughly Union States would require more time and greater preparation than one through Tennessee and Kentucky. I soon discovered that he was determined that he would make some forward movement.[26]

Skillful Use of Our Interior Lines

General Lee started planning the campaign that would lead him to Gettysburg. Longstreet's plan was more feasible than what Lee proposed in that many of the South's railroads converged in Tennessee, allowing for rapid transit and quick concentration. As there was no railroad going north into Pennsylvania, wagons had to be relied on to haul provisions and ammunition over a long and tenuous supply line and prevented the speedy movement of troops. Longstreet stated:

> It was manifest before the war was accepted that the only way to equalize the contest was by skillful use of our interior lines, and this was so impressed by two years' experience that it seemed time to force it upon the Richmond authorities. But foreign intervention was the ruling idea with the President, and he preferred that as the easiest solution of all problems.
>
> The only objection offered by the Secretary was that Grant was such an obstinate fellow that he could only be induced to quit Vicksburg by terribly hard knocks.
>
> On the contrary, I claimed that he was a soldier, and would obey the calls of his government, but was not lightly to be driven from his purpose.[27]

General Pemberton

On May 13, at the time Longstreet and Lee were discussing strategy to save Vicksburg, Longstreet wrote a letter to Texas senator Louis Wigfall of the Senate Military Affairs Committee—Longstreet's and Johnston's friend, confidant, and supporter. Longstreet imparted to Wigfall that Lee was considering an advance into Pennsylvania which would dash any plans of a western campaign. He intimated to Wigfall that Seddon had requested Lee release Pickett's division from Longstreet's corps to be sent directly to Pemberton in Vicksburg to bolster his force. Longstreet believed this was a waste of manpower, and that more than a division or two was needed: "We need all that we have and even the five thousand sent to Pemberton from Charleston. Grant seems to be a fighting man, and seems to be determined to fight. Pemberton seems not to be a fighting man. If he does not desire to fight the fewer troops he has the better." Longstreet did not want to lose any troops trying to hold Vicksburg which he perceived as worthless: "We would then be no worse cut off from the West than we are now."[28]

By the end of June, Johnston had formed an army of twenty-six thousand men:

> On the 28th, the necessary supplies and field transportation having been procured, the equipment of the artillery completed, and a serviceable floating-bridge finished (the first constructed having proved a failure), the army was ordered to march next morning toward the Big Black River.
>
> This expedition was not undertaken in the wild spirit that dictated the dispatches from the War Department, of the 16th and 21st of June. I did not indulge in "the sentiment" that it was better for me to waste the lives and blood of brave soldiers, "than, through prudence even" to spare them; and therefore intended to make such close and careful examination of the enemy's lines as might enable me to estimate the probability of our being able to break them; and, should the chances of success seem to justify it, attack in the hope of breaking them, and rescuing the army invested in Vicksburg. There was no hope of saving the place by raising the siege.
>
> In providing the means necessary for this expedition, I had looked to the employment of at least three days in reconnaissance, and thought it necessary to provide food and wagons for the Vicksburg troops, who, if the attempt to extricate them should prove successful, might be expected to join us with no other supplies than the ammunition in their cartridge-boxes.

Johnston wrote that reconnaissance between July 2 and 4 convinced him that no attack could be made against Federals position north of the railroad, confirming previous reports that the besiegers were protected by a series of fieldworks, extending from the railroad bridge to the Yazoo River. Roads leading to this line were found to be obstructed by felled trees, with strong forces of Federal infantry and cavalry guarding the river. Johnston continued:

> I determined to move on the morning of the 5th, by Edwards's Depot, to the south of the road—thinking, from the reports of the officers, who had reconnoitered on that side, that the Federal works there were less strong, and the river unguarded, and the chances of success, therefore, much better on that side; although the consequences of defeat would have been much more disastrous, as General Sherman's troops, in the line between the bridge and the Yahoo, might have intercepted retreat.
>
> On the 3d a courier from Vicksburg arrived, but without dispatches from General Pemberton. He had been in such danger of capture, he said, as to think it necessary to destroy the letter he was bringing. He had left Vicksburg on the 28th of June, and the letter had that date. In a note dispatched at night General Pemberton was informed of this; and told we were about to attempt to create a diversion, to enable him to cut his way out of the place, and hoped to attack the enemy, for this object, on the 7th.
>
> But, in the evening of the 4th, intelligence of the surrender of Vicksburg was received; in consequence of which the army fell back to Jackson, which it reached on the afternoon of the 7th.[29]

Vicksburg Surrenders

Pemberton had written to Johnston that his provisions would only last until July 10, and that he must surrender due to starvation if Johnston did not act by then. On July 3, Johnston replied that Pemberton's dispatches of June 28 had been destroyed by the messenger, but his account of conditions at Vicksburg had convinced Johnston that he should create a diversion to enable Pemberton's forces to cut their way out, if able to do so. Johnston wrote: "I hope to attack the enemy in your front [on] the 7th, and your co-operation will be necessary. The manner and the proper point for you to bring the garrison out must be determined by you, from your superior knowledge of the ground and distribution of the enemy's forces. Our firing will show you where we are engaged. If Vicksburg cannot be saved, the garrison must [be]."[30] Pemberton never received Johnston's letter, opening negotiations with Grant on July 3 to surrender Vicksburg. On July 1, Pemberton had sent a confidential note to his four division commanders—Major Generals John S. Bowen, Carter L. Stevenson, John H. Forney, and Martin Luther Smith—requesting their opinion as to the condition of their soldiers. He stated that unless the siege was raised or supplies were received, it would soon be necessary to mount an evacuation: "I see no prospect of the former, and there are many great, if not insuperable, obstacles in the way of the latter. You are, therefore, requested to inform me with as little delay as possible as to the condition of your troops, and their ability to make the marches and undergo the fatigues necessary to accomplish a successful evacuation." All answered in the negative, saying the soldiers were not in any shape for the exertion required. Pemberton thus surrendered Vicksburg on July 4.

Johnston wired the news of Vicksburg's surrender to Richmond after word of the capitulation reached him on July 4, and had his troops occupy the minor line of fieldworks constructed on Pemberton's orders for the defense of Jackson. These works consisted of a line of rifle pits, with occasional low embankments to cover fieldpieces, from north of the town and east of the Canton road to a point near the Pearl River to the south "These intrenchments were very badly located and constructed, and offered very slight obstacle to a vigorous assault," Johnston discerned.[31] With the fall of Vicksburg, Johnston knew Grant would turn his forces against his small army. The weather was hot and dry, it had not rained for weeks, and small streams and ponds had dried up. Johnston ordered his troops to foul the few wells in the area, depriving the Federals of water to carry on a siege. On July 9, while at Jackson, Johnston received information of the capitulation of Port Hudson. Early on the morning of July 9, Sherman arrived before the Confederate works at Jackson with an army of approximately fifty thousand soldiers, consisting of the IX, XIII, and XV Corps, with two additional divisions. Johnston expected the Federal army would be compelled to make an immediate assault and felt assured that his confident troops, fighting behind entrenchments, would decisively repel any attack. However, the Federals entrenched and began to construct battery emplacements. The Federal army was held at bay until heavy rains fell, providing a water ration, soon after which Grant assembled two hundred pieces of artillery to shell the city. On July 14, Johnston's scouts brought word that a large train, loaded with artillery ammunition, had left Vicksburg by the Jackson road to supply Grant's guns. Johnston sent out his cavalry under Brigadier General William H. Jackson to intercept the ammunition train, but the attempt failed. Unable to stand a siege for want of provisions, and recognizing that the position would become untenable under powerful artillery bombardment, Johnston evacuated Jackson on the night of July 16, marching his army to Morton, Mississippi, about 35 miles to the east, where they halted on July 20. Johnston's losses in Jackson were 71 killed, 504 wounded, and 25 missing. Federal casualties amounted to 129 killed, 762 wounded, and 231 missing.

On July 13, Senator Wigfall wrote to Senator C. C. Clay of Alabama that the criticism of Lee after his defeat at Gettysburg—just a day before the capitulation at Vicksburg—had created increased resentment in President Jefferson Davis, who was denouncing Johnston

> in the most violent manner … & attributing the fall of Vicksburg to him & to him alone, regretting that he had been sent to the West & accusing himself of weakness in yielding to outside influence etc. His opinion of Johnston had undergone no change. His utter want of capacity he had always known etc. Has it ever occurred to you that Davis' mind is becoming unsettled? No sane man would act as he is doing. I fear that his bad health & bad temper are undermining his reason & that the foundation is already sapped. God knows what is to become of us with such a man at the head of the government.

Edward Pollard, editor of the *Richmond Examiner*, wrote an open and ironic article on July 10 about rumors he heard around Richmond. He stated: "No one here is yet acquainted with the circumstances which attended and preceded the fall of Vicksburg, but the blame is Johnston's. He did it—Who can suppose, even for a moment, that the fortunate, victorious, heaven-born Pemberton could have done the wrong?"[32]

CHAPTER 15

Condemnation over the Surrender of Vicksburg

With the capitulation of Vicksburg and Lee's defeat at Gettysburg, July 1863 was a distressing month for the Confederacy. Robert Kean, head of the Bureau of War, wrote in his diary: "God help this unhappy country." Late in July, Adjutant General Samuel Cooper telegrammed Joseph Johnston that he was relieved from the command of the Department of Tennessee, which included Bragg's army, in accordance with his repeated requests. This reduced Johnston's responsibility to the Department of Mississippi, which encompassed the states of Alabama and Mississippi.

While Johnston was at Mobile, Alabama, to inspect its defenses on July 28, Colonel Frank Schaller, traveling from Richmond, handed him a 15-page letter written by President Davis on July 15 that harshly reviewed Johnston's connection with the Vicksburg campaign. Johnston replied on August 8, defending himself and refuting every charge Davis made. When Johnston's wife, Lydia, heard of this, she wrote to Mrs. Charlotte Wigfall—wife of Senator Wigfall—that the president's missive was "a letter of 15 pages of such insults as only a coward or a woman could write. I wish it could be published along with his pious proclamations."

Early in August, President Davis directed that a court of inquiry—composed of Generals Robert Ransom Jr., Howell Cobb, and John Echols—should assemble at Montgomery to "inquire into the events of the campaigns of Mississippi and eastern Louisiana during the months of May, June, and July last, and especially as to the surrender of Vicksburg, of Port Hudson, and the evacuation of Jackson."[1]

The court never convened, probably because the government knew its case was on shaky ground and blame would be placed on Davis and his administration.

In mid-September, Davis replied to Johnston's letter of August 8, writing in a conciliatory manner but holding to his earlier contentions that Johnston was at fault. Johnston described the letter as "the coolest piece of impudence I have ever read."[2] President Davis had telegraphed Pemberton on July 27 to make his official report "promptly and fully," which Pemberton did on August 25, sending it directly to Cooper and Davis, bypassing Johnston. Pemberton's report placed all responsibility for the surrender of Vicksburg on Johnston's bad decisions. Senator Wigfall wrote to Johnston from Richmond: "Let me warn you against Pemberton. The moment he was whipped at Edward's station he wrote to the President that he had made the fight against his own judgment & under positive orders from you."[3] After much difficulty, Johnston obtained a copy of Pemberton's report and responded on November 10. Johnston regretfully stated:

> It is a new military principle that, when an officer disobeys a positive order of his superior, that superior becomes responsible for any measure his subordinate may choose to substitute for that ordered; but had the battle of Baker's Creek not been fought, General Pemberton's belief that Vicksburg was his base rendered his ruin inevitable. He would still have been besieged, and, therefore, captured. The larger force he would have carried into the lines would have added to, and hastened, the catastrophe. His disasters were due not merely to his entangling himself with the advancing columns of a superior and unobserved enemy, but to his evident determination to be besieged in Vicksburg, instead of maneuvering to prevent a siege.
>
> In this report I have been compelled to enter into many details, and to make some animadversion upon the conduct of General Pemberton. The one was no pleasant task; the other a most painful duty. Both have been forced upon [me] by the official report of General Pemberton, made to the War Department instead of me, to whom it was due.
>
> General Pemberton, by direct assertion and by implication, puts upon me the responsibility of the movements which led his army to defeat at Baker's Creek and the Big Black Bridge; defeats which produced the loss of Vicksburg and its army.
>
> This statement has been circulated by the press in more or less detail, and with more or less marks of an official character, until my silence would be almost an acknowledgement of the justice of the charge.
>
> A proper regard for the good opinion of my Government has compelled me, therefore, to throw aside that delicacy which I would gladly have observed toward a brother officer suffering much undeserved obloquy, and to show that in his short campaign General Pemberton made not a single movement in obedience to my orders and regarded none of my instructions, and, finally, did not embrace the only opportunity to save his army—that given by my order to abandon Vicksburg.[4]

The responsibility for the fall of Vicksburg was not Johnston's, nor Pemberton's, but rested squarely on the Confederate administration, particularly on the shoulders of President Jefferson Davis. When Davis sent his secret dispatch to Pemberton, instructing him to hold both Vicksburg and Port Hudson; Pemberton—who allowed his army to be trapped inside Vicksburg—was compelled to obey Davis's superior command, which superseded and conspired against the authority of his commander in chief, General Joseph Johnston. Newspaper editor Edward Pollard asserted: "The latter [Johnston] was placed in the field to bear the responsibility of a campaign which he never ordered, and the secret history of which remained at Richmond, to be disclosed or to be retained, according as the result might make to the credit or discredit of the military genius of Mr. Davis."[5] Johnston knew nothing of this at the time.

Poor Strategy

Johnston reflected on the poor strategy devised by the Confederate Government which led to the loss of Vicksburg and Pemberton's army. In early July 1862, he stated, Federal general-in-chief General Halleck had transferred General Buell and his troops to central Tennessee, leaving Ulysses Grant in command of those holding northeast Mississippi and southwest Tennessee. Grant's forces, deployed around Corinth, Memphis, and Jackson, had, in President Davis's estimation, numbered about forty-two thousand men fit for duty. Johnston continued:

> Their wide dispersion put them at the mercy of any superior or equal force, such as the Confederacy could have bought against them readily; but this opportunity, such a one as has rarely occurred in war, was put aside by the Confederate Government, and the army which, properly used, would have secured to the South the possession of Tennessee and Mississippi was employed in a wild expedition into Kentucky, which could have had only resulted in a raid.
>
> Mr. Davis extols the strategy of that operation, which, he says, "manoeuvred the foe out of a large and to us important territory." This advantage, if it could be called so, was of the briefest. For this "foe" drove us out of Kentucky in a few weeks, and recovered permanently the "large and to us important territory." After General Bragg was compelled to leave Kentucky, the Federal army, which until then had been commanded by General Buell, was established at Nashville, under General Rosecrans. And General Bragg, by a very circuitous route through south-eastern Kentucky and north-eastern Tennessee, brought his troops to the neighborhood of Murfreesboro'.[6]

Johnston thought that instead of raiding Kentucky, Bragg's army could have been used more effectively in smashing up the Union garrisons in Tennessee, thus curtailing Grant's attack on Vicksburg and securing Tennessee with its vital resources so important to the Confederacy. Bragg's army consisted of forty-four thousand soldiers, while the Federal army was a little less than forty-two thousand and widely scattered.

Meanwhile, on August 16, General Rosecrans opened his offensive to take Chattanooga and successfully outmaneuvered General Bragg by threatening his communications along the Western and Atlantic Railroad to Atlanta, forcing

Bragg to abandon the city on September 7. In mid-August, Longstreet wrote to the Secretary of War, reiterating his call for a concentration in Tennessee to defeat Rosecrans, as he had advocated in May:

> While the army was lying idle on the south bank of the Rapidan my mind reverted to affairs in the West, and especially to the progressive work of the Union army in Tennessee towards the northern borders of Georgia. Other armies of the South were, apparently spectators, viewing those tremendous threatenings without thought of turning minds or forces to arrest the march of Rosecrans.
>
> To me the emergency seemed so grave that I decided to write the Honorable Secretary of War (excusing the informality under the privilege given in his request in May) expressing my opinion of affairs in that military zone. I said that the successful march of General Rosecrans's army through Georgia would virtually be the finishing stroke of the war; that in the fall of Vicksburg and the free flow of the Mississippi River the lungs of the Confederacy were lost; that the impending march would cut through the heart of the South, and leave but little time for the dissolution; that to my mind the remedy was to order the Army of Northern Virginia to defensive work, and send detachments to reinforce the army of Tennessee; to call detachments of other commands to the same service, and strike a crushing blow against General Rosecrans before he could receive reinforcing help; that our interior lines gave the opportunity, and it was only by skilful use of them that we could reasonably hope to equalize our power to that of the better-equipped adversary; that the subject had not been mentioned to my commander, because like all others he was opposed to having important detachments of his army so far beyond his reach; that all must realize that our affairs were languishing, and that the only hope of reviving the waning cause was through the advantage of interior lines.[7]

Longstreet was ordered to send two divisions, those of McLaws and Hood, and Alexander's battalion of artillery of 26 guns to Bragg, for which General Lee had the quartermaster general prepare transportation on September 6. Buckner arrived from East Tennessee with nine thousand men. General Johnston sent twelve thousand troops to assist Bragg, which included half of his infantry, comprised of two divisions commanded by Major Generals John C. Breckinridge and W. H. S. Walker—some 9,000 troops—leaving him only 8,700 to defend his department. Johnston, who felt that the War Department had finally accepted the principles of concentration of force for which he had long advocated, urged that he should be included in the coming battle.

Battle of Chickamauga

The battle of Chickamauga resulted in a Confederate victory but at a heavy cost, driving Rosecrans and his Army of the Cumberland in a hasty retreat back to Chattanooga. But Bragg did not follow Longstreet's sound advice to threaten Rosecrans's communications and force him out of Chattanooga and

Middle Tennessee; instead, he settled down for a siege of the city. The diarist Mary Chesnut lamented Bragg's methods:

> Bragg—thanks to Longstreet and Hood, he won Chickamauga. So we looked (for) results that would pay for our losses in battles, at least. Certainly they would capture Rosecrans. No! There sits Bragg—a good dog howling on his hind legs before Chattanooga, a fortified town—and some Yankee Holdfast grinning at him from his impregnable heights. Waste of time.
>
> How?
>
> He always stops to quarrel with his generals.[8]

After the battle, Bragg antagonized his generals and had a greater desire to wage war upon his own officers than Rosecrans's army at Chattanooga. Bragg targeted Hindman for failing to trap General James Negley's division at McLemore's Cove on September 11, and Polk for not attacking at daylight on September 20 at Chickamauga. On September 29, Bragg sacked Major General Thomas C. Hindman and Lt. Gen. Leonidas Polk from their commands and banished them to Atlanta to await further orders. Polk, Longstreet, D. H. Hill, and Buckner had met secretly on September 26 to oust Bragg, who they believed was incompetent to lead the Army of Tennessee in battle and had squandered the fruits of victory by not driving Rosecrans from Chattanooga. Polk and Longstreet, being the most influential in Richmond, were designated to initiate a letter-writing campaign. Longstreet wrote to Secretary of War Seddon on September 26:

> Sir: May I take the liberty to advise you of our conditions and our wants? On the 20th instant, after a very severe battle, we gained a complete and glorious victory—the most complete victory of the war, except perhaps, the first Manassas. On the morning of the 21st General Bragg asked my opinion as to our best course. I suggested at once to strike Burnside, and if he made his escape to march upon Rosecrans' communications in the rear of Nashville. He seemed to adopt the suggestion, and gave the order to march at 4 o'clock in the afternoon. The Right Wing of the army marched some 8 or 10 miles, my command following the next day at daylight. I was halted at the crossing of the Chickamauga, and on the night of the 22d the army was ordered to march for Chattanooga, thus giving the enemy two days and a half to strengthen the fortifications here already prepared for him by ourselves. Here we remained under instructions that the enemy shall not be assaulted. To express my convictions in a few words, our chief has done but one thing that he ought to have done since I joined his army. That was to order the attack upon the 20th. All other things that he has done he ought not to have done. I am convinced that nothing but the hand of God can save or help us as long as we have our present commander.
>
> Now to our wants. Can't you send us General Lee? The army in Virginia can operate defensively, while our operations here should be offensive—until we have recovered Tennessee, at all events. We need some such great mind as General Lee's (nothing more) to accomplish this. You will be surprised to learn that this army has neither organization nor mobility, and I have doubts if its commander can give it them. In an ordinary war I could serve without

> complaint under any one whom the Government might place in authority, but we have too much at stake in this to remain quiet under such distressing circumstance. Our most precious blood is now flowing in streams from the Atlantic to the Rocky Mountains, and may yet be exhausted before we have succeeded. Then goes honor, treasure and independence. When I came here I hoped to find our commander willing and anxious to do all things that would aid us in our great cause, and ready to receive what aid he could get from his subordinates. It seems that I was greatly mistaken. It seems he cannot adopt and adhere to any plan or course, whether of his own or of some one else. I desire to impress upon your mind that there is no exaggeration in these statements. On the contrary, I have failed to express my convictions to the fullest extent. All that I can add without making this letter exceedingly long is to pray you to help us, and speedily.[9]

On October 4, a formal petition was sent to President Jefferson Davis by Longstreet, Polk, Daniel Harvey Hill, Simon Buckner, and eight other generals commanding divisions or brigades, calling for Bragg's removal. The document was carefully worded to avoid mention of Bragg's military failings, which might be interpreted as mutinous. The petitioners said that "The fruits of victory at Chickamauga have now escaped our grasp" and the army was "stricken with complete paralysis." They blamed "the condition of his health unfits him for the command of an army in the field." Bragg got wind of the petition, which, in the words of Brigadier General William Whann Mackall, his chief of staff, "caused him much distress and mortification."

In exile at Atlanta, General Polk, the Episcopal Bishop of Louisiana, wrote Davis a letter on October 6, expounding on the dissatisfaction with Bragg:

> I wrote you on the 27th renewing the expression of my opinion of the incapacity of General Bragg for the responsible office of commander-in-chief of the Army of Tennessee, and asking that he should be replaced by General Lee or some other. It is proper to add that that letter was written after a meeting by appointment of Lieutenant-Generals Longstreet, Hill, and myself to consider what should be done in view of the palpable weakness and mismanagement manifested in the conduct of the military operations of this army. It was agreed that I should address you, sir, and General Longstreet the Secretary of War on the subject. These letters were written and forwarded, and, I need not add, after mature deliberation. General Hill concurred in the necessity of this measure.

Polk claimed that had an attack been launched at daybreak then Chattanooga would have been taken after the Federal army was defeated, blaming Bragg's failure to do so for all subsequent delays and problems. He continued:

> To make this affirmation good, it must be shown that at the close of the battle that night, a condition of things was developed which made pursuit impossible, and that it was equally hopeless next morning. This will not be pretended, inasmuch as the troops at the close of the fight were in very high spirits, ready for any service, and the moon, by whose guidance the enemy fled the field, was never brighter—as bright to guide us in pursuit as the enemy in their flight. Besides, if the commanding general, under a delusion he took no pains to dispel,

> thought the troops were fatigued and chose to put off pursuit until the morning, why did he not attempt it then? Was it because he had made the discovery that the enemy had made his retreat into Chattanooga in good order, and that he was secure behind fortifications? No, sir; General Bragg did not know what had happened, and allowed the whole fruits of this great victory to pass from him by the most criminal negligence, or, rather, incapacity, for there are positions in which weakness is wickedness. If there be a man in public service who should be held to a more rigid accountability for failures, and upon the largest scale, than another, that man is General Bragg, that I may have the opportunity not only vindicating my own conduct, but of establishing the truth and justice of what I have written of his lack of capacity as a commanding general.[10]

President Davis was disturbed by the suspension of Polk and Hindman, and by Bragg's refusal to drop the charges and reinstate them. Davis sent his aide-de-camp, Colonel James Chesnut—husband of famed diarist Mary Chesnut—on a tour of the western theater to check out the situation. Chesnut stopped in Atlanta on October 3 to talk with Polk, then went north near Chattanooga to speak with Longstreet. On October 5, Chesnut, finding intense feeling against Bragg, telegraphed Davis: "Your immediate presence in this army is urgently demanded. Come, if possible." On the same day, Bragg telegraphed Davis to intercede.

President Davis Detested General Johnston

Mary Chesnut recorded in her diary: "J. C. [James Chesnut] said he told Mr. Davis that every honest man he saw out west thought well of Joe Johnston. He knows the president detests Joe Johnston for all the trouble he has given him. And General Joe returns the compliment with compound interest. Joe Johnston advancing, or retreating, I may say with more truth, is magnetic. He does draw the goodwill of those by whom he is surrounded."[11]

President Davis decided to board a train and see for himself, arriving at Bragg's headquarters on October 9. Davis was completely out of touch with affairs in the western theater, for he brought with him Lt. Gen. John C. Pemberton, who had just surrendered Vicksburg, as Polk's replacement. Davis met with Bragg in private on the afternoon of October 9. Bragg offered his resignation, which Davis refused to accept, assuring Bragg that he would not be relieved of command. That night, Davis called a meeting of the corps commanders at Bragg's headquarters, ostensibly to discuss future military operations. Davis went off topic and asked each to comment on Bragg's fitness to command. Longstreet spoke first and made some biting remarks about Bragg, who was present, saying that he "was incompetent to manage an army or put men into a fight," adding that he "knew nothing of the business" and "that our commander could be of greater service elsewhere than at the head of the Army of Tennessee."[12] The other commanders gave similar opinions. Lieutenant Colonel Moxley Sorrel set the tone of the meeting:

> Mr. Davis made his celebrated visit to the camp to see and hear for himself. It is difficult, even now, to recall and realize that unprecedented scene. The President, with the commander-in-chief, and the great officers of the army, assembled to hear the opinion of the General's fitness for command. In the presence of Bragg and his corps commanders he asked each his opinion, and his reasons if adverse. This was eye to eye with the President, the commander-in-chief and the generals. There was no lack of candor in answer to such challenge with men like Longstreet, Cheatham, Hill, Cleburne, and Stewart. Some very plain language was used in answer, but it seems that one and all were quite agreed as to Bragg's unfitness for command of that army. These opinions were received by the President and his general without comment, and Mr. Davis got more than he came for.[13]

On the next day, October 10, Davis had a lengthy private conversation with Longstreet, to whom he wished to offer command of the army, but Longstreet felt the time for handling the army as an independent force had passed, believing it should come under Johnston's command:

> Regarding this question, as considered in Virginia, it was understood that the assignment would be made at once, and in time for opportunity to handle the army sufficiently to gain the confidence of the officers and soldiers before offering or accepting battle. The action was not taken, a battle had been made and won, the army was then seriously entangled in a quasi siege, the officers and soldiers were disappointed, and disaffected in morale. General Grant was moving his army to reinforce against us, and an important part of the Union army of Virginia was moving to the same purpose.
>
> In my judgment our last opportunity was lost when we failed to follow the success at Chickamauga, and capture or disperse the Union army, and it could not be just to the service or myself to call me to a position of such responsibility. The army was part of General Joseph E. Johnston's department, and could only be used in strong organization by him in combining its operations with his other forces in Alabama and Mississippi. I said that under him I could cheerfully work in any position. The suggestion of that name only served to increase his displeasure, and his severe rebuke.[14]

Longstreet's suggestion to have Johnston in command was supported by Bragg's chief of staff, Brigadier General Mackall, who wrote to his wife shortly after Chickamauga: "If Mr. D. [Davis] would send [Johnston] here, his presence here would be worth ten thousand men to this army, but [Davis] won't see with his eyes. With an empire at stake, and the happiness of the whole people, he will indulge like a spoiled child his prejudices."[15]

Fortunately, Davis did not press for Pemberton's reinstatement to command. Hardee warned Davis in August that Pemberton was too unpopular to serve with the Mississippi army, and Governor John Pettus of Mississippi forwarded a report that the parolees from Vicksburg and Port Hudson would not serve under Pemberton. John B. Jones, a senior clerk in the War Department, made this entry in his diary: "October 12th. Hon. G. A. Henry, Senator from Tennessee writes to the Secretary [Seddon] that it is rumored that Gen. Pemberton is to command Gen. Polk's corps in Tennessee. He says if this be true, it will be disastrous; that the Tennessee troops will not serve under him, but will mutiny and desert."[16] On October 13, Mackall gave Joseph Johnston an update on Davis's visit:

> Mr. D. [Davis] arrived on Friday, and goes to-day, it is said by his staff, on a visit to you.
>
> He has decided to retain Bragg, though he must have been fully satisfied of his unpopularity and the decided opposition of the mass of the generals. I think Longstreet has done more injury to the general than all the others put together. You may understand how much influence with his troops a remark from a man of his standing would have to the effect that B. was not on the field and Lee would have been.
>
> Pemberton consulted me about staying here in command of a corps. I told him that there was not a division in this army that would be willing to receive him; that I was sorry to be obliged to tell him so unpleasant a truth, but so it was. He told me Mr. B. wanted him to stay. I told him that B. ought to understand the temper of his army better than I did, but that we did not always agree upon the point. He goes away, however.[17]

Missionary Ridge

Davis and Bragg purged the army of the malcontents, sending some to other areas and practically relegating a few to retirement. Longstreet, with fifteen thousand infantry and five thousand cavalry—a third of Bragg's army—was sent away, heading for Knoxville to destroy Burnside. Bragg was left with only thirty-six thousand men to besiege the Federal army at Chattanooga that had grown to nearly eighty thousand. On November 24, a division under Major General Joseph Hooker seized Lookout Mountain on the Confederate left. The next day, General Grant had Sherman assail the Confederate right as Major General George H. Thomas's army overran the center of the Confederate line on Missionary Ridge, inflicting a loss of 6,700 men in killed, wounded, and prisoners, and capturing 40 pieces of artillery. Bragg's badly defeated army headed for shelter at Dalton, Georgia, on the Atlanta Railroad just east of Taylor's Ridge. On November 28, Bragg submitted his resignation to Richmond, and two days later he was ordered to temporarily turn over command to General William Hardee.

Soldier-historian Porter Alexander, at the time serving as Longstreet's chief of artillery, made the following comments on these events:

> As it was now beginning to become apparent that our victory at Chickamauga would be a fruitless one, there began to spring up all over the South many evidences of great

> dissatisfaction with Gen. Bragg as the commander of the army; and, although our generals in the field kept their own counsel, I am sure that very few, if any of them, were sanguine of any success under his leadership.
>
> But Gen. Bragg had one strong hold. He had the thorough confidence of President Davis, than whom no man was ever a more persistent friend, through evil report or good.
>
> And now, when the feeling against Gen. Bragg was rising & spreading on every hand, Mr. Davis paid a visit to the army & exercised his best influence to allay it there, &, after his return, he made public addresses, calculated to have similar effect upon the press throughout the country.
>
> As will soon appear, however, he only succeeded in postponing Gen. Bragg's removal for a few weeks. For before the end of November the general received at Missionary Ridge the most complete, thorough, & disgraceful defeat which ever befell a Confederate army, & after that it was only possible [to] let him down easy, with a few weeks' command in winter quarters, & then Gen. Jos. E. Johnston replaced him.
>
> But, even then. Mr. Davis found a soft place for him, & took him into the War Department as sort of general advisor, & kept him there until the close of the war.[18]

Robert Hughes, Johnston's biographer, wrote that after the severe defeat at Missionary Ridge—also known as the battle of Chattanooga—President Davis could no longer retain Bragg in command of the of Tennessee, "though he could not entirely forego his society or dispense with his counsel." Hughes wrote: "He therefore called him to Richmond and made him a sort of military director, under General Orders No. 23, dated February 24, 1864, as follows: 'General Braxton Bragg is assigned to duty at the seat of the Government, and, under the direction of the President, is charged with the conduct of military operations in the armies of the Confederacy.'" In this position, Hughes added, Bragg could, "under the direction of the President," supervise both Lee and Johnston in the coming campaign.[19] Bragg, as one of Jefferson Davis's "pets," was always protected by the president. Bragg can be seen as a classic example of the Peter Principle, being continually promoted until he reached a level at which he was totally incompetent.

CHAPTER 16

The Army of Tennessee

There was heated debate over who would replace Bragg in command of the Army of Tennessee. Pressure from the press, from Congress, and from the general population urged Johnston's appointment, and the army clamored that he was the proper successor to assume command. General Polk wrote to President Davis: "General Joe Johnston is the person to whom you should offer that command." Mackall, Bragg's chief of staff, told Johnston: "I never did believe Mr. D. would give you your place as long as he can help it, but he can't. The army wants you … he will be forced to yield." Senator Louis Wigfall met with Secretary of War Seddon and several other Johnston supporters in the Secretary's office, where they advocated for Johnston. At a Cabinet meeting in December, where the matter of a successor for commander in chief of the Army of Tennessee was decided, Seddon proposed Johnston. After much discussion, the sentiment of the meeting turned to Johnston as the only viable candidate; a majority of the Cabinet recommended him for the position. According to Seddon's account, the "President after doubt and with misgivings to the end, chose him, and not as due exaltation on this score, but as the best on the whole to be obtained." Wigfall wrote to Johnston, stressing Robert E. Lee's part in winning Davis's reluctant approval: "Genl. Lee came to Richmond at once &—you were appointed. You owe your appointment to Genl. Lee & doubtless fully appreciate his kindness."[1] Mary Chesnut reiterated Lee's intervention in Johnston's selection: "Joe Johnston made commander in chief of the Army of the West. General Lee had this done."[2]

President Davis sent Johnston the following order from Richmond on December 16:

> General J. E. Johnston: You will turn over the immediate command of the Army of Mississippi to Lieutenant-General Polk, and proceed to Dalton and assume command of the Army of Tennessee … A letter of instruction will be sent you at Dalton.

Johnston proceeded to Dalton in obedience to this order and assumed command, issuing the following dictate on December 27:

> In obedience to the orders of his Excellency the President, the undersigned has the honor to assume command of the Army of Tennessee.
>
> J. E. Johnston, General.[3]

Two Letters

When Johnston reached Dalton, he found two letters awaiting him. One was from Secretary of War Seddon and the other from Jefferson Davis. Seddon's letter, dated December 20, read as follows:

> General: It is apprehended the army may have been, by recent events, somewhat disheartened, and deprived of ordinance and material. Your presence, it is hoped, will do much to reestablish hope and inspire confidence, and through such influence, as well as by the active exertions you are recommended to make, men who have straggled may be recalled to their standards, and others, roused to the dangers to which further successes of the enemy must expose the more Southern States, may be encouraged to recruit the ranks of your army. It is desired that your early and vigorous efforts be directed to restoring the discipline, prestige, and confidence of the army, and to increasing its numbers; and that at the same time you leave no means unspared to restore and supply its deficiencies in ordnance, munitions, and transportation. It is feared also that under grave embarrassments to which the commissariat is exposed, both from deficiencies of supplies in the country, and the impediments which unfortunately the discontents of producers and the opposition of State authorities to the system of impressment established by the law of Congress have caused, you may find deficiencies in and have serious difficulties in providing the supplies required for the subsistence of the army. You will use all means in your power to obtain supplies from the productive States around you, and strong confidence is entertained that you may be enabled to rouse among the people and authorities a more willing spirit to part with the means of subsistence for the army that defends them. Meantime the efforts of the Commissary Bureau will be directed to aid in your supply, and General Polk will be instructed to afford from your late department such resources as can be spared.
>
> As soon as the condition of your forces will allow, it is hoped you will be able to resume the offensive.

Johnston was confounded by this letter, writing: "Although unable at the time to discover the Honorable Secretary's object in addressing such a letter to one thought competent, apparently, to the second military position in importance in the Confederacy, or to find in it much that was instructive, I replied immediately, and gravely." Johnston's reply stated:

> Sir: The duties of military administration that you point out to me shall be attended to with diligence. The most difficult of them will be the procuring supplies of food. Foreseeing this before leaving Mississippi, I applied for permission to bring Major W. E. Moore with me, to be chief commissary of the army. The reply of the adjutant and inspector general was,

that Major Moore has been collecting supplies in Mississippi so long that it was deemed inexpedient to transfer him. General Cooper was mistaken. Major Moore has not served long in Mississippi, nor collected large supplies there. He made his reputation in this army. Major Dameron directs the purchase and impressment of provisions in Mississippi. So that Major Moore's position is not an important one. Therefore Lieutenant-General Polk, from interest in this army, is anxious that he should be its chief commissary. I therefore most respectfully repeat my application.

This army is now far from being in condition to "resume the offensive." It is deficient in numbers, arms, subsistence stores, and field transportation.

In reference to the subsistence of the army, you direct me to "use all means in my power to obtain supplies from productive States around me." Let me remind you that I have little if any power to procure supplies for the army. The system established last summer deprives generals of any control over the officers of the quartermaster's and subsistence departments detailed to make purchases in the different States. I depend upon three majors in each State, neither of whom owes me obedience. Having no power to procure means of feeding, equipping, and moving the army, I am also released from the corresponding responsibilities. I refer to this matter in no spirit of discontent—for I have no taste, personally, for the duties in question—but to beg you to consider if the responsibility for keeping the army in condition to move and fight ought not to rest upon the general, instead of being divided among a number of officers who have not been thought by the Government competent to the duties of high military grades.

President Davis's letter, dated December 23, was received by Johnston on the 31st. The letter was a status report on the Army of Tennessee since the battle of Missionary Ridge:

In a letter written to me after the battle, General Bragg expressed his unshaken confidence in the courage and morale of the troops. He says: "We can redeem the past."

The official reports made to my aide-de-camp, Colonel Ives, who has just returned from Dalton, presented a not unfavorable view of the material of the command.

The effective condition of your new command, as thus reported to me, is a matter of much congratulations, and I assure you that nothing shall be wanting on the part of the Government to aid you in your efforts to regain possession of the territory from which we have been driven.

Johnston was astounded by the president's assertions, declaring that he could see no military object for which the letter could have been written, "especially by one whose time was supposed to be devoted to the most important concerns of the government." He was dumfounded how Davis might have believed "that I was to be taught the moral and material condition of the army around me by him, from the observations of his aide-de-camp, who had never seen military service," rather than learning it from his own scrutiny:

Nor could he have believed that the army which he so described was competent to recover "the territory from which we have been driven." As I had much better means of information on the subjects of this paper than its author, it could not have been written for my instruction.

> The two high executive officers expressed in their letters very different opinions of the effect of its recent defeat, upon the army. The Secretary of War expressed plainly his consciousness of the great losses it had suffered in men, morale, and material. The President on the contrary, regarded, "the effective condition" of the army as "a matter of much congratulation."[4]

General Johnston found he had to deal with various major challenges in the army he now commanded, and it was not quite the rosy picture Davis presented. On January 2, 1864, Johnston replied to the president, expressing his views on the best strategy under the current circumstances:

> Your Excellency well impresses upon me the importance of recovering the territory we have lost. I feel it deeply, but difficulties appear to me in the way.
>
> The Secretary of War has informed me that I must not hope for reenforcements. To assume the offensive from this point, we must move either into Middle or East Tennessee. To the first, the obstacles are Chattanooga, now a fortress, the Tennessee River, the rugged desert of the Cumberland Mountains, and an army outnumbering ours more than two to one. The second course would leave the way into Georgia open. We have neither subsistence nor field transportation enough for either march. General Bragg and Lieutenant-General Hardee, in suggesting the offensive, proposed to operate with a powerful army formed upon this as a nucleus. The former was unable to advance before the arrival of Sherman had added twenty-five thousand men to the Federal army, and the march of Longstreet into East Tennessee had reduced ours by twelve thousand. The latter, in his letter to you of the 17th ultimo, expresses the opinion that this army is too weak to oppose the enemy should he advance.
>
> There would be much less difficulty, I think, in advancing from Northern Mississippi, avoiding the mountains.
>
> I can see no other mode of taking the offensive here, than to beat the enemy when he advances, and then move forward. But, to make victory probable, the army must be strengthened.[5]

"The Very Picture of a General"

Joseph Johnston wanted the soldiers to become acquainted with him, and he with them, so he conducted an informal review by riding through the camps on December 27 after announcing he was the new commander of the Army of Tennessee. One of the soldiers, Private Sam R. Watkins of the 1st Tennessee, gave his impression of the new general:

> Fancy, if you please, a man about fifty years old, rather small of stature, but firmly and compactly built, an open and honest countenance, and a keen but restless black eye, that seemed to read your very inmost thoughts. In his dress he was a perfect dandy. He ever wore the very finest clothes that could be obtained, carrying out in every point the dress and paraphernalia of the soldier.
>
> ... His hat was decorated with a star and feather, his coat with every star and embellishment, and wore a bright new sash, big gauntlets, and silver spurs.
>
> He was the very picture of a general.

Johnston acknowledged the cheers of the soldiers "by darting out on his bright bay horse in front of the line & lifting his hat, not merely off his head, but down to his stirrup," one officer recalled.[6]

General Johnston took stock of the Army of Tennessee and made the following evaluation of his new command:

> In the inspections, which were made as soon as practicable, the appearance of the army was very far from being "a matter of much congratulations." Instead of a reserve of muskets there was a deficiency of six thousand and as great a one of blankets, while the number of bare feet was painful to see. The artillery horses were too feeble to draw the guns in fields, or on a march, and the mules were in similar condition; while the supplies of forage were then very irregular, and did not include hay. In consequence of this, it was necessary to send all these animals not needed for camp service to the valley of the Etowah, where long forage could be found, to restore their health and strength.
>
> The last return of the Army was on December 20th, and exhibited an effective total of infantry and artillery 36,826, 6,000 infantry were without arms and as many without shoes, and 5,613 cavalry.[7]

Furloughs

To deal with problems of morale and desertions, Johnston proclaimed a general amnesty to all men who were absent without leave if they returned to the ranks. To prevent further unauthorized absences, he granted furloughs—one-third of the army at a time—that enabled every man in the army to go home for a visit. Furloughs were drawn by lot and the winners could give or sell their draw to a family man. One officer commented that "these furloughs were the most charming stroke in the management of soldiers that was ever tried."[8]

Another challenge Johnston had to attend to was deficiencies in supplies for his army. One of his first acts was to have two days' rations issued to the troops at once. The area around Dalton was a mountainous wilderness, with few farms. The Army of Tennessee depended upon the Western and Atlantic Railroad from Atlanta, which was owned by the State of Georgia, as its lifeline for supplies. Due to mismanagement and the shortage of rolling stock, a single trainload of supplies sometimes took up to 36 hours to make the 85-mile run from Atlanta to Dalton. Johnston wrote to the feisty governor of Georgia, Joseph E. Brown: "The railroad from Atlanta does not supply our needs." By the end of January 1864, Johnston told Governor Brown, who had intervened to greatly improve the management of the railroad, with "great satisfaction" that "the daily receipts of provision and fodder from Atlanta are now fully equal to the consumption." Johnston contrived to have beef cattle driven to Dalton and slaughtered there, rather than being butchered in Atlanta and shipped salted in barrels, which was so rancid and slippery that the men called it "blue beef." In the meantime, he ordered the commissary to distribute the small reserves of bacon and sugar, and had tobacco and whiskey issued twice a week. Another issue was that officers, who by law could not draw rations, were having difficulty affording food since their salaries had not kept pace with rising prices. Officers from Breckinridge's division petitioned Richmond to allow them to draw rations, Johnston noting that "at the present prices of provisions the pay of company officers is worth less than privates." By February, the government allowed officers to draw rations. In a letter to a friend, President Davis was dismissive of Johnston's efforts to keep his soldiers well fed: "To consult the soldiers as to what they would eat was to play the part of a tavern keeper rather than that of a general." However, the men were delighted with their new general, as one soldier recalled: "A new era had dawned. He was loved, respected, admired; yea, almost worshipped by the troops. I do not believe there was a soldier in his army but would gladly have died for him." Private Watkins of the 1st Tennessee added: "We knew we had a Gen. that would take care of his men."[9]

To instill discipline, order, and confidence in the men, Johnston drafted a detailed general order decreeing reveille at dawn, breakfast at sunrise, three hours of drill per day, and dress parade at sunset. He insisted that soldiers on guard duty require positive identification of all individuals. In mid-March, a soldier on guard duty arrested Johnston; "He took it good-humoredly," the soldier wrote home, "while little colonels and majors become very indignant and wrathy under such circumstances." Johnston insisted that during inspections, "the quarters are to be in perfect order, knapsacks properly packed, and bedding neatly folded." He informed his officers: "The test of their fidelity is in the condition of the troops which they command. Men well disciplined, well instructed, and well cared for point out the honest officer and true patriot." General Johnston rode his horse at a gallop through the camps. "He passed through the ranks of the common soldiers, shaking hands with everyone he met," wrote Sam Watkins. Johnston emphasized to President Davis that whatever the shortcomings of numbers, equipment, and materiel in the Army of Tennessee, he had "no doubt of the spirit of the soldiers" and "full confidence in their courage." Of his success in this, an intelligent writer, who visited Dalton in April 1864, wrote:

> Gen. Johnston is unquestionably a great captain in the science of war. In ninety days he has so transformed this army that I can find no word to express the extent of the transformation but the word regeneration. It is a regenerated army. He found it, ninety days ago, disheartened, despairing, and on the verge of dissolution. By judicious measures he has restored confidence, reestablished discipline, and exalted the heart of his army.[10]

Necessity to increase the strength of the Army of Tennessee became of the most importance. At a meeting of the general officers on January 2, one week after Johnston's arrival, Major General Patrick R. Cleburne suggested that the Confederacy should enlist the enslaved for military service in exchange for their freedom. This proposal met opposition in the army and was strongly disapproved by the government. Nevertheless, Johnston took a more realistic approach by substituting Black enslaved people "for all soldiers on detached or daily duty, as well as company cooks, pioneers, and laborers for engineer service." He believed this would free between ten and twelve thousand men for fighting, and would strengthen other armies of the Confederacy in the same proportion. "The plan is simple and quick," he explained. "It puts soldier and negro each in his appropriate place—the one to fight, the other to work." Johnston urged Wigfall to enlist other members of Congress to support the measure, and on February 17 a bill authorizing the use of previously enslaved Black people and up to twenty thousand enslaved people was approved by Congress. Within a month, General Samuel Cooper placed responsibility for enrolling and assigning previously enslaved Black people with the Bureau of Conscription, but the enslaved could only be impressed after consultation with the state authorities, as in the past, which diluted the effectiveness of Johnston's design.[11]

General Johnston also started to reorganize the Army of Tennessee to make it a more effective fighting force. He appointed as his chief of staff Brig. Gen. William Whann Mackall, an old friend of Johnston's who had served with him in the Mexican War. Mackall was an efficient and capable administrator and had been Bragg's chief of staff since April 1863; he had been a West Point classmate of Bragg's. Colonel Benjamin S. Ewell, who had an eloquent style of writing, was retained as Adjutant General. The Army of Tennessee was divided into two infantry corps and a cavalry brigade; Johnston advocated to Davis for the addition of a third corps which he believed would make the army more efficient in battle, but the president refused. Lieutenant General William Joseph Hardee, nicknamed "Old Reliable," who had written the U.S. Army's principal book on light infantry tactics, was his senior corps commander. Hardee's corps was composed of the divisions of Cheatham, Breckenridge, Cleburne, and Walker. The other corps commander was Maj. Gen. Thomas C. Hindman, his command comprising his own, Stevenson's, and Stewart's divisions. However, Hindman's corps properly belonged to a lieutenant general. Johnston appealed to Richmond to send him an officer of the appropriate rank, asking for the promotion of Major General Mansfield Lovell for the assignment. Eventually, Davis sent Lieutenant General John Bell Hood, who arrived on the same day Davis appointed Bragg as his military adviser. Hood, who had his left arm shattered at Gettysburg and his right leg amputated at Chickamauga, could hardly mount a horse and had to be strapped into the saddle. Hood began a prearranged clandestine letter campaign with President Davis in March and April, which undermined Johnston's credibility and generalship.

Joseph Wheeler (1836–1906) was appointed colonel of the 19th Alabama Infantry on September 4, 1861, and led the regiment at Shiloh in April 1862. Braxton Bragg made Wheeler the chief of cavalry of the Army of Mississippi on October 13, 1862. (Library of Congress)

The cavalry arm was commanded by 27-year-old Major General Joseph Wheeler, who had a poor relationship with Johnston, simply because Johnston had replaced Bragg, who had sponsored Wheeler for the rank of major general only four years out of West Point and had advocated for his appointment as his cavalry commander. By January 1864, Davis was having trouble getting Wheeler's nomination confirmed by the Senate because the nomination was opposed by old pro-Johnston partisans, especially the Texas and Kentucky delegations, who wanted General John Wharton to receive the post. On January 23, Davis asked Johnston to make a statement of Wheeler's abilities, to which Johnston immediately replied and sent a separate note to Wigfall exalting Wheeler's experience. Wheeler secured the assignment but did not show appreciation for Johnston's efforts on his behalf; indeed, he wrote secretive damaging letters to the government, beginning in February. Wheeler's cavalry amounted to about sixteen hundred, those being the fittest for active service. The long arm of artillery currently had no commander. Johnston applied to Richmond for General E. Porter Alexander, but General Lee objected that he was too valuable in his present position. Bragg proposed Brigadier General William N. Pendleton as chief of artillery for the Army of Tennessee, but again Lee objected. Instead, Richmond sent Brigadier General Francis A. Shoup.

"This is Old Joe"

In another effort to improve morale, Joseph Johnston restored the composition of specific units and placed them under the command of their original officers. As part of his vendetta against the officers who had opposed him, Bragg had decided to break up the powerful Tennessee and Kentucky cliques in the army and disperse the opposition. A case in point was Major General Benjamin F. Cheatham's division, which had contained 22 Tennessee regiments, but now had only six from the state. Johnston reversed Bragg's decision and brought the division back to its former configuration. This move "created unbounded enthusiasm" among the men. After a formal announcement, the division marched out of camp to Johnston's headquarters, led by Cheatham and with a band playing at the head of the column, and called for the army commander. Cheatham threw an arm around Johnston's shoulder, patted him on his balding pate two or three times, and said to his men: "Boys, this is Old Joe."[12]

Edward A. Pollard, editor of the *Richmond Examiner* during the war, remarked how General Joseph Eggleston Johnston reinvigorated the Army of Tennessee after its disaster on Missionary Ridge:

> On the 1st May, the effective artillery and infantry of the Army of Tennessee amounted to 40,900; the effective cavalry to about four thousand. Gen. Johnston was thus greatly overmatched in numbers; and he had no prospect of compensation, but in superiour skill and strategy. But the condition of his army was excellent in every respect, and had been made so by the admirable skill and inspiration he had brought to the work of its regeneration. It was well-fed, well-clad, in high and hopeful spirits; and for the first time in its history there was no barefoot soldier in its ranks. Ninety days before, the army left by Bragg was disheartened, despairing and on the verge of dissolution. By judicious measures Gen. Johnston had restored confidence, re-established discipline, and exalted the hearts of his army. There was reason now to hope that the Army of Tennessee, the most ill-starred and successless of all our armies, had seen its worst days.[13]

CHAPTER 17

Dalton Realities and Richmond's Castles in the Air

Having first seen his new command on December 27, 1863, General Johnston trained, refitted, and reorganized the Army of Tennessee at Dalton. He wrote that Bragg's occupation of Dalton had been "accidental," having encamped there for a night during his retreat from Missionary Ridge and only remaining when it was seen the following morning that the Federal pursuit had ceased. Johnston commented:

> The position of Dalton had little to recommend it as a defensive one. It had neither intrinsic strength nor strategic advantage. It neither fully covered its own communications nor threatened those of the enemy. The railroad from Atlanta to Chattanooga passes through Rocky-Faced Ridge by Mill-Creek Gap, three miles and a half beyond Dalton, but very obliquely, the course of the road being about thirty degrees west of north, and that of the ridge about five degrees east of north. As it terminates but three miles north of the gap, it offers little obstacle to the advance of a superior force from Ringgold to Dalton. Between Mill-Creek and Snake-Creek Gaps, this ridge protects the road to Atlanta on the west, but at the same time covers any direct approach from Chattanooga to Resaca or Calhoun-points on the same route from Dalton to Atlanta—or flank movement in that direction, by an army in front of Mill-Creek Gap. These conditions would have induced me to draw the troops back to the vicinity of Calhoun, to free our left flank from exposure, but for the earnestness with which the President and Secretary of War, in their letters of instructions, wrote of early assumption of offensive operations and apprehension of the bad effect of a retrograde movement upon the spirit of the Southern people.
>
> During the previous winter Major-General Gilmer, chief engineer, had wisely made an admirable base for our army by intrenching Atlanta.
>
> As a road leads from Chattanooga through Snake Creek Gap to the railroad bridge at Resaca, a light intrenchment to cover 3,000 or 4,000 men was made there; and to make quick communication between that point and Dalton, two rough country roads were so improved as to serve that purpose.[1]

On February 3, Sherman marched out of Vicksburg with a force of thirty-five thousand infantry toward Jackson, which was guarded by a single Confederate brigade. Davis suspected Sherman was part of a plan to capture Mobile.

By February 14, Sherman had reached Meridian. Placed in command of the Mississippi-Alabama department was Lieutenant General Polk, who had only ten thousand infantry and cavalry to counter this threat. Polk appealed for aid from the government and Johnston. Johnston asked Polk for information about the numbers and position of the two forces, wanting to clarify the true state of affairs. Davis pushed Johnston to send troops to assist Polk, since there was no reported aggressive action in the Dalton area. Johnston resisted, saying that to send sufficient troops to Polk would weaken the army at Dalton and allow the Federals to "seize Atlanta before our return." He added: "If General Polk has assembled his cavalry it ought to prevent the enemy from marching to Mobile. I have asked information from General Polk."[2] By February 17, the president became so apprehensive that he ordered Johnston to dispatch General Hardee with three divisions of about seventeen thousand to Polk's assistance. Longstreet thought this strategy was faulty, and that instead of being reinforced, Polk should have been sent to bolster Johnston:

> That would have drawn General Sherman to General Thomas, but Polk, having interior lines of transit, could have been in time for Johnston to strike and break up the road and bridge behind Thomas before Sherman could reach him. The break could have forced Thomas to care for his own position, and the want of the bridge behind him might have forced him to abandon it, in search of safe communication with his supplies. But the authorities could not be induced to abandon the policy of placing detachments to defend points to which the enemy chose to call us. We had troops enough in Tennessee, Georgia, Alabama, and Mississippi, if allowed to use them in co-operative combination, to break the entire front of the Federal forces and force them back into Kentucky before the opening of the spring campaign, when we might have found opportunity to "dictate" their campaign. The enemy was in no condition for backward move at the time of my advance upon Knoxville, so simultaneous advance of many columns could have given him serious trouble, if not confusion.[3]

Meanwhile, Maj. Gen. George H. Thomas, having learned that Confederate troops were leaving Dalton for Mobile, recommended to Grant that he make a "formidable reconnaissance" toward Dalton with the hope the Confederates might be caught off balance, to which Grant consented. On the night of February 22, Johnston was informed by scouts of the advance by Thomas and mobilized his army to meet the threat. But the strategic picture had changed in Mississippi; Sherman's army turned around and headed back to Vicksburg on February 21, having accomplished its mission to destroy Meridian. On February 23, Johnston heard from Davis that Hardee was too late and would return. Johnston telegrammed Hardee: "The enemy is advancing; is now in force at Tunnel Hill. Lose no time."[4] Some of Hardee's troops arrived in time by train to repel the Federal incursion. Johnston wrote to Davis in his report of February 25: "We have been skirmishing most of the day in the gap through which the railroad passes, 3½ miles from Dalton, and in the valley east of the same mountain easily holding our ground in the gap and driving back the enemy in the valley. His forces and plans not developed."[5] On the night of February 26, convinced the Confederates outnumbered his forces, Thomas retired, Johnston concluding the Federals had converted the movement into a reconnaissance.

Bragg's Plan

General Johnston had not heard from President Davis concerning military operations since the suggestions he made on December 23. Johnston wrote to General Bragg, military advisor to Jefferson Davis, on February 27 to get some clarification on policy:

> Letters received from the President and Secretary of War soon after my assignment to this command gave me the impression that a forward movement by this Army was intended to be made in the spring. If I am right in that impression, and the President's intentions are unchanged, I respectfully suggest that much preparation is necessary—large additions to the number of troops, a great quantity of field transportation, subsistence stores and forage, a bridge equipage, and fresh artillery horses. Few of those we have are fit for a three day's march, as they have not recovered from the effects of the last campaign. To make our artillery efficient, at least 1,000 fresh horses are required, even should we stand on the defensive. Let me suggest that the necessary measures be taken without delay.[6]

Bragg replied on March 4 and affirmed that Richmond expected a forward movement. Three days later, Bragg reiterated the government's desire that Johnston make preparations for aggressive action, writing: "The enemy is not prepared for us, and if we can strike him a blow before he recovers success is almost certain. The plan which is proposed has long been my favorite, and I trust our efforts may give you the means to accomplish what I ardently desired but never had the ability to undertake."[7] In the meantime, Lieutenant General Longstreet heard that a plan for a joint offensive with Johnston was in the offing and communicated this to him on March 5:

> I have received a verbal message from the President, through General Alexander, to confer with you upon the propriety and practicality of uniting our armies at or near Madisonville, East Tenn., with a view to a move into Middle Tennessee upon the enemy's line of communication. My transportation is so limited that I cannot take more than enough to supply us on the road. There is nothing in the country through which I must pass, or so little that we could place no reliance upon the country for supplies. I shall be obliged to depend upon you for food and forage when we are united.[8]

Longstreet wrote again to Johnston on the same date, advising against the movement: "I have just finished an official letter setting forth the projected campaign of the President and General Bragg. It does not look very inviting to me, and from here it looks very much less to you. Your facilities for rapid movement may have been so much improved, however, since I was with that army, that you may be able to accomplish the object in view." He continued that he could see one serious objection to the move:

> If the enemy should slip in behind you and fortify strongly, both armies (yours and mine) will be obliged to disperse in the mountains and many of us perish, or surrender to the enemy without a fight. It may be that this would be sport to some people, but I confess that I should not enjoy it at all. However, the idea may be beyond my comprehension. I shall wait, therefore, for your opinions upon the matter.[9]

On March 8, Longstreet left his command in East Tennessee to travel to Richmond for a conference, for plans or suggestions that could anticipate the movements of the enemy, disconcert his plans, and move him to new combinations." The conference was scheduled for March 14, to discuss military options, as Longstreet related:

> Forced to extremities, the Richmond authorities began to realize the importance of finding a way out of our pent-up borders before the Union commander could complete his extensive arrangements to press on with his columns. They called upon General Lee, General Johnston, and myself for plans or suggestions that could anticipate the movements of the enemy, disconcert his plans, and move him to new combinations. In front of General Lee and on his right and left the country had been so often foraged by both Union and Confederate armies that it was denuded of supplies. Besides, a forced advance of Lee's army could only put the enemy back a few miles to his works about Washington. General Johnston's opportunities were no better, and in addition to other difficulties, he was working under the avowed displeasure of the authorities, more trying than his trouble with the enemy.

Longstreet's military perspective had materialized into a strategic plan to win back Tennessee and Kentucky:

> I was under the impression that we could collect an army of twenty thousand men in South Carolina by stripping our forts and positions of all men not essential for defence; that that army could be quietly moved north by rail through Greenville to the borders of North Carolina, and promptly marched by Abingdon, Virginia, through the mountain passes, while my command covered the move by its position in East Tennessee. That army passing the mountains, my command could drop off by the left to its rear and follow into Kentucky—the whole to march against the enemy's only line of railway from Louisville, and force to loose his hold against General Johnston's front, and give the latter opportunity to advance his army and call all of his troops in Alabama and Mississippi to like advance, the grand junction of all of the columns to be made on or near the Ohio River—General Beauregard to command the leading column, with orders not to make or accept battle until the grand junction was made. That General Johnston should have like orders against battle until he became satisfied of fruitful issues. The supplies and transportation for Beauregard to be collected at the head of the railroad, in advance of the movement of troops, under the

ostensible purpose of hauling for my command. The Arrangements perfected, the commander of the leading column to put his troops on the rail at or near Charleston and march with them as they arrived at the head of the road.

Longstreet arrived in Virginia and met privately with Gen. Robert E. Lee, who approved his plans and asked him to take it to the authorities in Richmond:

> I objected that the mere fact of its coming from me would be enough to cause its rejection, and asked, if he approved, that he would take it and submit it as his own. He took me with him to Richmond, but went alone next morning, to see the President. He met besides the President, the Secretary of War and General Bragg. Conference was held during the forenoon, but was not conclusive. In the afternoon he called me with him for further deliberation.
>
> At the opening of the afternoon council it appeared that General Bragg had offered a plan for early spring campaign, and that it had received the approval of the President—viz.:
>
> "General Johnston to march his army through the mountains of Georgia and East Tennessee to the head-waters of Little Tennessee River; my command to march through the mountains east of Knoxville to join General Johnston. The commands united, to march west, cross the river into Middle Tennessee, and march for the enemy's line of supplies about Nashville."
>
> When asked an opinion of this, I inquired as to General Johnston's attitude towards it, and was told he objected; that he thought the sparsely-settled country of the mountains through which he would move could not supply his army; that he would consume all that he could haul before turning westward for the middle country, and would be forced to active foraging from his first step between the two armies of the enemy.
>
> General Lee inquired if General Johnston had maturely considered the matter. I thought that he had, and that the objections of the officer who was to conduct the campaign were, of themselves, reasons for overruling it; but its advocates were not ready to accept a summary disposal of their plans, and it began to transpire that the President had serious objections to General Beauregard as a commander for the field.
>
> But General Lee called us back to business by asking if there was anything more to be added than General Johnston's objections. I called attention to General Bragg's official account of the battle of Chickamauga, in which he reported that a similar move had been proposed for him through Middle Tennessee towards the enemy's line of communication at Nashville early on the morning after the battle; that he rejected it, reported it "visionary"; said that it would leave his rear open to the enemy, and alluded to the country through which the march was proposed as "affording no subsistence to men and animals." This at harvest season, too! the enemy demoralized by the late battle, and the Confederates in the vigor of success! Now, after a winter of foraging by the Union armies, the country could not be so plethoric of supplies as to support us, while an active army was on each flank, better prepared to dispute our march.[10]

The conference ended without reaching a conclusion. Johnston considered Bragg's plan foolhardy. The enemy forces were closer to each other and connected by railroad, while Johnston and Longstreet would be in rugged country, further separated from each other than to the enemy. The enemy could easily concentrate against either of them and crush them one at a time. Bragg and Davis had not considered the value of the all-important railroad as a vital link for men and supplies for the Army of Tennessee. In addition, it would allow the enemy to seize Johnston's base at Atlanta and fortify it, which would open up other areas of the South to further Federal incursions. Longstreet's plan envisioned a grand turning movement aimed at the enemy's communications to force a retrograde movement. But the most attractive feature was that it left Johnston's Army of Tennessee in place at Dalton on the railroad guarding Atlanta, where it could be heavily reinforced. It avoided a direct confrontation with the enemy in pitched battle to achieve the objectives, instead proposing a leisurely pursuit of a retreating enemy trying to protect its communications.

Johnston's Strategic Plan

Johnston always favored concentration and wanted to bring the troops from Mississippi, those from Beauregard's department, and Longstreet's soldiers to Dalton. Johnston told Davis: "I can see no other mode of taking the offensive here than to beat the enemy when he advances and then move forward."[11] Longstreet also favored this approach to "re-enforce General Johnston in his present position."

On March 18, Colonel John B. Sale, General Bragg's military secretary, arrived at Dalton with a "confidential" letter dated the 12th providing detailed instructions of Bragg's proposed offensive operations. Bragg apprised Johnston that "the following forces, it is believed, will be available, if nothing shall occur to divert them": a force of seventy-five thousand men would be gathered at Dalton, which included Johnston's own command, General Martin's cavalry of three thousand, five thousand contributed by Lieutenant General Polk, ten thousand by General Beauregard, plus Longstreet's entire command. But Bragg added a caveat: "It is proposed to hold the reenforcements ready, and to put them in motion just as soon as you may be able to use them. To throw them to the front now, would only impede the accumulation of supplies necessary for your march." Bragg asked for Johnston's views on the subject; Johnston expressed them by telegraph, mail, and in a lengthy discussion with Colonel Sale. On March 19, Sale issued a memorandum delineating Johnston's objections to Bragg's plan for a forward movement.

> First. He thinks Kingston too far east for union with Longstreet. The enemy could unite their Knoxville and Chattanooga forces four days sooner than we by keeping the north side of the Tennessee River, and could attack us in detail before our union.
>
> Second. It would require more transportation than can be had, or than it would be politic to cumber an army with, to carry our subsistence and other stores to that point.

Third. He does not think the army could subsist itself till it should get far west or north of Sparta. The country has been exhausted by the enemy, and did not abound even while we held McMinnville and Tullahoma.

Fourth. A battle fought on the proposed route on the north side of the Tennessee would make victory to us indispensable as the only way of avoiding the other alternative of utter destruction or loss of our army.

Fifth. The re-enforcements should assemble at once, instead of awaiting the other preparations, so as to prepare to resist an attack in force on us here. They can be easily subsisted here.

Let this army be still further strengthened as proposed, and then a part of it thrown into East Tennessee, near Chattanooga, and far enough in advance to cut communication with Knoxville and Chattanooga, and virtually isolate the former. Let the part thus thrown forward into East Tennessee be near enough to the main body for them to unite in the event of the battle; and let our communications with Dalton be still kept open, so that we may continue to draw our supplies from south as now. We will thus hold the enemy at Chattanooga in observation and isolate Knoxville at the same time, thus forcing an engagement to relieve the latter, while at the same time our subsistence is divided, as heretofore, and the road to Atlanta protected. Should we meet with disaster, we can fall back along our present line to the rear; but should we beat them, we can then (being already previously prepared to do so) follow them into Middle Tennessee. The enemy, if beaten, will have the further disadvantage of the river in his rear.

He thinks that, if it be determined to go first into Middle Tennessee at all hazards, it would be best to cross the river in North Alabama, advancing by way of Rome, Gadsden, & c. The road is less mountainous; supplies will be sooner reached, and the distance is less over which we would have to haul subsistence—say from Gadsden to Decatur, about seventy-six miles.[12]

Ultimatum

Bragg responded to Johnston on March 21: "General Bragg replied that my answer did not indicate acceptance of the plan proposed, and the troops could be drawn from other points only to advance. As the idea of advancing had been accepted by me, it was evident his strategy was the ultimatum."[13]

At the time, Johnston did not have a commander for his artillery, so Richmond ordered Brigadier General William Nelson Pendleton, Johnston's former chief of artillery, to make an inspection of the Army of Tennessee's artillery. Pendleton arrived in Dalton on March 12, reported to General Johnston and began his job. Pendleton made personal observations and inquiries to officers as to the effectiveness of the artillery and left Dalton on March 21. On March 29, Pendleton made a written report to General Samuel Cooper, Adjutant and Inspector General of the Confederate States Army, and stated it in person at a meeting with Davis, Seddon, Bragg, and Cooper:

The armament I found less strong than desirable. The 6-pounders, of which there are fifteen, are, in the present state of firearms, nearly useless, if not indeed worse, employing and

> exposing as they do a number of men and animals, while they can scarcely ever accomplish anything against the more powerful guns or even the long-range muskets of the enemy. The 12-pounder howitzers, of which there are twenty-seven, are scarcely more valuable; a few batteries of these for special service in that broken and wooded country may be useful, but the proportion is obviously too large. As rapidly as possible these deficiencies will be remedied; perhaps by 10th April nearly all the 6-pounders will be substituted by the more efficient 12-pounder Napoleon, and within a few weeks, the Chief of Ordnance assures me, several rifle batteries will be furnished in place of so many howitzers.
>
> The prevalent condition of the forces is nearly, if not quite, up to the average seen at this season in most of our artillery animals on the fronts, where hard service and hard fare occur together. With the addition of about 500, soon to be furnished, I was assured by the chief quartermaster, they will be capable at an early day, I am satisfied, of effective service.[14]

Johnston complained of a lack of transport for an offensive operation, upon which Richmond sent another envoy, Lieutenant Colonel Arthur H. Cole, to ascertain his transportation shortages. On April 11, after 10 days' work, Cole produced a report for Major Gibbons, Chief Inspector General Transportation at Richmond:

> This army to move, owing to the distance it will have to travel before reaching a country furnishing supplies, will have to start with twenty days' supplies. This will involve extra supply reserve trains, over and above that now on hand, 900 wagons and teams, and for which the chief quartermaster has never estimated; all he has called on Major Smith for is 600 artillery horses and wagons and teams for a pontoon train consisting of 135 wagons and teams—540 mules. On my arrival here I found that no one in this army knew what transportation was on hand, nor what was needed for a campaign. I had therefore to go to work and inspect and ferret out everything in order to arrive at some calculation as to the deficiency. I have been here now ten days, and by hard labor night and day am prepared to show General Johnston what he has, what he requires, and what we may possibly be able to do for him.

On April 6, Cole had been told by Major Norman W. Smith, Chief Inspector at Augusta, Georgia: "I really do not believe that in sixty days 1,000 mules can be obtained from all sources in this district."[15] These reports upheld Johnston's convictions concerning his army's incapacity to perform an offensive campaign, aggravated by the sparse animal supply in Johnston's Georgia and Alabama command.

Johnston had received no answer from his letter of March 18 or telegram of the 22nd General Bragg, and was apprehensive that President Davis was not apprised of his correspondence relating to the spring campaign. Johnston decided to send to Richmond on April 8 his personal friend, Colonel Benjamin Ewell, Adjutant-General of the Army of Tennessee, a trusted staff officer, to confer with Davis and Bragg to remove any misunderstanding. Johnston stated:

> He was instructed to show the President that in my correspondence with the Government I had not declined to assume the offensive—as General Bragg charged—but, on the contrary,

> was eager to move forward whenever the relative forces of the opposing armies should justify me in such a measure; to point out the difference between the plan of operations proposed through General Bragg and that which I advocated, and in that connection to explain that I had been actively engaged in preparations to take the field—those over which I had control being in a satisfactory state of forwardness. But in the important element of field-transportation, the need of which had several times been represented to the Government, and which I had neither the means or authority to collect, nothing had been done, while steps to collect the large number of artillery-horses necessary, had just been taken; and that the surest means of enabling us to go forward was to send the proposed reenforcements to Dalton at once; then, should the enemy take the initiative, as was almost certain, we might defeat him on this side of the Tennessee, where the consequences of defeat would be so much more disastrous to the enemy, and less so to us, than if the battle were fought north of that river.[16]

On the morning of April 14, Ewell met Bragg first because he wanted to mollify any bad feeling between Bragg and Johnston. Bragg was conciliatory, saying nothing could interfere with "his friendly relations with General Johnston." Bragg portrayed himself as a moderator between Davis and Johnston to prevent "any interruption of harmonious relations." When Ewell alleged that Johnston's views on the offensive had been misunderstood, that Johnston was willing to go on the offensive but only opposed the plan Richmond had presented, Bragg maintained that such an interpretation "had been done by the President and Secretary of War; that he himself had not so understood them." Bragg expressed sympathy for Johnston's transportation problems and hoped to reinforce him. He proposed that if Johnston initiated an offensive, the government would supply him with fifteen thousand troops from Polk's and Beauregard's commands. Bragg told Ewell that because of new pressure in Virginia and North Carolina, the troops could only be sent to Dalton if Ewell could assure Davis at their interview the next day that Johnston would take the offensive. Ewell sent a telegram to Johnston asking for a reply, informing him of Longstreet's departure from Tennessee to join Lee in Virginia. Although he did not get an answer in time for his meeting with Davis on April 15, Ewell gave the president a "decided affirmative answer." On April 19, Ewell received an answer from Bragg that no substantial aid would be sent to Dalton because "the pressure at Richmond" was too great. Bragg could only send a single brigade from Mobile and a few regiments from Beauregard. Johnston, discouraged, wrote to Senator Wigfall on April 1: "I fear that the government does not intend to strengthen the army." In late April, Johnston sent another letter to Wigfall: "The U.S. have the means of collecting two great armies—here & in Virginia. Our government thinks they can only raise but one, that of course in Virginia."[17]

While Ewell was conferring in Richmond, Jefferson Davis ordered Pendleton back to confer with Johnston on April 7 "respecting the principal facts relative to the enemy and to our own condition and as to the operations of the Army of Tennessee." Robert E. Lee was intimating to Davis that "the great effort in this campaign will be made in Virginia" and heavy reinforcements "daily arriving to the Army of the Potomac," were probably coming from Johnston's front, though Lee lacked substantiated proof. On April 16, Pendleton issued a lengthy memorandum of his meeting with Johnston:

> Reaching Dalton about midnight of the 14th, I had the privilege of an extended interview with General Johnston at his headquarters during the greater part of the 15th instant, and the advantage of General Wheeler's presence for several hours, he being conversant with the strength and distribution of the enemy's forces in Tennessee, and with the contour and resources of the country. As desired by the President, I endeavored to present to the general's mind what I understood to be the President's views, and what were my own convictions, concerning the importance—indeed, necessity—of the earliest and most efficient aggressive operations possible by the Army of Tennessee, on about the following grounds:
>
> First. To take the enemy at disadvantage while weakened, it is believed, by sending troops to Virginia, and having others absent still on furlough.
>
> Second. To break up his plans by anticipating and frustrating his combinations.
>
> Third. So to press him here as to prevent his heavier massing in Virginia.
>
> Fourth. To beat him, it is hoped, and greatly gain strength in supplies, men, and productive territory.
>
> Fifth. To prevent the waste of the army incident to inactivity.
>
> Sixth. To inspirit it and the country, and to depress the enemy, involving the greatest results.
>
> Seventh. To obviate the necessity of falling back likely to occur if the enemy be allowed to consummate his own plans.
>
> To these considerations, received by the general with courteous attention, he replied, in effect, that no one could more thoroughly appreciate them than he did, nor could the demands of the country be more sensibly felt by any than by himself; that he cordially approved of an aggressive movement, sanctioned by his judgment, and would make it the very moment he was reasonably strengthened therefor, that movement being, however, different from the advance into Tennessee, which had been previously suggested to him, and promising fair results without the hazard of ruin involved in the other. In the existing state of facts his judgment could not approve the proposal immediately to advance into Tennessee, so as to encounter the enemy far beyond Chattanooga, for these reasons:
>
> First. The enemy is, in fact, not weakened in Tennessee, but is, if anything, stronger than at Missionary Ridge. General Wheeler estimated their force to be—Fifteenth Corps (McPherson's), from Decatur to Bridgeport, 15,000; First (Hooker's), from Nashville to Chattanooga, 14,000; Fourteenth (Palmer's), at Chattanooga and Ringgold, 18,000; Fourth (Howard's), at Cleveland, 18,000; making of infantry proper, 65,000; also Twenty-third (Schofield's mounted infantry), at Knoxville, 12,000 and Hovey's division, Ringgold, 6,000; cavalry, 15,000, and artillery, 5,000; making an effective total of 103,000, besides about 15,000 negro troops, and 5,000 unassigned (but armed) Tennesseans.
>
> Second. This army—34,500 infantry, 2811 artillery, 2085 effective cavalry, making in all 39,396, with additions now contingently proposed from General Polk—will not be strong enough to advance at once into Tennessee.

Third. The immense trains essential for supporting the army through such a wilderness must be greatly exposed, and would render the force needed for their protection powerless against the enemy.

Fourth. Transportation for these [is] not adequately available for a month. This Lieutenant-Colonel Cole, superintendent transportation C. S. Army, stated in my presence.

Fifth. Means for securing supplies in presence of the enemy would be inadequate, even if the abundant country of Middle Tennessee were reached.

Sixth. The enemy is apparently preparing to advance before we can.

Seventh. Disaster beyond the Tennessee would probably prove ruinous—this army destroyed, Georgia occupied, the Confederacy pierced in its vitals, and all the Southwest lost.

On these grounds he deems it wisest and his duty—

First. To stand on the defensive till strengthened; to watch, prepare, and then strike as soon as possible.

Second. To have sent him immediately all the troops that can be furnished from other points.

Third. At the earliest day possible to advance to Ringgold, attack the enemy there, and, if successful, as expected, if it be done promptly, strike at Cleveland; then cut the railroad, control the river, and thus isolate East Tennessee. This would probably force the enemy to a general battle this side the Tennessee.

Fourth. Simultaneously send large cavalry force (General Polk's) to enemy's rear in Middle Tennessee. These operations might enforce the evacuation of the Tennessee Valley and render safely practicable an advance into the heart of the State.

Fifth. Should the enemy ultimately succeed against this course, in penetrating to Rome, or in some similar move, to take position where he could be met and probably beaten, and then press him back to the Ohio.

In these views thus presented I understood General Wheeler, who was present most of the time, mainly to concur. An immediate advance into Middle Tennessee with, say, 15,000 additional troops, if be had, via Washington, toward McMinnville, and successful assault upon the enemy be regarded, perhaps, as not quite so hazardous as did General Johnston, though he considered it a critical question, and, like the general, looked upon disaster there as probably fatal.

In view of the facts exhibited and reasons urged I did not feel justified in pertinaciously advocating the particular movement into Tennessee, and could not but admit that the mode of attack preferred by General Johnston might on the whole, prove most proper.

The enemy's force here is evidently greater than has been supposed. A result differing by only about 2,000 as to his numbers was reached by data from time to time derived by an officer (not consulting scout reports) from the enemy's papers respecting regiments, brigades, divisions, and corps, so that the estimate is probably not far from the truth.

From reports of scouts just sent by General Wheeler, and shown me by General Johnston, it seems clear that the enemy is preparing for a great effort here. If so, it will no doubt be wise to have everything at once ready for the most telling blow that can be dealt with.

This memorandum has been read to General Johnston and approved by him as correct.

General Bragg communicated to President Davis on April 22 that Johnston overrated Union strength, and only sixty-thousand Federals faced Johnston at Dalton. Bragg proposed to throw Loring's division and one more brigade, about seven thousand troops, from General Polk's department to Dalton to reinforce Johnston and recommended Nathan Forrest threaten Middle Tennessee.[18]

Johnston wrote to Wigfall not to believe any reports that he had refused proposals to take the offensive with a large army: "The truth is that in proposing the offensive, a plan of operations was suggested which I regard as impracticable. My saying so was treated in a telegram from Genl. Bragg as a refusal to do anything but stand still."

Review

On April 19, Joseph Johnston held a review of his army while sat astride his horse dressed in one of his finest uniforms. Johnston went down the line, stopping at each brigade to receive salutes from the officers, who raised their swords then dropped them in Johnston's honor. A young captain of Wheeler's cavalry told his new bride: "I doubt whether a volunteer army could be more perfect in its organization than the Army of Tennessee. General Johnston seems to have infused a new spirit into the whole mass, and out of chaos brought order and beauty." Johnston felt the soldiers respected and loved him. "If this army thought of me & felt towards me as some of our high civil functionaries do it would be necessary for me to leave the military service," he told Wigfall, "But thank heaven, it is my true friend." Johnston's Army of Tennessee would soon be put to the test, as the Federal army under General Sherman was about to launch its expected spring offensive. A chaplain in Lt. Gen. John Bell Hood's corps confided to his diary: "We are doubtless on the eve of important events."[19]

CHAPTER 18

Opposing Sherman's Campaign to Atlanta

On March 18, 1864, Major General William Tecumseh Sherman was appointed as commander of Union forces in the West. Sherman accompanied Grant, who was newly commissioned as lieutenant general and general in chief of all Union armies, on a train from Nashville, Tennessee, to Cincinnati, Ohio, where Grant described his strategic plan for the spring offensive, a concerted effort against the major Confederate forces. On April 4 and 19, at his headquarters in Nashville, Sherman received two letters from Grant formalizing a joint offensive: "I will stay with the Army of the Potomac and operate directly against Lee's army, wherever it may be found. You I propose to move against Johnston's army, to break it up, and to get into the interior of the enemy's country as far as you can, inflicting all the damage you can against their war resources."[1]

William Tecumseh Sherman (1820–91) was made commander of the military division of the Mississippi and began his invasion of Georgia in May 1864. On September 2, Sherman's forces occupied Atlanta. The Union war effort was faltering in the east, and Sherman's capture of Atlanta was a much-needed victory. (Library of Congress)

Sherman made extensive preparations for the coming campaign, overlooking nothing. Sherman's supply line ran along a single railroad—under

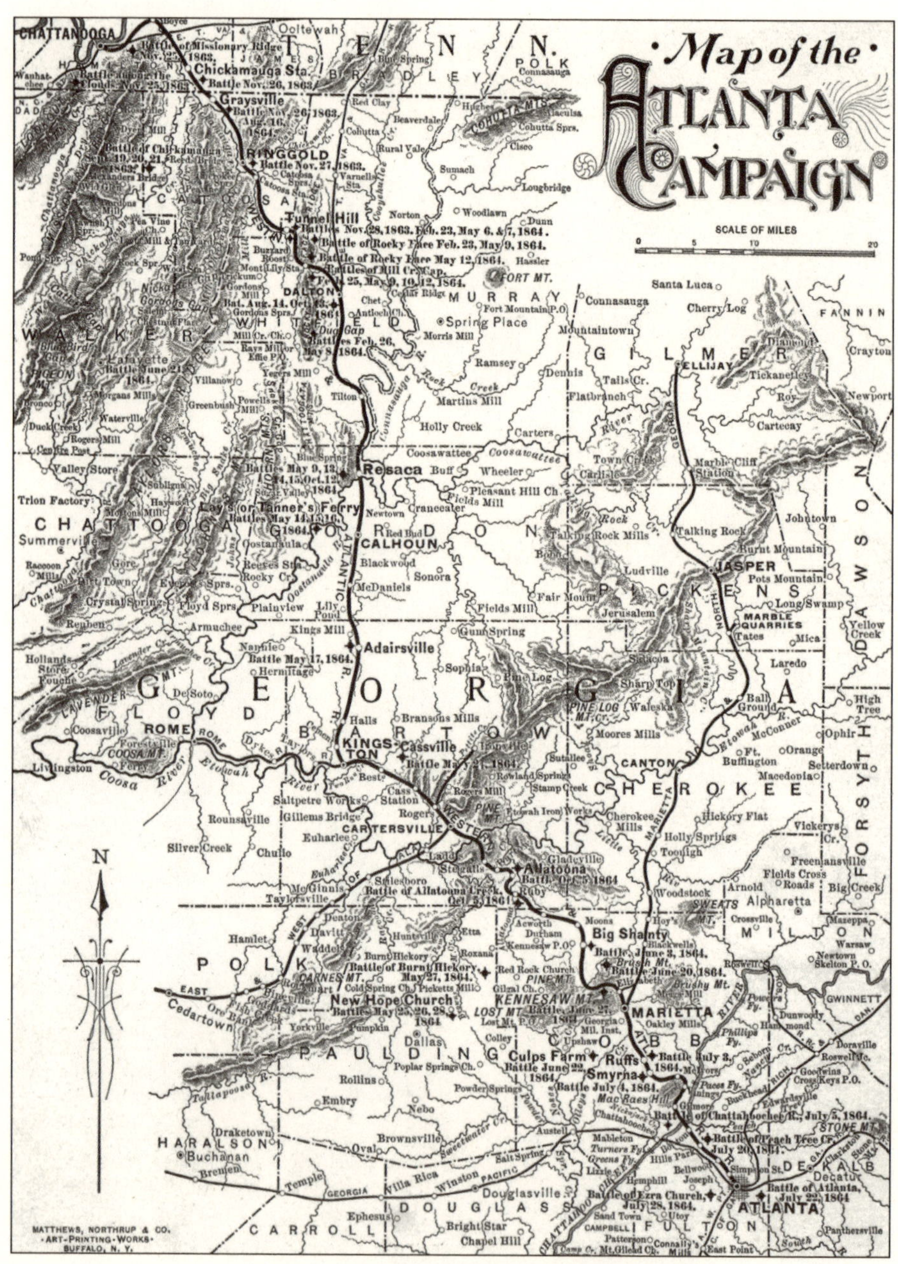

Atlanta Campaign. (Library of Congress)
Map shows railroads and roads leading to Atlanta.

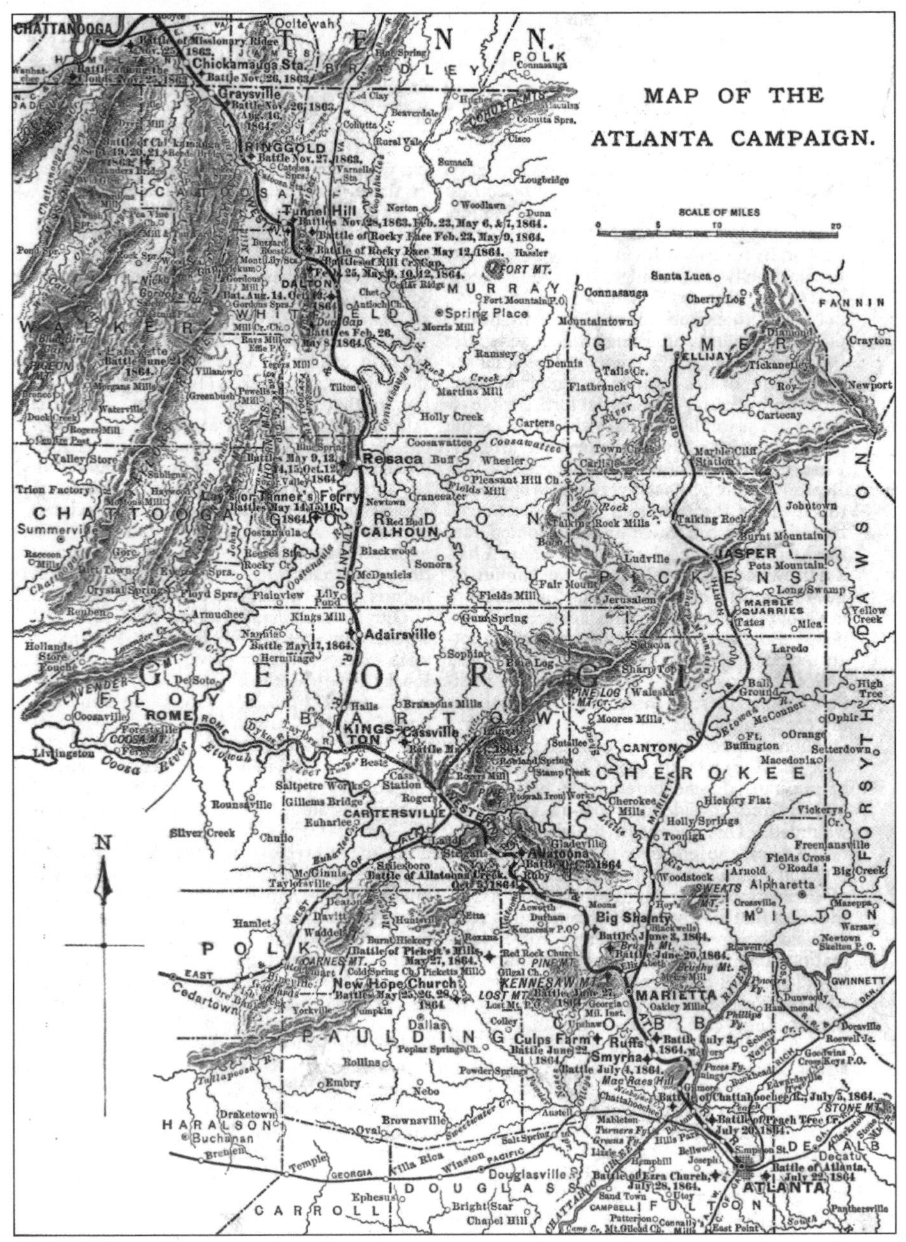

Atlanta Campaign. (Library of Congress)
Map shows the lay of the land from Dalton to Atlanta

strict military control—starting at his main depot at Louisville, running 185 miles to Nashville and from there 150 miles through mid-Tennessee to Chattanooga. In readiness for the offensive, repairs were done on two stretches of railroad, the Western & Atlantic from Chattanooga to Ringgold and the East Tennessee & Georgia to Red Clay. To protect his lifeline, Sherman ordered the construction of blockhouses at bridges and tunnels to ward off attacks by local guerrillas and Confederate cavalrymen, especially, Brig. Gen. Nathan Bedford Forrest, whom Sherman referred to as "that devil Forrest." Also, at 8-mile intervals, sidings were constructed to expedite traffic, each having a telegraph operator ready to report enemy attacks. Sherman instituted a training program for a rail-repair crew of two thousand men and had a government-built and operated rolling mill erected on the Tennessee River at Chattanooga ready to repair twisted railroad ties. He provided a light wagon train to carry wire and other equipment to string and maintain telegraph lines on trees from his headquarters, to keep in contact with his subordinate commanders in the field. Sherman stockpiled rations and munitions—enough to sustain his armies in the field for four months—at Chattanooga and Nashville, where 12 new warehouses were under construction. An amazed brigadier described Nashville as "one vast storehouse—warehouses covering city blocks, one a quarter of a mile long; stables by the ten and twenty acres, repair shops by the fieldful." Pens were built near the army to house thousands of cattle moved overland from Nashville. Before the end of April, enough food was accumulated at Nashville to feed two hundred thousand men for four months, and sufficient grain to sustain fifty thousand animals for the rest of the year, due to the efforts of Quartermaster General Montgomery Meigs.[2]

General Sherman had three armies under his orders: the Army of the Cumberland, with 60,733 men under Maj. Gen. George H. Thomas, concentrated around the rail station at Ringgold, Georgia; the Army of the Tennessee, with 24,465 men under Maj. Gen. James B. McPherson, moving from northern Alabama to the Federal right flank next to Thomas; and the Army of the Ohio, with 13,559 men under Major General John M. Schofield, marching south from Cleveland, Tennessee, to be on the Federal left flank along the East Tennessee & Georgia railroad, which joined the Western & Atlantic railroad at Dalton. His total strength at the time when he moved forward was 110,123 men, consisting of 93,131 infantry, 12,455 cavalry, and 4,537 artillery. The artillery had 254 guns, the pick of 530 pieces available in the three armies, nothing under a 10-pounder, a large proportion of them rifled, and the supply of ammunition was unstinted.

On May 4, Johnston wired Bragg:

> The movements of the enemy in our front, who is now establishing his picket-line as low down on the Cleveland Road as Varnell's Station, within nine miles of Dalton, the concurring reports of every scout that he has for some days past been drawing all his forces from both flanks to Cleveland and Ringgold, and is now bringing them up from North Alabama, satisfy me that he will immediately attack with his united forces. I urge you to send Loring's division and Reynold's brigade, now between Selma and Rome, at once to Rome, and put them at my disposal till the enemy can be met.

On the same day, Cooper telegrammed Lieutenant General Polk: "The President directs, in consequence of the movements of the enemy in front of General Johnston (concentrating his forces from North Alabama), that you move Loring's division, and any other available force at your command, to Rome, Ga., and there unite with General Johnston to meet the enemy." Polk was told that Maj. Gen. S. D. Lee would command in his department. On May 6, Polk replied to Cooper: "My troops are concentrating and moving as directed. I shall take to General Johnston, exclusive of what has been already ordered from this department, about 10,000 infantry and 4,000 cavalry, excluding Roddey, whose strength I do not know."[3] Johnston had anticipated this advance; on May 2, he notified the wives of officers of his headquarters staff to leave Dalton and said goodbye to his wife, Lydia, who went by train to Atlanta. Johnston made his headquarters in a two-story wooden-frame house near the center of Dalton, where he lived and worked.

According to its return of May 1, Johnston's Army of Tennessee had an effective strength of 37,652 infantry, 2,392 cavalry, and 2,812 artillerymen, with 144 guns, which included 36 pieces in the reserve and 18 belonging to the cavalry. The artillery were inferior to their Federal foes in caliber, range, and equipment, with a meager supply of ammunition, and still had a large number of the 6-pounders and 12-pound howitzers that had been condemned by General Pendleton. Johnston commented on the disparity of his artillery to Sherman's: "Mr. Davis descants on the advantages I had in mountains, ravines, and streams, and General Sherman claims that those features of the country were equal to the numerical difference between our forces. I would gladly have given all the mountains, ravines, rivers, and woods of Georgia for such a supply of artillery ammunition, proportionally, as he had."[4]

Dalton was laid out on a grid near the western edge of the broad valley of the Connasauga River, where Johnston expected Sherman's advance and prepared accordingly:

> Dalton is in a valley so broad so as to give ample room for the deployment of the largest American army. Rocky-face, which bounds it on the west, terminates as an obstacle three

> miles north of the railroad gap, and the distance from Chattanooga to Dalton around the north end exceeds that through the railroad gap less than a mile; and a general with a large army, coming from Chattanooga to attack an inferior one at Dalton, would follow that route and find in the broad valley a very favorable field.
>
> Until that day I regarded a battle in the broad valley in which Dalton stands as inevitable. The greatly superior strength of the Federal army made the chances of battle altogether in its favor. It had also places of refuge in case of defeat, in the intrenched pass of Ringgold and in the fortress of Chattanooga; while we, if beaten, had none nearer than Atlanta, 100 miles off, with three rivers intervening. General Sherman's course indicating no intention of giving battle east of Rocky-face, we prepared to fight on either side of the ridge. For that object A. P. Stewart's division was placed in the gap, Cheatham's on the crest of the hill, extending a mile north of Stewart's and Bate's also on the crest of the hill, and extending a mile south of the gap. Stevenson's was formed across the valley east of the ridge, his left meeting Cheatham's right; Hindman in line with Stevenson and on his right; Cleburne behind Mill Creek and in front of Dalton. Walker's division was in reserve.[5]

Sherman began his campaign on May 2 when Thomas moved on Tunnel Hill as Federal cavalry pushed back Confederate units from Ringgold Gap to Tunnel Hill. Schofield advanced upon Varnell's Station. McPherson moved upon Villanow and Snake Creek Gap with orders to seize and break up the railroad between Resaca and Tilton, then withdraw to Snake Creek Gap and prepare to strike the flank of the Confederate army as it retreated. Sherman wanted a decisive battle while he was near his base and Johnston was far from his. In a letter to McPherson on May 5, he expounded on this strategy: "Do not fail in that event to make the most vigorous attack possible, as it may save us from what we have most reason to apprehend—a slow pursuit, in which he gains strength as we lose it."[6] Sherman preferred to fight the battle west of Rocky Face Ridge to cover his base at Chattanooga.

"Terrible Door of Death"

On May 7, Thomas's Army of the Cumberland attacked the Confederate outpost at Tunnel Hill manned by three brigades of dismounted Southern cavalry and horse artillery fighting behind breastworks. They delayed the Federals for several hours but retreated so rapidly that they failed to destroy the tunnel. The Federals pressed on and encountered the main Confederate line at Rocky Face Ridge on the morning of May 8. One major pass, Mill Creek Gap, breached the ridge's craggy wall of quartz, and Confederate engineers had constructed dams with sluice gates across Mills Creek, creating a reservoir 16 feet deep in some places. The attackers were thus forced to advance across a narrow field surrounded by earthworks and dominated by rebel artillery perched on cliffs ominously named Buzzard's Roost. When Sherman peered at Mill Creek Gap through a glass from atop Tunnel Hill, he pronounced it a "terrible door of death." That afternoon, around 4.00 p.m., a division of Hooker's corps commanded by Brigadier General John W. Geary assailed the outpost at Dug Gap, a slight depression gouged out of the mountain for the passage of a country road. The outpost was only guarded by a thousand men from two regiments, commanded by Colonel Williamson, of Reynold's Arkansas brigade. They were soon joined by a small brigade of Kentucky cavalry led by Colonel J. Warren Grigsby. Johnston requested his corps commander, Lieutenant General Hardee, to hurry two brigades from Cleburne's division to bolster the outpost, and accepted Hardee's offer to direct the defense. Cleburne rode ahead of his troops, accompanied by Hardee. The contest came to an end at nightfall, when Hooker's men withdrew.

On the same day, Brigadier General John Newton's division of IV Corps attacked the angle where the Confederate right and center joined. Pettus's brigade held the angle and repulsed the bluecoats. Brown's brigade moved to Pettus's left for support, and both were vigorously assaulted on May 9, but the Confederates offered a stout defense and once more drove back the assailants. General Johnston knew the value of fieldworks with the introduction of the rifled musket with its long-range accuracy prior to the Civil War:

> The Confederate troops suffered little in these engagements, for they fought under the protection of intrenchments. But we had reason to believe that the enemy, who were completely exposed, often at short range and in close order, sustained heavy losses. This belief was strengthened in my mind by the opinion, long entertained, that the soldiers of the United States never give way without good reason.[7]

Meanwhile, Schofield pressed on from Red Clay to Varnell's Station, but was harassed on May 7 and 8 by small groups of Confederate horsemen, which slowed his progress. To eliminate the annoyance, he detached a division of his cavalry on May 9 to deal with it. Major General Wheeler, with Dribrell's and Allen's brigades, recoiled, luring the Federal cavalry away from the main body and then dismounting all his troops. However, two Federal regiments sprung upon them in a combined attack of infantry and cavalry, killing or capturing some 150, a standard, and many small arms and putting them to flight. Among the captives was Colonel La Grange, commanding a brigade, along with three captains and five lieutenants.

Resaca

While these demonstrations were going on, McPherson's Army of the Tennessee was moving to reach the Confederate rear at Resaca via Snake Creek Gap to interrupt Johnston's communications. On May 8, McPherson occupied the gap with no opposition and camped there overnight. During the night, Confederate headquarters realized that Snake Creek Gap was not defended and assigned Colonel Grigsby's Kentucky troopers, who had helped defend Dug Gap. Yet when they arrived, they were brushed aside by McPherson's infantry and fell back to Resaca. In his official report, Maj. Gen. Patrick R. Cleburne stated:

> At about 1 a. m. on the 10th, I received orders to move to the junction of the Sugar Valley and Dug Gap roads. At that point further orders were communicated to me to move toward Resaca. This movement was rendered necessary by the untoward circumstances of Snake Creek Gap not being adequately occupied to resist the heavy force thrown against it, under the sagacious and enterprising McPherson. How this gap, which opened upon our rear and line of communication, from which it was distant at Resaca only five miles, was neglected I cannot imagine. General Mackall, Johnston's chief of staff, told me it was the result of a flagrant disobedience of orders, by whom he did not say. Certainly the commanding general never could have failed to appreciate its importance.[8]

General Sherman, at his headquarters near Tunnel Hill, was taking an early supper late in the afternoon of May 9 when a courier delivered McPherson's first dispatch. The dispatch was sent by messenger at 12.30 p.m. with news that McPherson was 5 miles from Resaca, facing no serious opposition. Sherman banged his fist on the table, rattling the supper dishes, and shouted: "I've got Joe Johnston dead!" Nevertheless, Johnston had anticipated such a move. Brigadier General James Cantey's brigade (1,395 troops), recently sent from the vicinity of Mobile, Alabama, by Major General Maury, had just arrived at Rome. On May 7, Johnston had ordered Cantey to stop at Resaca and keep close observation on all routes leading from La Fayette to Resaca or to Oostenaula on his left. Cantey reported on May 8 that cavalry scouts had observed Yankees in the vicinity of Villanow that day. On May 9, Johnston sent Cantey another brigade—that of Alfred J. Vaugn—promising to come to his aid if attacked. Johnston emphasized to Cantey "the importance of the bridges you guard and the absolute necessity of their being held."[9]

McPherson and his Army of the Tennessee encountered some of Cantey's skirmishers on a hill about a mile west of Resaca. Once Federal skirmishers had cleared the hill after 5.00 p.m., McPherson rode up the hill and scanned the Confederate works through a glass atop a tree stump before ordering an attack. He saw that the Confederates had constructed strong fortifications on the heights in front of Resaca manned by over four thousand troops, supported by artillery and protected by the swampy Camp Creek. McPherson decided to withdraw to Snake Creek Gap and began entrenching there. Johnston felt that this was McPherson's best course of action:

> So if McPherson had attacked on the 9th, according to General Sherman's plan, Resaca could easily have been held against him until next morning, when the army, having left Dalton the night before, without the enemy's knowledge, would be ready to fall upon him from the rear, while holding his line of retreat. With twice his number on one side, and Resaca on the other, he could not have escaped. If the other course, suggested for McPherson by General Sherman, had been taken—that of "placing his whole force astride the railroad above Resaca"—Johnston must have marched against and assailed him in the same manner, with the same advantages. Either course suggested, taken by McPherson, would have compelled Johnston to attack him, and with such advantages of numbers and position as to secure his destruction. We never found it difficult to leave the presence of the Federal army at night without its knowledge. In his report, General Sherman expresses the opinion that nothing saved the Confederate army from the effects of his first manoeuvre "but the impracticable nature of the country, which made the passage of the troops across the valley almost impossible."
>
> This obstacle to a rapid march by the United States army was not unknown to the Confederates. We had examined the country very minutely; and learned its character thoroughly. We could calculate with sufficient accuracy, therefore, the time that would be required for the march of so great an army from Tunnel Hill to Resaca, through the long defile of Snake-Creek Gap, and by the single road beyond that pass. We knew also in how many hours our comparatively small force, moving without baggage trains and in three columns, on roads made good by us, would reach the same point from Dalton.[10]

Bradley Tyler Johnson, who wrote a memoir of Johnston, made the following insight: "The country from Chattanooga to Atlanta is mountainous, traversed by mountain ranges running north and south, with numerous ridges across the valleys and bold streams affording positions for defense. Since Johnston had assumed command of the Army of Tennessee, he had caused careful surveys to be made of the country behind him, and had selected positions for defense to be fortified and prepared."[11]

When General Johnston received reports of McPherson's march on Resaca, he ordered Lieutenant General Hood to move to Resaca with three divisions—those of Hindman, Cleburne, and Walker. On May 10, Hood reported that McPherson had retired to Snake Creek Gap, whereupon Johnston recalled Hood. Via telegram, Hood asked Johnston whether he should halt his troops halfway between Dalton and Resaca; Johnston decided to withdraw Hindman's division, but left Cleburne's and Walker's divisions at Tilton Station, betwixt Dalton and Resaca. In the meantime, Maj. Gen. William W. Loring's division arrived at Resaca on the night of May 10, which "prevented any immediate apprehension for the place." Johnston ordered Loring to assume command until Polk arrived. Two hundred railroad cars, the bulk of the rolling stock in

Georgia, were sent to Rome to transport the rest of Polk's forces to Resaca. On Wednesday, May 11, Lieutenant General Polk reached Resaca and took charge of the defenses. That night, "bishop-general" Polk of the Episcopal Church of Louisiana rode the train up to Dalton to meet with Johnston, accompanied by John Bell Hood, who confided he wished to be baptized. The meeting ended a little before midnight. Before Polk boarded a train back to Resaca, he went to Hood's headquarters, where the one-legged general, unable to kneel, leaned on his crutches in the dim candlelight to be baptized by Polk, who used a bucket of water obtained from a horse trough.

Johnston, wanting to know what Sherman was up to, directed Major General Wheeler to move at dawn on Thursday, May 12, around the north end of Rocky-Face Ridge. Major General Hindman was instructed to support the cavalry with his division of infantry. General William T. Martin's cavalry surveyed the roads west of Resaca. Wheeler encountered Stoneman's Federal cavalry and drove it back, killing, wounding, or capturing 150 men. The reconnaissance confirmed what Johnston suspected, that the main body of Sherman's army was marching toward Snake Creek Gap. Twice on May 12, Johnston wired Polk: "Have you received any information from General Martin, require it at once." Finally, Polk responded that three Union corps were opposite Resaca, with prisoners reporting that "Sherman is at Snake Creek Gap." Johnston, with conclusive evidence that the main Union thrust was in his rear at Resaca, decided to abandon Dalton that night and started his withdrawal. Sam Watkins of Hardee's corps recalled that there was "no excitement" as they moved "as if on review." They passed "old Joe" and his staff, Watkins noting that Johnston was wearing a hat adorned with a black feather: "He is listening to the firing going on at the front. One little cheer, and the very ground seems to shake with cheers. Old Joe smiles as blandly as a modest maid, raises his hat in acknowledgement, makes a polite bow, and rides toward the firing."[12]

Johnston gave an account of the action:

> About one o'clock a.m. on the 13th the Confederate infantry and artillery were withdrawn from the position they had been holding in and near Mill-Creek Gap, and marched to Resaca—the cavalry being ordered to follow after daybreak as rear-guard, and to observe any body of Federal troops that might advance through Dalton.
>
> The Federal army, approaching Resaca on the Snake-Creek Gap road, was met about a mile from the place by Loring's division, and held in check long enough to enable Hardee's and Hood's corps, then just arriving to occupy their ground undisturbed. As the army formed (in two lines), Polk's and Hardee's corps were west of the place and railroad, facing to the west; the former on the left, with its left resting on the Oostenaula. Hood's corps extended from Hardee's right across the railroad to the Connesauga, facing to the northwest.

> There was brisk skirmishing all the afternoon of May 13th on Polk's front, and that of Hardee's left division-Cheatham's.[13]

John Schofield's Army of the Ohio on the Federal left launched two divisions abreast against Maj. Gen. Thomas C. Hindman's Confederate division fortified behind Camp Creek. All of Schofield's attacks were repulsed, with great loss. Meanwhile, Major General Wheeler was directed to ascertain the position and formation of the Federal left flank. Wheeler's cavalry scouts reported that Sherman's left wing was in the air, indicating an opportunity to gain the initiative. Lieutenant General Hood was directed to make an attack with Stewart's and Stevenson's divisions, to which Johnston added four brigades from Hardee's front to strengthen the assault. Hood engaged the Federals about 6.00 p.m., slamming into the right flank of Brigadier General David S. Stanley's division, exposed on the left near the railroad. Thomas Deavenport, one of Hood's regimental chaplains, wrote that "a grand charge and the enemy were driven hastily back from their entrenched position, leaving knapsacks, haversacks, guns." After dark, Johnston sought out Hood to discuss plans to continue the attack at dawn, hoping to turn the enemy's left and break through to Snake Creek Gap. However, a courier brought news that Martin's cavalry patrols had discovered that a Federal division under Brigadier General Thomas Sweeny had rafted over the Oostanaula River at Lay's Ferry, 6 miles west of Resaca. Johnston sent Walker's division to drive the Federals back across the river and cancelled Hood's attack. Further bad news arrived at the same time; after dark Lieutenant General Polk's advanced troops had been driven from a piece of high ground in front of his left and Federal troops were bringing up artillery, which commanded the railway and turnpike bridges at short range. Johnston directed his chief engineer, Colonel Prestman, to make a road during the night and assemble a pontoon bridge a mile above and out of range of the Federal artillery.

Johnston rode to the right to talk to Hood about renewing the attack on the Federal left flank. In front of Hindman's position, Hood had a redoubt constructed about 80 yards in front of the Confederate main line, where it could enfilade advancing Federals. Hood put four 12-pounder Napoleons of Captain Max Van Den Corput's Georgia battery into the redoubt. Work was still going on in the redoubt when General Hooker instructed Major General Daniel Butterfield's division to seize the earthworks. At 11.00 a.m., Federal infantrymen overwhelmed the redoubt and captured the guns, but the position was untenable as Confederate sharpshooters and counterbattery fire from the Confederate main line targeted the earthworks, making it impossible to haul off the guns. The four guns remained in the fort between the lines until after dark, when they were removed by the Federals. Hood commented that they were "four old iron pieces, not worth the sacrifice of the life of even one man."

While Johnston and Hood were discussing the tactical situation, a courier from Walker arrived with news that the report of Union troops south of the Oostanaula was false. Johnston thus ordered Hood to renew the attack: "Less resistance was encountered than had been expected; this encouraged me, during the engagement, to hope that Hood's corps, and the second line of Polk's and Hardee's, might constitute a force strong enough to defeat the left of the Federal army, while its right was held in check by the remaining third of ours, protected by intrenchments."[14] Hours later, though, Walker sent word that the Federals were back across the river in force. Thomas Sweeny had withdrawn his troops back across the river at the approach of Walker's division, but had returned on boats under Sherman's orders and had laid a pontoon bridge and begun erecting earthworks. Walker was unable to dislodge them and Sweeny was reinforced the next morning. Again, Johnston countermanded the orders for Hood to attack, but corps headquarters did not send this on to Stewart's division in time; consequently, Stewart attacked unsupported and suffered before being recalled.

Johnston decided to pull out of Resaca to protect his line of communications, ordering the army to cross the river around midnight. To mask the rumble of the wagons and gun carriages moving over the bridges, Confederate pickets made a racket with rifle fire and artillerists laid green cornstalks over the bridges to muffle the sound. Polk and Hardee used the turnpike and railway spans, while Hood crossed on the new pontoon bridge. After Johnston's army was safely across, the rearguard burned the railroad bridge, took up the pontoons, and loaded them onto wagons, but overlooked the turnpike bridge in the last-minute confusion.

One Confederate soldier wrote in his diary: "I consider Genl. Johnston the best General in the Confederacy, not even excepting Robt. E. Lee, but this is one time that old Sherman came near over-reaching him. I will always consider it a mere chance if he gets well away from Resaca."[15]

Johnston's Strategy

Joseph Johnston laid out his strategy for the coming campaign to oppose Sherman's advance to Atlanta, declaring that his movements "were determined by the relative forces of the armies, and a higher estimate of the Northern soldiers than our Southern editors and politicians were accustomed to express, or even the Administration seemed to entertain. It was not to be supposed that such troops, under a sagacious and resolute leader, and covered by intrenchments, were to be beaten by greatly inferior numbers." He said he thus determined to switch to the defensive, "to spare the blood of our soldiers by fighting under cover habitually, and to attack only when bad position or division of the enemy's forces might give us advantages counterbalancing that of superior numbers." Johnston added that all positions were held until their communications were seriously threatened, whereupon his forces "fell back only far enough to secure them, watching for opportunities to attack, keeping near enough to the Federal army to assure the Confederate Administration that Sherman could not send reenforcements to Grant, and hoping to reduce the odds against us by partial engagements." He also hoped that the Federal army might be weakened before the end of June due to the expiring of terms of service of regiments that had not reenlisted. "I was confident, too, that the Administration would see the expediency of employing Forrest and his cavalry to break the enemy's railroad communications, by which he could be defeated."[16] Johnston recognized the tactical supremacy of defense supplemented by entrenchments, especially since the advent of the rifled musket, thus safeguarding his troops and protecting his communications.

Although Johnston hoped to find a good defensive position to cover the roads south of the Oostanaula River near Calhoun, none could be found. Late in the afternoon of May 16, he and his staff reached Calhoun and set up headquarters at Curtin House. The troops rested for up to 20 hours near Calhoun, then on the 17th marched some 7 or 8 miles to Adairsville. It was thought a stand could be made there in the valley of the Oothealoga Creek, but the breadth of the valley exceeded the front of Johnston's army properly formed for battle. While at Adairsville, Polk's cavalry—a division of about 3,700 troopers commanded by Brigadier General William H. "Red" Jackson—joined the army. Federal troops began pushing back the cavalry, but Hardee sent Cheatham's division to support Wheeler's troopers and kept the Federals at bay until nightfall. The troops rested 18 hours and were ordered to march to Cassville.

Cassville

Johnston received a telegraphic dispatch from Brigadier General Stephen Dill Lee, who was in charge of the Mississippi Department, announcing that Forrest, with a force of 3,500 picked horsemen and two batteries of artillery, would set out on May 20 to disrupt Sherman's line of communications in central Tennessee. When Wheeler's scouts reported that Sherman was pursuing in three widely separated columns, Johnston devised a plan to ambush part of his army:

> Two roads lead southward from Adairsville—one following the railroad through Kingston, and, like it, turning almost at right angles to the east at that place; the other, quite direct

> to the Etowah Railroad-bridge, passing through Cassville, where it is met by the first. The probability that the Federal army would divide—a column following each road—gave me a hope of engaging and defeating one of them before it could receive aid from the other. In that connection the intelligent engineer-officer who had surveyed that section, Lieutenant Buchanan, was questioned minutely over the map as to the character of the ground, in the presence of Lieutenant-Generals Polk and Hood, who had been informed of my object. He described the country on the direct road as open, and unusually favorable for attack. It was evident, from the map, that the distance between the two Federal columns would be greatest when that following the railroad should be near Kingston. Lieutenant Buchanan thought that the communications between the columns at this part of their march would be eight or nine miles, by narrow and crooked country roads.
>
> In the morning of the 18th, Hardee's corps marched to Kingston; Polk's and Hood's, followed the direct road, halted within a mile of Cassville—the former deployed in two lines, crossing the road and facing Adairsville; the latter halted on the right. Jackson's division observed the Federal column on the Kingston road, and Wheeler's troops that [were] moving toward Cassville. Those two officers were instructed to keep me accurately informed of the enemy's progress.
>
> Next morning, when Brig.-General Jackson's reports showed the head of the Federal Column following the railroad was near Kingston, Lieutenant-General Hood was directed to move with his corps to a country road about a mile to the east of that from Adairsville, and parallel to it, and to march northward on that road, right in front. Polk's corps, as then formed, was to advance to meet and engage the enemy approaching from Adairsville; and it was expected that Hood's would be in position to fall upon the left flank of those troops as soon as Polk attacked them in front. An order was read to each regiment, announcing that we were about to give battle to the enemy. It was received with exultation.[17]

Johnston had the following general order, which he composed, read at the head of each regiment next morning, May 19:

> Soldiers of the Army of Tennessee:
>
> You have displayed the highest qualities of the soldier—firmness in combat, patience under toil. By your courage and skill you have repulsed every assault of the enemy. By marches by day and marches by night you have defeated every attempt upon your communications. Your communications are secured. You will now turn and march to meet his advancing columns. Fully confiding in the conduct of the officers, the courage of the soldiers, I lead you to battle. We may confidently trust that the Almighty Father will still reward the patriots' toil and the patriots' banners. Cheered by the success of our brothers in Virginia and beyond the Mississippi, our efforts will equal theirs. Strengthened by His support, these efforts will be crowned with the like glories.[18]

Baptism

After discussing matters concerning the coming battle, Hood, Hardee, and Polk went with General Johnston to his tent to fulfill a request his wife, Lydia, had made in a letter two days previously to bishop-general Polk:

> You are never too occupied, I well know, to pause to perform a good deed, and will, I am sure, even whilst leading you soldiers on to victory, lead my soldier nearer to God. General Johnston has never been baptized. It is the dearest wish of my heart that he should be, and that you should perform the ceremony would be a great gratification to me. I have written to him on the subject, and am sure he only waits your leisure. I rejoice that you are near him in these trying times. May God crown all your efforts with success, and spare your life for your country and friends.[19]

Polk donned his surplice and performed the rite of baptism in front of an improvised altar, with candlelight glistening, as Johnston knelt to receive the sacrament.

Meanwhile, on the afternoon of May 19, Major General Samuel French's division of Polk's corps—consisting of 4,174 men—arrived from Rome, Georgia. Johnston had repeatedly urged French to join his army, even though it meant abandoning Rome with its factories and the Noble Brothers Iron Works, which had been the South's second-largest cannon foundry. However, Johnston felt it was vital to protect his base at Atlanta and his lifeline, the railroad, which brought supplies for his army and reinforcements.

Brigadier General Stephen Dill Lee advised Johnston that Federal threats from Memphis had forced him to call off Nathan Bedford Forrest's raid on Sherman's communications. General Washburn at Memphis had dispatched a major Federal cavalry expedition of eight thousand men under Brigadier General Samuel D. Sturgis into Mississippi to distract Forrest. Sherman had recommended such moves, directing "great and constant activity" for "diverting the enemy's attention as far as possible from the operations in Georgia."[20]

Johnston rode with his corps commanders to show Hood where to form his line of battle, then after seeing Polk and Hardee to their positions he returned to his headquarters. Hardee moved on the Kingston road to divert Thomas's Army of the Cumberland and McPherson's Army of the Tennessee along the line of the railroad. Schofield's Army of the Ohio and Hooker's XX Corps were advancing along the Cassville road, where Polk's corps would encounter their front while Hood's corps would fall upon the left flank of the column.

About 10.00 a.m., Johnston sent his aide-de-camp, Brig. Gen. William Whann Mackall, to ride out to direct Hood "to make quick work" and "not to make too wide a movement; not to separate himself too far from the left of the army, but if the enemy advanced upon him to strike him promptly and hard." The official record notes:

> On reaching General Hood, who was in a field in rear of one of his divisions, I informed him that the enemy was advancing in force on Hardee. He instantly said, "And they are on me too. The cavalry gave me no warning. I only learned the fact through officers of my own

> staff, and am now falling back to form a line farther to the rear." I asked him, "What road are the enemy moving on?" He replied, "On both the Canton and Spring Place road; and did you not see them?" I answered that I had seen no enemy. I then rode back. I returned to General Johnston and reported the information and the fact that General Hood was then forming on a range of hills crossing the Canton road. I tell the general, who says it can't be. Mackall had sent a courier to Johnston with a report that "enemy in heavy force close to Hood on Canton road."[21]

Hood described the incident in his official report to General Cooper, saying he was at the head of his troops and found the road to be held by Confederate dismounted cavalry, with no enemy initially in sight:

> While in motion a body of the enemy, which I supposed to be cavalry, made its appearance on the Canton road, in rear of the right of my original position. Major-General Hindman was then in that direction with his division to ascertain what force it was keeping the other two divisions in the vicinity of the Canton road. It was not a mistake (as General Johnston states) that the force appeared as is shown from the fact that Major-General Hindman had men wounded from the small-arms and artillery fired from this body. Maj. James Hamilton, of my staff, was sent to report to General Johnston the fact that the enemy had appeared on the Canton road. During Major Hamilton's absence Brigadier-General Mackall, chief of staff, rode up in great haste and said that General Johnston directed that I should not separate myself so far from General Polk. I called his attention to where General Polk's right was resting, and informed him that I could easily form upon it, and orders were given to that effect, throwing back my right to look after this body, which turned out to be the enemy's cavalry.[22]

Indeed, the "heavy force" was a unit of General Alexander McCook's cavalry, which had been separated from the main Federal body and was not enough of a threat to thwart the plans for the day's attack. Johnston stated: "I heard of this erratic movement after it had caused such a loss of time as to make the attack intended impracticable; for its success depended on accuracy in timing it. The intention was therefore abandoned."[23]

Sounds of artillery fire on the Kingston road from the Federals pressing Hardee's corps, and skirmishing by Wheeler's cavalry on the Cassville road, indicated that Sherman's army was about to attack the Army of Tennessee. Johnston's engineers had found a ridge near Cassville to make a stand. Johnston rode out with Polk and Mackall to examine this new line of defense and check if it would suffice to receive Sherman's attack. Johnston was pleased with the new position:

> To be prepared for it, the Confederate army was drawn up in a position that I remember as the best that I saw occupied during the war—the ridge immediately south of Cassville, with a broad, open, elevated valley in front of it completely commanded by the fire of the troops occupying its crest.
>
> The eastern end of this ridge is perhaps a mile to the east of Cassville. Its southwest end is near the railroad, a little to the west of the Cassville Station. Its length was just sufficient for

> Hood's and Polk's corps, and half of Hardee's, formed as usual in two lines, and in that order from right to left. The other half of Hardee's troops, prolonging this line, were southwest of the railroad, on undulating ground on which they had only such advantage as their own labor, directed by engineering, could give them. They worked with great spirit, however, and were evidently full of confidence. This gave me assurance of success on the right and in the centre, where we had very decided advantage of ground.
>
> Brigadier-General Shoup, chief of artillery, had pointed to me what he thought a weak point near General Polk's right, a space of a hundred and fifty or two hundred yards, which, in his opinion, might be enfiladed by artillery placed on a hill more than a mile off, beyond the front of our right—so far, it seemed to me, as to make the danger trifling. Still, he was requested to instruct the officer commanding there to guard against such a chance by the construction of traverses, and to impress upon him that no attack of infantry could be combined with a fire of distant artillery, and that his infantry might safely occupy some ravines immediately in rear of this position during any such fire of artillery.[24]

Traverses are stubby earth walls running perpendicular to the main trench wall at regular intervals, comparting the trenches, protecting the defenders from lateral blast and shrapnel flying in all directions from improved artillery shells discharged by the more accurate long-range rifled Federal cannon. They were an innovative design that Longstreet had incorporated in a system of fieldworks known as the "line" of the Rappahannock.

The area where Brigadier General Shoup believed there would be a problem was a salient that jutted out where Polk's right met Hood's left. It was occupied by the Mississippi battery of Captain James A. Hoskins. The Federal artillery opened an artillery barrage on Hood's and Polk's troops as they moved into position, which lasted until nightfall. The Federal line curved in a gentle arc across the valley, allowing their guns to commence a concentrated crossfire on Hoskin's battery, which was exposed due to a lack of vegetation around its portion of the line.

Johnston inspected his line and went to his tent after dark to take supper. Waiting for him was Colonel William D. Gale, Polk's staff aide, with an invitation to meet the lieutenant generals at Polk's headquarters to discuss the army's plans. Johnston had his dinner and asked Maj. Gen. Samuel French to accompany him to Polk's quarters, arrived at about 8.00 p.m. Johnston found Polk and Hood waiting for him, but Hardee was absent from the conference.

To Johnston's surprise, General Hood, who was the chief spokesman, expressed the opinion that he and Polk believed the position was untenable. He said Polk would not be able to hold his line for three-quarters of an hour, nor his corps for two hours, due to enfilading fire by Federal artillery. Hood argued that the weakness of the salient compromised the whole position. They urged Johnston to abandon the position at once and withdraw south of the Etowah. Johnston objected, asserting that the Confederate army was in a commanding position on the ridge, with clear lines of fire. French recalled: "Johnston insisted on fighting."

Johnston, after debating the matter with Hood for two hours, conceded:

> Although the position was the best we had occupied, I yielded at last, in the belief that the confidence of the commanders of two of the three corps of the army, of their inability to resist the enemy, would inevitably be communicated to their troops, and produce that inability. Lieutenant-General Hardee, who arrived after this decision [around 10.00 p.m.], remonstrated against it strongly, and was confident that his troops could hold their ground, although less favorably posted. The error was adhered to, however, and the position abandoned before daybreak.

Lieutenant Thomas B. Mackall, cousin and aide-de-camp to Brigadier General Mackall, who kept a journal of operations of the Army of Tennessee, wrote: "Feeling in army: One lieutenant-general talks about attack and not giving ground, publicly, and quietly urges retreat."[25] The lieutenant general Thomas Mackall was referring to was John Bell Hood. Prior to arriving at Dalton on February 24 to take command of one of Johnston's corps, Hood played up to Jefferson Davis during the winter while recovering from his wound received at Chickamauga. Before leaving Richmond, Hood agreed to send clandestine correspondence to the president. After his arrival, Hood wrote a series of private letters to Davis, Bragg, and Seddon during March and April on the condition of the Army of Tennessee and emphasized his willingness to take the offensive. On March 7, Hood wrote to Davis:

> We should march to the front as soon as possible, so as not to allow the enemy to concentrate and advance upon us. The addition of a few horses for our artillery will place this army in fine condition. It is well clothed, well fed, and the transportation is excellent and the greatest possible quantity required. I never before felt that we had it so thoroughly in our power. He is at present weak, and we are strong. I am eager for us to take the initiative.

In April, Hood wrote to Bragg:

> I received your letter, and am sorry to inform you that I have done all in my power to induce General Johnston to accept the proposition you made to move forward. He will not consent, as he desires the troops to be sent here and it is left to him as to what use should be made of them.
>
> I regret this exceedingly, as my heart was fixed upon our going to the front and regaining Tennessee and Kentucky. When we are in better condition to drive the enemy from our country I am not able to comprehend.
>
> How unfortunate for our country it is for the Generals in the field to fail to cooperate with the authorities of the Government.[26]

Johnston wired a report to Davis on May 20 at Etowah, stating that over the previous eight days the Federals had pressed his forces back 32 miles:

> We kept near him to prevent his detaching to Virginia, as you directed, and have repulsed every attack he has made. On the 12th at Resaca my arrangements for an attack were defeated by his crossing a column close to my communications, and yesterday, having ordered a general attack, while the officer charged with the lead was advancing he was deceived by a false report that a heavy column of the enemy had turned our right and was close upon him, and took a defensive position. When the mistake was discovered it was too late to resume the movement.

On May 21 near Allatoona, Johnston reported to Davis:

> I know that my dispatch must of necessity create the feeling you express. I have earnestly sought an opportunity to strike the enemy. The direction of the railroad to this point has enabled him to press me back by steadily moving to the left and by fortifying the moment he halted. He has made an assault upon his superior forces too hazardous, and in making this retrograde march we have [not] lost much by straggling or desertion.[27]

Colonel Henry P. Brewster

On May 21, Hood dispatched an intermediary with a letter of introduction to the president, Colonel Henry P. Brewster, a Texas lawyer, who was a close friend and advocate for Hood. Hood wrote to Davis: "Colonel Brewster has been with us since we left Dalton, and can give you an account of the operations of this army since the enemy made their appearance in our immediate front. He leaves for Richmond today and I think it would be well for you to have a conversation with him in relation to our affairs." It is not known what Brewster told President Davis, but it must have been slanted in Hood's favor and denigrated Johnston. Mary Chesnut's diary sheds some light on Brewster's distortions. On June 4, she wrote: "He [Brewster] said Joe Johnston was kept from fighting at Dalton by no plan—by no strategy. Hood and Polk wanted to fight. He resisted their council. It is said he is afraid to trust them because they do not hate Jeff Davis enough—maybe at all—and all the delay is breaking Hood's heart. Hood's is in the reserved corps. So much retreating would demoralize General Lee's army."[28]

Johnston ordered the army to withdraw south of the Etowah River on the night of May 20 and take a position at the head of Allatoona Pass. After the army crossed the river about noon, Johnston had Wheeler's cavalry placed above the infantry and Jackson's below to observe the enemy. Major General Wheeler was directed to make a reconnaissance on the 22nd by crossing the river 5 or 6 miles to the right to determine in what direction the Federal army was moving and to inflict damage by breaking the railroad and capturing or destroying trains and detachments. Near Cassville Station on May 24, General Wheeler came upon a large Federal supply train. After defeating the brigade of cavalry guarding it, he captured 250 loaded wagons, hauled off 80 with their teams, plus three hundred equipped horses and mules, and burned the rest. In addition, he captured 158 prisoners.

Johnston needed to ascertain where Sherman's drive was headed so that he could counter it:

> No movement of the enemy was discovered until the 22d, when General Jackson reported their army moving toward Stilesboro', as if to cross the Etowah near that place; they crossed on the 23d. On the 24th Hardee's and Polk's corps encamped on the road from Stilesboro' to Atlanta, south-east of Dallas, and Hood's four miles from New Hope Church, on the road from Allatoona. On the 25th the Federal army was a little east of Dallas, and Hood's corps was placed with its center at New Hope Church, Polk's on his left, and Hardee's prolonging the line to the Atlanta road, which was held by its left. A little before 6 o'clock in the afternoon Stewart's division in front of New Hope Church was fiercely attacked by Hooker's corps, and the action continued two hours without lull or pause, when the assailants fell back. The canister shot of the sixteen Confederate field-pieces and the musketry of five thousand infantry at short range must have inflicted heavy loss upon General Hooker's, as is proved by the name "Hell Hole," which General Sherman says, was given the place by the Federal soldiers.

Johnston said that the following day, Federal troops worked "vigorously" to extend their defenses toward the railroad, and thus there was little skirmishing. Meanwhile, Confederate forces "labored strenuously" to keep up with the Federal entrenching work, but struggled to do so due to their inferior numbers and a lack of entrenching tools. Johnston continued:

> On the 27th, however, the fighting rose above the grade of skirmishing, especially in the afternoon, when at half-past 5 o'clock the Fourth Corps (Howard) and a division of the Fourteenth (Palmer) attempted to turn our right, but the movement, after being impeded by the cavalry, was met by two regiments of our right division (Cleburne's), and two brigades of his second line brought up on the right of the first. The Federal formation was so deep that its front did not equal that of our two brigades; consequently those troops were greatly exposed to our musketry—all but the leading troops being on a hillside facing us. They advanced until their first line was within 25 or 30 paces of ours, and fell back only after at least 700 men had fallen dead in their places. When the leading Federal troops paused in their advance, a color-bearer came on and planted his colors eight or ten feet in front of his regiment, but was killed in the act. A soldier sprang forward to hold up or bear off the colors [and] was shot dead as he seized the staff. Two others who followed successively fell like him, but the fourth bore back the noble emblem. Some time after nightfall the Confederates captured above two hundred prisoners in the hollow before them.
>
> In the afternoon of the 28th Lieutenant-General Hood was instructed to draw his corps to the rear of our line in the early part of the night, march around our right flank, and form it facing the left flank of the Federal line and obliquely to it, and attack at dawn—Hardee and Polk to join in the battle successively as the success on the right of each might enable him to do so. We waited next morning for the signal—the sound of Hood's musketry—from the appointed time until 10 o'clock, when a message from that officer was brought by an aide-de-camp to the effect that he had found R. W. Johnson's division intrenching on the left of the Federal line and almost right angles to it, and asked for instructions. The message proved that there could be no surprise, which was necessary to success, and that the enemy's intrenchments

would be completed before we could attack. The corps was therefore recalled. It was ascertained afterward that after marching eight or ten hours Hood's corps was than at least six miles from the Federal left, which was little more than a musket-shot from his starting-point.

The extension of the Federal intrenchments toward the railroad was continued industriously to cut us off from it or to cover their own approach to it. We tried to keep pace with them, but the labor did not prevent the desultory fighting, which was kept up while daylight lasted. In this the great inequality of force compelled us to employ dismounted cavalry. On the 4th or 5th of June the Federal army reached the railroad between Ackworth and Allatoona. The Confederate forces then moved to a position carefully marked out by Colonel Presstman, its left on Lost Mountain, and its right, of cavalry, beyond the railroad and somewhat covered by Noonday Creek, a line much too long for our strength.

On the 8th the Federal army seemed to be near Ackworth, and our position was contracted to cover the roads leading thence to Atlanta. This brought the left of Hardee's corps to Gilgal Church, Polk's right near Marietta and Ackworth road and Hood's corps massed beyond the road. Pine Mountain, a detached hill, was held by a division. On the 11th of June the left of the Federal army was on the high ground beyond Noonday Creek, its center a third of a mile in front of Pine Mountain and its right beyond the Burnt Hickory and Marietta road.

In the morning of the 14th General Hardee and I rode to the summit of Pine Mountain to decide if the outpost there should be maintained. General Polk accompanied us. After we had conducted our examination and the abandonment of the hill that night had been decided upon, a few shots were fired at us from a battery of Parrott guns a quarter of a mile in our front; the third of these passed through General Polk's chest, from left to right, killing him instantly. This event produced a deep sorrow in the army, in every battle of which he had been distinguished. Major-General W. W. Loring succeeded to the command of the corps.

A division of Georgia militia (about three thousand eventually increased to five) under Major-General G. W. Smith, transferred to the Confederate service by Governor Brown, was charged with the defense of the bridges and ferries of the Chattahoochee, for the safety of Atlanta.[29]

Death of General Polk

Johnston had rushed to Polk's lifeless body, which lay face-up having been propelled to the top of the hill by the force of the impact. Johnston and Hardee knelt by Polk's body, and Johnston tearfully said: "We have lost much! I would rather anything but this." He found three bloodstained copies of a little book of religious inspiration entitled *Balm for the Weary and Wounded*, inscribed with the names of Johnston, Hardee, and Hood, which he meant to give them as gifts. On June 14, Johnston wrote an emotional message to the army mourning the loss:

> Comrades, you are called to mourn your great captain, your oldest companion in arms. Lieutenant-General Polk fell today at the outpost of this army, the Army he raised and commanded, in all of whose trials he shared, to all of whose victories he contributed. In this distinguished leader we have lost the most courteous of gentlemen, the most gallant of soldiers. The Christian patriot soldier has never lived nor died in vain. His example is before you; his mantle rests with you.

After Bate's division withdrew from Pine Mountain that night, Yankee soldiers occupying the position before dawn the next day found a message chalked on the door of a log cabin: "You damned Yankees, you have killed our old General Polk."[30]

On May 26, General Johnston received the addition of William Quarles's brigade of 2,500 men, who arrived from Mobile. This was a small accession to his forces, whereas Sherman could not only get replacements to replenish his loses but even augment his army.

Leonidas Polk (1806–64) graduated from West Point in 1827. He later left the Army for the Church and became the first Episcopal Bishop of Louisiana in 1841. At the outbreak of the Civil War, he offered his services to the Confederate army and was made a major general in June 1861. He was killed at the battle of Pine Mountain, near Kennesaw, Georgia, on June 14, 1864. (Library of Congress)

Value of the Railroad

Joseph Johnston constantly implored Bragg to send Forrest's or Morgan's cavalry to interrupt Sherman's communications. He realized the value of the new technology of the railroad, which allowed large armies to operate in the field, and that interruption in the railroad's operation would result in their ruin. On June 16 Johnston wired Bragg: "Since my last dispatch the enemy has, as usual, been approaching by fortifying. I can find no mode of preventing this. I repeat the suggestion that the cavalry in Alabama be put in the enemy's rear." On June 26, he again emphasized this strategy: "The enemy is gradually pressing us back. To defeat his design it is necessary to break the railroad this side of Dalton. We have not cavalry enough. Can you not send such an expedition from East Tennessee or Mississippi?"[31]

Governor Joseph E. Brown

His plea was seconded by Governor Joseph E. Brown of Georgia on June 28 at Atlanta in a communication with Jefferson Davis. Brown believed it vital that the Confederacy hold on to Atlanta, which he said was "almost as important as the heart is to the human body." He continued:

> I have done all in my power to reenforce and strengthen General Johnston's army. As you know, further reenforcements are greatly needed on account of the superior numbers of the enemy. Is it not in your power to send more troops? Could not Forrest or Morgan, or both, do more now for our cause in Sherman's rear than anywhere else? He brings his supplies from Nashville, over nearly three hundred miles of railroad, through a rough country, over a great number of bridges. If these are destroyed, it is impossible for him to subsist his large army, and he must fall back through a broad scope of country destitute of provisions, which he could not do without great loss, if not annihilation. I do not wish to volunteer advice, but so great is our anxiety for the success of arms, and the defense of the State, that I trust you will excuse what may seem to be an intrusion.

President Davis replied from Richmond on June 29, although Governor Brown did not receive the message until July 4:

> Your dispatch of yesterday received. I fully appreciate the importance of Atlanta, as evinced by my past action. I have sent all available reenforcements, detaching troops even from points that remain exposed to the enemy. The disparity of force between the opposing armies in Northern Georgia is less, as reported, than at any other point. The cavalry of Morgan is on district service, and may fulfill your wishes. Forrest's command is now operating on Sherman's line of communication and is necessary for other purposes in his present field of service. I do not see that I can change the disposition of our forces so as to help General Johnston more effectually than by the present arrangement.

To this Governor Brown replied on July 4:

> I received your dispatch last night. I regret exceedingly that you cannot grant my request, as I am satisfied Sherman's escape with his army would be impossible if ten thousand good cavalry under Forrest were thrown in his rear this side of Chattanooga, and his supplies cut off. The whole country expects this, though points of less importance should, for a time, be overrun. Our people believe that General Johnston is doing all in his power with the means at his command, and all expect you to send the necessary force to cut off the enemy's subsistence. We do not see how Forrest's operations in Mississippi, or Morgan's raids as conducted in Kentucky, interfere with Sherman's plans in this State, as his supplies continue to reach him.
>
> Destroy these, and Atlanta is not only safe, but the destruction of the army under Sherman opens up Tennessee and Kentucky to us. Your information as to the relative strength of the two armies in North Georgia cannot be from reliable sources. If your mistake should result in the loss of Atlanta and the occupation of other strong points in this State by the enemy, the blow may be fatal to our cause and remote posterity may have reason to mourn over the error.

This rejoinder angered Davis, who sent a sarcastic reply on July 5:

> I am surprised to learn from you that the basis of the comparison I made on official reports and estimates is unreliable. Until your better knowledge is communicated I shall have no means of correcting such errors, and your dicta cannot control the disposition of troops in different parts of the Confederate States. Most men in your position would not assume to

decide on the value of the service to be rendered by the troops in distant positions. When you give me your reliable statement of comparative strength of the armies, I will be glad also to know the source of your information as to what the whole country expects and posterity will judge.

On July 7, Brown answered back with even greater sarcasm than Davis displayed:

I regret the exhibition of temper with which I am met in your dispatch refusing to grant my request to send Forrest or Morgan, or both, with their commands, to cut off Sherman's supplies and relieve my State. I have not pretended to dictate, but when Georgia has forty to fifty regiments defending Richmond and Atlanta is in great danger, probably no one but yourself would consider the anxiety of the efforts of her Governor to use every argument in his power to obtain re-enforcements just cause of rebuke, while the defense of the Gulf States depends upon the strength of one of the armies now in front of Atlanta and the Western States upon the other. If you continue to keep our forces divided, and our cavalry raiding and meeting raids while the enemy's line of communication, nearly 300 miles from his base, is uninterrupted, I fear the result will be similar to those which followed a like policy of dividing our forces at Murfreesborough and Chattanooga. If Atlanta is sacrificed and Georgia overrun while our cavalry is engaged in distant raids, you will have no difficulty in ascertaining, from correct sources of information, what was expected of you by the whole people, and what verdict posterity will record from your statements as to the relative strength of the two armies. I venture, at the hazard of further rebuke, to predict that your official estimates of Sherman's numbers are as incorrect as your official calculations at Missionary Ridge were erroneous.

General Johnston noted in his *Narrative* that cutting off Sherman's supplies had both military and political implications:

It can scarcely be doubted that five thousand cavalry directed by Forrest's sagacity, courage, and enterprise, against the Federal railroad communications, would have been at least so far successful as to prevent as much food as was absolutely necessary for its subsistence, from reaching the Federal army. Such a result would have compelled General Sherman to the desperate resource of a decisive battle on our terms, which involved attacking excellent troops entrenched, or to that abandoning his enterprise. In the first event, the chances of battle would have been greatly in our favor. In the second, a rout of the Federal army could scarcely have been prevented.

The importance to the Confederacy of defeating the enterprise against Atlanta was not to be measured by military consequences alone. Political considerations were also involved, and added much to the interest of that campaign.

The Northern Democrats had pronounced the management of the war a failure; and declared against its being continued; and the presidential election, soon to occur, was to turn upon the question of immediate peace or continued war. In all the earlier part of the year 1864, the press had been publishing to the Northern people most exaggerated ideas of the military value of Atlanta, and that it was to be taken, and that its capture would terminate the war. If Sherman had been foiled, these teachings would have caused great exaggeration of the consequences of his failure, which would have strengthened the peace party greatly; so much, perhaps, as to have enabled it to carry the presidential election, which would have brought the war to an immediate close.[32]

President Davis treated Johnston's pleas for assistance with derision. The decisive theater of the war was at the time in northern Georgia, but Davis failed miserably in dealing with it. He could not see that the fate of the Confederacy was intertwined with Johnston's Army of Tennessee.

One of Johnston's biographers, Robert M. Hughes, expressed the opinion that reinforcing Johnston as he and Governor Brown requested could have turned the tide of the campaign:

> Had Johnston's suggestion been acted upon, and a strong body of horse under the gifted Forrest been sent upon such an expedition, the story of that campaign might have been reversed. In the view of the Administration, the protection of Mississippi and Alabama from raids was of more importance than the defeat of this invasion. It was but another phase of the old question on which President Davis and General Johnston had differed from the outbreak of the war, each with equal sincerity and positiveness—the question of the relative wisdom of concentration for decisive operations or diffusion to protect territory.[33]

After abandoning Pine Mountain on June 16, General Johnston withdrew Cleburne's division behind Mud Creek, which was found to be enfiladed by a Yankee battery on a small hill. Consequently, on the following day, Johnston had Colonel Presstman prepare another position, which the army occupied on June 19. Hardee's corps was on the left, between the railroad and along the road from Lost Mountain to Marietta; Loring's corps in the center occupied the crest of Big Kennesaw Mountain, a prominence of 700 feet, then Little Kennesaw, some 400 feet in height, and finally a 200-foot knoll known as Pigeon Hill; and Hood was on the right. Johnston relocated his headquarters to a small cottage called Fair Oaks at Marietta. On June 20, Wheeler's cavalry on the right flank was attacked by cavalry under General Garrard, who were repulsed. As Garrard was retiring, General Wheeler charged with over a thousand troopers and routed Garrard's cavalry, capturing one hundred men and horses and two standards. Garrard lefty 50 dead on the field, while the Confederates lost just 15 killed and 50 wounded. On June 21, Sherman extended his right and entrenched, compelling the transfer of Hood's corps to Hardee's left, while Wheeler's cavalry replaced Hood's men on the right.

Kolb's Farm

On June 22, in the pre-dawn darkness, Hood deployed his three divisions in a blocking position on Powder Springs road near a plantation called Kolb's Farm, where they dug in. That afternoon, Hood's skirmishers encountered two Federal regiments, which fell back, whereupon Hood decided to launch an attack with the divisions of Hindman and Stevenson. However, Hood had not scouted the terrain nor what forces were in front of him, and did not consult Johnston about his assault. Hood attempted to capture some artillery crowning a high, bare hill but ran into the Federal entrenched front line manned by Schofield's Army of the Ohio and Hooker's XX Corps, about fourteen thousand men and nearly 40 cannons to Hood's eleven thousand troops. The Confederates suffered over a thousand casualties, while the Federals lost only 350; the attempt was abandoned. Johnston was angry, Hood having lost men the Confederacy found impossible to replace.

On June 24, Senator Wigfall, his wife, and two daughters stopped at Atlanta on their way to Texas to touch base with his constituents. Charlotte and the girls stayed with Lydia Johnston in her small house on the outskirts of Atlanta, while Wigfall went to Marietta to see Johnston. Wigfall told Johnston that, on good authority, he had heard rumors in Richmond suggesting that Davis was disappointed and was considering removing Johnston from command. Wigfall mentioned that John Bell Hood was frequently suggested as Johnston's replacement. Wigfall had come to investigate if the people of Georgia and the army had lost faith in Johnston. The senator talked with friends in the army and people and officials in Georgia, finding that Johnston was well respected and that stories in Richmond to the contrary were untrue. Johnston explained his strategic plan in detail to Wigfall. He said that Sherman would be most vulnerable after crossing the Chattahoochee; a defeat with the river at his back would be decisive, and the best opportunity for attack was when the Federal army tried to cross Peachtree Creek. If unsuccessful, Johnston could fall back into the fortifications of Atlanta. Wigfall, impressed, hurried to Governor Brown's office in Atlanta and wrote a letter to Senator B. H. Hill, at the governor's suggestion, to come to Atlanta to meet with them.

Kennesaw Mountain

Due to the wet weather that made a flanking movement difficult, Sherman decided on June 24 to launch a frontal attack in three days on Johnston's Kennesaw Mountain defenses, hoping to split the Confederate army in half. His plan was to feint on the Confederate flanks to draw out Johnston's troops, then smash through the center. On June 27, a Confederate soldier wrote: "The heavens seemed made of brass and the earth of iron, and as the sun began to mount toward the zenith, everything became quiet and no sound was heard save a peckerwood on a neighboring tree, tapping on its old trunk, trying to find a worm for its dinner." At 8.00 a.m., the silence was broken as over 50 Federal artillery pieces opened a bombardment on

Kennesaw Mountain. One Southern soldier yelled: "Hell has broke loose in Georgia, sure enough!" After the artillery barrage ceased about 8.30 a.m., 5,500 soldiers of McPherson's Army of the Tennessee—Brigadier-General Morgan Smith's division, reinforced by another brigade of Major General John A. Logan's XV Corps, started forward to break through and split the Confederate line between Little Kennesaw and Pidgeon Hill. Logan's attack struck the 12th Louisiana, which was deployed as skirmishers. They withdrew to the main line as the Federals advanced upon them, the Confederates opening up a withering fire from musketry, enfilading artillery from French's batteries posted on Little Kennesaw, and even rolling stones on the Yankees. Within two hours, the attack was stalled and the Federals withdrew.

Meanwhile, Thomas's Army of the Cumberland launched an assault with two divisions simultaneously—Jefferson Davis's division of Palmer's XIV Corps on the right and Brig. Gen. John Newton's division of Howard's IV Corps on the left—against Cheatham's division. They reached within 40 yards of the Confederate line before stalling, the position becoming known as the "Dead Angle" from the number of dead Federals lying there. A massed Confederate volley struck the Federal ranks as French's batteries, a quarter-mile away, added their fire to Cheatham's defense. The attack was so threatening that part of Cheatham's reserve, Vaughn's brigade, had to be brought up to prevent a breakthrough. The attack was repulsed with great loss to the Federals. During the fighting, the gunfire ignited the underbrush and flames were threatening the Federal wounded as they lay between the lines. Lieutenant Colonel William H. Martin, commander of the consolidated 1st and 15th Arkansas, tied his handkerchief to a ramrod as a flag of truce and jumped onto the rampart, calling to the Federals to rescue their wounded. "Come and remove your wounded; they are burning to death," Martin shouted. "We won't fire a gun until you get them away. Be quick." Soldiers from both sides then carried the wounded to safety in the Federal rear. After the area was cleared and the flames put out, a Federal major approached Martin and presented him with a pair of Colt revolvers as tokens of appreciation. Major James T. Holmes of the 52nd Ohio best described the battle here: "The wonder was that any lived through such a storm of shot and shell and grape and canister and musket balls. It was a very costly experiment, and, judged by the event, without a single, actual, compensating return." Major General Oliver O. Howard of IV Corps reflected: "Our losses in this assault were heavy indeed and our gain was nothing. We realized now, as never before, the futility of direct assault upon intrenched lines already well prepared and well manned."

Senator Benjamin H. Hill

Senator Benjamin H. Hill of Georgia arrived at Johnston's headquarters on July 1 after meeting with Governor Brown and Senator Wigfall at Atlanta. Brown and Wigfall had explained the military situation and urged Hill to write to Davis to support Johnston's request for cavalry to break Sherman's supply line. But Hill decided against writing: "The matter is too important, time is too precious, and letters are too inadequate." "Mr. Wigfall was on bad terms with B. H. Hill Senator from Georgia," stated Edward A. Pollard in his book *Secret History of the Southern Confederacy*, "but he knew him to be an obsequious politician and to some extent, a favorite of Mr. Davis, well-qualified to influence the President by his adroit servility, and to exercise an influence over him denied to wiser and purer counsellors." Pollard said Senator Wigfall was "willing to lay aside his private feelings, and to use a medium to which he was personally averse to accomplish a public benefit." He thus suggested Senator Hill for the mission to Richmond, which was agreed. Pollard continued:

> Mr. Hill was called into council with Johnston and some of his corps commanders; the clear-headed General submitted to him all his plans, assured him of the safety of Atlanta, pointed out the opportunity of operating on Sherman's rear; and at the close of the conference, the Senator expressed himself as fully satisfied with all that Johnston proposed and requested. He left with the promise warmly expressed that he would go at once to Richmond and use all the influence he had or could assemble to persuade the President to sustain General Johnston, and especially to give him command of Forrest's cavalry for the critical operation he designed.
>
> The promise was never kept. The confidence with General Johnston was not only violated but betrayed. Senator Hill went to Richmond; but the gossip was that he "went back" upon Johnston, and joined his enemies and detractors who he found had secured the ear of Mr. Davis. The fact may be that Senator Hill was at first sincere in what he had undertaken in behalf of the injured General, but that coming to Richmond, he found the President so impatient of anything said in favor of Johnston, and so well-disposed towards those who brought him any tale to the discredit of this commander, that weak and servile as he was, a man always anxious to court favor for himself than for others, he was easily led away from his first intentions and by another step of descent in sincerity was involved in the intrigue which he found busy in Richmond to depose Johnston, and to make a pretext on which Mr. Davis might gratify the malice he had nursed against this great and good commander. Whatever the explanation, it is certain that Senator Hill, a short time after reaching Richmond, was active in the intrigue referred to; that he circulated stories to alarm the more foolish of the public for the safety of Atlanta; that he was in frequent conversation with General Bragg, whom the President had, previous to this occasion, sent as a well-disguised spy into Johnston's camp; and that he was in correspondence with one of the corps commanders of the Army of Tennessee whom Mr. Davis had already designated as one of his favorites.[34]

Hill had arrived in Richmond on July 10; Johnston awaited the result of Hill's mission. Hearing nothing from Hill, Johnston sent a special messenger with full and detailed dispatches to be submitted to Jefferson Davis, but the messenger waited two weeks and could not obtain an audience with the president. On July 15, Johnston received a curt wire from Hill written on the 14th: "You must do the work with your present force. For God's sake do it."[35]

CHAPTER 19

Chattahoochee River

Observers atop Kennesaw Mountain and outposts of Wheeler's cavalry reported a movement by McPherson's corps to the right towards the Chattahoochee on July 1 and 2. Johnston moved his army to new lines prepared by Colonel Presstman on the 3rd near New Smyrna, 10 miles south of Marietta. However, on July 4, Hood reported the Yankees were again turning the Confederate left, so Johnston sent Cheatham's division to hold them in check. Two days later, Sherman's army continued to flank and entrench. This forced General Johnston to abandon New Smyrna that night and move his three corps 6 miles to the north bank of the Chattahoochee River on a line selected by Major General Lovell. Here on the high ground, Brigadier General Shoup was directed to construct formidable bridgehead fortifications known as a "*tête-du-pont*," defenses that were 6 miles long and a mile deep. Over the previous two weeks, more than a thousand enslaved people were pressed into work on the structure. The works had a line of redoubts, 80 feet apart, made of logs and packed earth up to 12 feet thick. The redoubts were linked by a stockade of vertical logs. There were numerous rifle pits, artillery batteries, and heavy rifled guns from Mobile. The line covered the railroad bridge, three pontoon bridges, and Turner's Ferry. Johnston sent his cavalry to the south bank, those under Wheeler to observe the river above the position and Jackson's troopers below. An incredulous Sherman thought it "one of the strongest pieces of field fortifications I ever saw," but told General Thomas that "no general, such as he, would invite battle with the Chattahoochee behind him." Yet this is what Johnston intended to do; one corps was to defend the "*tête-du-pont*" while the other two were free to counter Sherman's efforts to cross the river. Simultaneously, Captain Grant, an engineer officer who had supervised the construction of entrenchments around Atlanta since the beginning of June, was directed to impress enslaved laborers to strengthen the fortifications.

Use Your Own Cavalry

On July 7, Lieutenant General Alexander P. Stewart, appointed by President Davis, was promoted to the command vacated by the death of Lieutenant General Polk. On the same date, Davis sent a wire to Johnston: "The announcement that your army has fallen back to the Chattahoochee renders me more apprehensive for the future. Hopeful of results in Northern Georgia, other places have been stripped to re-enforce your army until we are unable to make further additions, and are dependent on your success." The next day, Johnston sent a reply:

> We have been forced back by the operations of a siege, which the enemy's extreme caution and greatly superior numbers have made me unable to prevent. I have found no opportunity for battle except by attacking intrenchments. It is believed here that there are 16,000 cavalry for defense of Mississippi and Alabama, and, therefore, that the enemy cannot make a detachment able to invade that department. Might not 4,000 of this cavalry prevent the danger by breaking up the railroad between the enemy and Dalton, thus compelling Sherman to withdraw?

Davis suggested Johnston use his own: "If it is practicable for distant cavalry, it must be more so for that which is near."[1]

After having made a personal reconnaissance of the "*tête-du-pont*," Sherman thought it would be foolhardy to try to carry the bastion. He had Thomas's Army of the Cumberland dig in front of the fortified bridgehead while his cavalry and the armies of McPherson and Schofield searched for suitable crossings. On July 7, Schofield found a crossing where Soap Creek emptied into the Chattahoochee, a spot that was only lightly guarded by Confederate cavalry. The next morning, Schofield sent a detail across on piled-up rocks on a submerged fish dam a half-mile above the mouth of Soap Creek. Nearer the creek, he also sent an advance party on 20 pontoon boats for an amphibious landing. Before midnight, the area was secured and two pontoon bridges were in place, over which an entire division crossed the river and entrenched. On July 9, Johnston was alerted to Schofield's mile-deep bridgehead 8 miles upriver. Rather than attack the entrenched position, which Johnston felt was risky, since his assault might be held up while Federal forces crossed the river and came up behind him, he decided to evacuate the "*tête-du-pont*" on the night of the 9th. The three corps withdrew, each having two bridges to use. To muffle the sound of retreat, green cornstalks were strewn on the bridges. The artillery moved out at dusk, then at 10.00 p.m. the infantry left the trenches, and the skirmishers withdrew at 1.00 a.m., after which rearguards dismantled the pontoon bridges and burned the railroad trestle. By Sunday,

July 10, the army was encamped 2 or 3 miles south of the river on a ridge at Peachtree Creek. Johnston sent Bragg a message from Atlanta on July 11: "I strongly recommend the distribution of the U.S. prisoners, now at Andersonville, immediately." Since Davis had ordered Bragg to Georgia on July 9 to interview Johnston, Davis answered for Bragg that guarding Andersonville was Johnston's responsibility. Johnston feared a cavalry raid by the Federals on Andersonville, 125 miles south of Atlanta, would liberate some thirty thousand Union prisoners in his rear. Davis interpreted Johnston's concern as indicating he planned to abandon Atlanta. The next day, the president wired Gen. Robert E. Lee: "General Johnston has failed, and there are strong indications that he will abandon Atlanta. He urges that prisoners should be removed from Andersonville. It seems necessary to relieve him at once. Who should succeed him? What think you of Hood for the position?" That same day, Lee responded: "Telegram of today received. I regret the fact stated. It is a bad time to release the commander of an army situated as that of Tennessee. We may lose Atlanta and the army too. Hood is a bold fighter. I am doubtful as to other qualities necessary." Later that day, General Lee sent a longer reply to Davis:

> I am distressed at the intelligence conveyed in your telegram of today. It is a grievous thing to change commander of an army situated as is that of the Tennessee. Still if necessary it ought to be done. I know nothing of the necessity. I had hoped that Johnston was strong enough to deliver battle. We must risk much to save Alabama, Mobile & communication with the Trans Mississippi. It would be better to concentrate all the cavalry in Mississippi & Tennessee on Sherman's communications. If Johnston abandons Atlanta I suppose he will fall back on Augusta. This loses us Mississippi & communication with Trans Mississippi. We had better therefore hazard that communication to retain the country. Hood is a good fighter, very industrious on the battlefield, careless off, & I have had no opportunity of judging of his action, when the whole responsibility rested upon him. I have a high opinion of his gallantry, earnestness & zeal. Genl. [William J.] Hardee has more experience in managing an army.[2]

General Lee was advocating the very strategy that Johnston had proposed, using the cavalry in Mississippi and Tennessee on Sherman's communications. Before expressing his opinion regarding Johnston's removal, Lee consulted with Major General John B. Gordon, a native Georgian who had served with Johnston in Virginia. Gordon gave this evaluation:

> When President Davis asked General Lee for an opinion as to the wisdom of removing General Johnston from the command of that army, General Lee did me the honor, as I presume he honored other corps commanders, to counsel with me as to the policy of such an act. I had served under General Johnston while he commanded the Army of Northern Virginia. I had learned by experience and observation how he could retreat day after day and yet retain the absolute confidence of his officers and men, who were ready at any moment to about

face, and, with enthusiasm born of that confidence, assume the offensive at his command. I therefore expressed the opinion that there was no one except General Lee himself who could take General Johnston's place without a shock to the morale of his troops that would greatly decrease the chances of checking General Sherman. Hood and others were discussed, and I ventured the suggestion that if the time should ever come for the removal of General Johnston, it would be after he had lost and not while he still retained, as he clearly did, the enthusiastic confidence of his army, from the commanders of corps to the privates in the ranks. I may here remark that General Lee was perhaps the most unassuming of great commanders. I cannot be mistaken, however, as to his opinion of the suggested removal of General Johnston and the promotion of General Hood or any one else to the chief command. While he avoided any direct reply to my suggestions, he said enough to indicate his opinions. I could not forget his expressions, and I give, I believe, the exact words he used. He said: "General Johnston is a patriot and an able soldier. He is upon the ground, and knows his army and its surroundings and how to use it better than any of us."[3]

Bragg's Visit

On July 13, Bragg arrived in Atlanta. Johnston stated: "His visit to me was unofficial, he assured me. At the same time Governor Brown promised to bring ten thousand more State militia into the army; he was confident that it would be done in ten days. The promise gave me great satisfaction, for such a force might be made very valuable in operations about Atlanta."[4] But Bragg was there to spy on Johnston, discover his plans, and report back to Davis. Upon his arrival in Atlanta, Bragg immediately wired Davis: "Our army all south of the Chattahoochee, and indications seem to favor an entire evacuation of this place. Shall see General Johnston immediately." At 1.00 p.m., Bragg telegraphed again: "Our army is sadly depleted, and now reports 10,000 less than the return of 10th June. I find but little encouraging."[5] Johnston later disputed Bragg's claims:

When General Bragg was at Atlanta, about the middle of July, we had no conversation concerning the Army of Tennessee than such as I introduced. He asked me no questions regarding its operations, past or future, made no comments upon the one, nor suggestions for the other, and, so far from having reason to suppose that Atlanta would not be defended, he saw the most vigorous preparations for its defense in progress. Supposing that he had been sent by the President to learn and report upon the condition of military affairs there, I described them to him briefly, when he visited me, and proposed to send for the lieutenant-generals, that he might obtain from them such minute information as he desired. He replied that he would be glad to see other officers as friends, but only in that way, as his visit was unofficial. He added that the object of his journey was to confer with Lieutenant-General Lee, and from his headquarters to communicate with Lieutenant-General E. Kirby Smith, to ascertain what reenforcements for me could be furnished by their departments. He talked much more of military affairs in Virginia than of those in Georgia, asserting, what I believed, that Sherman's army exceeded Grant's in fighting force; and impressed upon me distinctly that his visit was merely personal. His progress to Lieutenant-General Lee's

> headquarters terminated in Montgomery; and his communications with the commanders of two departments, concerning military aid to me, subsided into a visit to that city.[6]

Bragg had no intention to get reinforcements for Johnston's army, only to find fault. Johnston surely realized Bragg's purpose. A Congressional delegation came to warn Johnston that Davis was dissatisfied and wanted to relieve, him stating the president's conviction "as a military man ... that if he were in your place he could whip Sherman now." Johnston said that President Davis thought he could "do a great many things that other men would hesitate to attempt. For instance, he tried to do what God failed to do. He tried to make a soldier of Braxton Bragg and you know the result. It couldn't be done." Johnston's chief of staff, Mackall, guessed Bragg's mission, writing to his wife on July 13:

> Joe looks uneasy this morning. I am sorry to see him so fretted. I fancy it is the design of Mr. D. [Davis] to take advantage of the discontent he has sensed in Richmond and the temporary excitement in Ga. produced by our own near approach to Atlanta, to make a display of his distrust of Johnston & if he finds he can infuse it into the army, to relieve him. I think he will signally fail.[7]

Although Johnston offered to send for his lieutenant generals to supply information, Bragg only talked to two general officers, Hood and Wheeler, both of whom had sent secret letters critical of Johnston and undermining his credibility. Bragg disregarded Hardee and Stewart, nor did he seek out Cleburne, Cheatham, or the other division or brigade commanders, all of whom he felt were his "enemies" when he was in command, and never visited the camps of the army. During Bragg's visit, Hood sent him a subversive letter on July 14, exalting himself and portraying Johnston as ineffective, which violated both military regulations and protocol. Hood wrote:

> During the campaign from Dalton to the Chattahoochee River it is natural to suppose that we have had several chances to strike the enemy a decisive blow. We have failed to take advantage of such opportunities, and find our army south of the Chattahoochee, very much decreased in strength. Our present position is a very difficult one, and we should not, under any circumstances, allow the enemy to gain possession of Atlanta, and deem it excessively important, should we find the enemy intends establishing the Chattahoochee as their line, relying upon interrupting our communications and again virtually dividing our country, that we should attack him, even if we should have to recross the river to do so. I have, general, so often urged that we should force the enemy to give us battle as to almost be regarded reckless by officers high in rank in this army, since their views have been so directly opposite. I regard it a great misfortune to our country that we failed to give battle to the enemy many miles north of our present position.[8]

Bragg telegraphed Davis from Atlanta on July 15, saying he had made two visits to Johnston, being received "courteously and kindly." He continued:

> He has not sought my advice, and it was not volunteered. I cannot learn that he has any more plan for the future than he has had in the past. It is expected that he will await the enemy on a line some three miles from here, and the impression prevails that he is now more inclined to fight. The enemy is very cautious, and intrenches immediately on taking a new position. The morale of our army is still reported good.

Later that day, Bragg sent a longer letter by special messenger, enclosing Hood's letter with it:

> As far as I can learn we do not propose any offensive operations, but shall await the enemy's approach and be governed, as heretofore, by the development in our front. All valuable stores and machinery have been removed, and most of the citizens able to go have left with their effects. There is but one remedy—offensive action. We should drive the enemy from this side of the river, follow him down by an attack in flank, and force him to battle, at the same time throwing our cavalry on his communications.
>
> Generals Hood and Wheeler agree in this opinion and look for success. The enemy's morale has no doubt improved as ours has declined, but his losses have been heavy, and he operates with great caution. His force has always been overestimated. During the whole campaign, from and including our position in front of Dalton, General Hood has been in favor of giving battle, and mentions to me numerous instances of opportunities lost. He assures me that Lieutenant-General Polk, after leaving Dalton, invariably sustained the same views. On the contrary, General Hardee generally favored the retiring policy, though he was frequently non-committal. Lieutenant-General Stewart, since his promotion, has firmly and uniformly sustained the aggressive policy. The commanding general, from the best information I can gain, has ever been opposed to seeking battle, though willing to receive it on his own terms in his chosen position.
>
> You will see at once that the removal of the commander, should such a measure be considered, would produce no change of policy, and it would be attended with some serious evils. A general denunciation by the disorganizers, civil and military, would follow. I do not believe the second in rank has the confidence of the army to the extent of the chief. If any change is made Lieutenant-General Hood would give unlimited satisfaction, and my estimate of him, always high, has been raised by his conduct in this campaign. Do not understand me as proposing him as a man of genius, or a great general, but as far better in the present emergency than any one we have available.
>
> As General J. has not sought my advice, nor ever afforded me a fair opportunity of giving my opinion, I have obtruded neither upon him. Such will continue to be my course.[9]

Hood's Lies

Hood had not only shaded the facts, but had outright lied, and Bragg was complicit. Hood had distorted the roles he and Johnston had played in the campaign, exaggerating his aggressiveness and Johnston's reluctance to take the offensive. Bragg never verified Hood's interpretation with other general officers, nor with Johnston's staff.

On July 16, Davis sent Johnston a blunt telegram to learn his plans for Atlanta: "A telegram from Atlanta of yesterday announces that the enemy is extending intrenchments from river toward railroad to Augusta. I wish to hear from you as to present situation, and your plans of operations so specifically as will enable me to anticipate events." On the very same day, Johnston sent back a pithy reply: "As the enemy has double our number, we must be on the defensive. My plan of operations must, therefore, depend upon that of the enemy. It is mainly to watch for an opportunity to fight to advantage. We are trying to put Atlanta in condition to be held for a day or two by the Georgia militia, that army movements may be freer and wider."[10]

Johnston was always reluctant to divulge his plans to Richmond, believed that there were leakers in the administration there.

CHAPTER 20

Relieved of Command

This message pushed Davis over the edge, and he sent word that Joseph Johnston was to be replaced by John Bell Hood. On July 17, at 10.00 p.m., as General Johnston was instructing Colonel Presstman regarding his work the next day on the entrenchments of Atlanta, he received a telegram from Adjutant and Inspector General Cooper:

> Lieut. Gen. J. B. Hood has been commissioned to the temporary rank of general under the late law of Congress. I am directed by the Secretary of War to inform you that you have failed to arrest the advance of the enemy to the vicinity of Atlanta, far in the interior of Georgia, and express no confidence that you can defeat or repel him, you are hereby relieved from the command of the Army and Department of Tennessee, which you will immediately turn over to General Hood.[1]

Evidence of Competency

On the morning of July 18, Johnston responded with a forceful defense of his campaign, ending with a sarcastic comment about Hood's generalship:

> Your dispatch of yesterday received and obeyed. Command of the Army and Department of Tennessee has been transferred to General Hood. As to the alleged cause of my removal, I assert that Sherman's army is much stronger compared with that of Tennessee than Grant's compared with that of Northern Virginia. Yet the enemy has been compelled to advance much more slowly to the vicinity of Atlanta than to that of Richmond and Petersburg, and has penetrated much deeper into Virginia than into Georgia. Confident language by a military commander is not usually regarded as evidence of competency.[2]

There is no question that Davis panicked and acted out of desperation; he should have waited until the campaign for Atlanta had been resolved. Johnston was one of his top commanders and should have been given the support he deserved and a chance to prove himself. There was no public clamor for his removal, in fact, many citizens, politicians, and the army had confidence in him. Nonetheless, Davis disliked Johnston and viewed everything he did with a prejudiced eye.

Davis wanted General Lee's Approval

Davis desperately wanted Robert E. Lee's approval and had Secretary of War Seddon travel to Lee's headquarters for a personal interview to receive his favor. General Lee had a conversation with General Hampton about this meeting, Hampton then writing to Johnston that Lee had expressed "great regret" about his removal and "had done all in his power to prevent it." Hampton continued: "General Lee assured me that he had urged Mr. Seddon not to remove you from command, and had said to him that if you could not command the army we had no one who could. He was earnest in expressing not only his regret at your removal, but his entire confidence in yourself."[3] Indeed, Lee spoke openly and expressed his disapproval to the Secretary of War: "That if General Johnston was not a soldier, America had never produced one. That if he was not competent to command that army, the Confederacy had no one who was competent."[4]

The Federal army, meanwhile, was elated by the change, General Sherman writing:

> No officer or soldier who ever served under me will question the generalship of Joseph E. Johnston. His retreats were timely, in good order, and he left nothing behind. [Johnston] was a sensible man and only did sensible things.
>
> We feigned to the right, but crossed the Chattahoochee by the left, and soon confronted our enemy behind the first line of intrenchments at Peach Tree Creek, prepared in advance for this very occasion. At this critical moment the Confederate Government rendered us most valuable service. Being dissatisfied with the Fabian policy of General Johnston, it relieved him, and General Hood was substituted to command the Confederate army [on July 18]. Hood was known to be a "fighter," a graduate of West Point of the class of 1853, No. 44, of which class two of my army commanders, McPherson and Schofield, were No. 1 and No. 7. The character of a leader is a large factor in the game of war, and I confess I was pleased at this change, of which I had early notice. I knew that I had an army superior in numbers and morale to that of my antagonist; but being so far from my base, and operating in a country devoid of food and forage, I was dependent for supplies on a poorly constructed railroad back to Louisville, five hundred miles. I was willing to meet the enemy in the open country, but not behind well-constructed parapets.

Major General Oliver O. Howard wrote: "Just at this time, much to our comfort and to his surprise, Johnston was removed, and Hood placed in command of the Confederate Army. Johnston had planned to attack Sherman at Peachtree Creek, expecting just such a division between our wings as we made."

General Jacob D. Cox, who took part in the operations, also spoke of Johnston's removal in his monograph on the Atlanta campaign, stating that news of the change "was learned with satisfaction by every officer and man" in the Federal army. Cox added: "The patient skill and watchful intelligence and courage with which Johnston had always confronted them with impregnable fortifications had been exasperating. They had found no weak points in the harness, and no wish was so common or so often expressed as that he would only try our works as we were trying his."[5]

John Bell Hood (1831–79) criticized Joseph E. Johnston for his overly cautious and defensive strategy, particularly during Sherman's march on Atlanta, believing Johnston was retreating too much and allowing the Union forces to gain ground without sufficient resistance. Hood advocated for a more aggressive offensive approach, which ultimately led to his replacement of Johnston as commander of the Army of Tennessee. (Library of Congress)

President Davis's "Superior Military Genius"

President Jefferson Davis considered himself an expert on military matters due to his background. He graduated from West Point, was an officer in the regular army for seven years on active duty, and had served as a regimental commander in the Mexican War with a distinguished combat record. He had served in the Senate as chairman of the Committee of Military Affairs during the 1850s, and from 1853– 57 held the office of Secretary of War in the administration of President Franklin Pierce. General Ulysses S. Grant, however, did not hold Davis in high regard: "Mr. Davis had an exalted opinion of his own military genius. On several occasions during the war he came to the relief of the Union army by means of his superior military genius."[6]

On the night of July 18, Johnston wrote a farewell to his soldiers:

> In obedience to orders of the War Department, I turn over to General Hood the command of the Army and Department of Tennessee. I cannot leave this noble army without expressing

> my admiration of the high military qualities it has displayed. A long and arduous campaign has made conspicuous every soldierly virtue, endurance of toil, obedience to orders, brilliant courage. The enemy has never attacked but to be repulsed and severely punished. You soldiers have never argued but from your courage, and never counted your foes. No longer your leader, I will watch your career, and will rejoice in your victories. To one and all I offer assurances of my friendship, and bid an affectionate farewell.[7]

Johnston indicated in his *Narrative* his desire to hold Atlanta:

> The proofs that I intended to defend Atlanta, seen by General Bragg and recognized by General Hood are: that under my orders the work of strengthening its defenses, begun several weeks before was going on vigorously; that I had just brought heavy rifled cannon from Mobile, to mount on the intrenchments; the communication made on the subject to General Hood, and the fact that my family was residing in the town; the removal of the machinery and workmen of the military shops, and prohibition to accumulate large supplies in the town, alleged by General Bragg to be evidence of the intention not to defend it, were measures of common prudence, and no more indicated that it was to be abandoned, than sending the baggage of the army to the rear in time of battle proves a foregone determination to fly from the field.[8]

Johnston's Plan to Defend Atlanta

Johnston had a sound strategic plan to defend Atlanta. Although the flanking operations by the Northern forces had pushed the Confederate armies back to Atlanta, they could do no more. Johnston said that outside Atlanta, the Southern troops were safely entrenched in defenses far stronger than any they had previously held, and too extensive to be laid siege to. As three railroads converged on the city, each of which could supply the army, he believed they could have maintained themselves there indefinitely, and even won the campaign with only light losses. Johnston wrote:

> If the enemy should give us a good opportunity in the passage of Peach Tree Creek, I expected to attack him. If successful, we should obtain important results, for the enemy's retreat would be on two sides of a triangle and our march on one. If we should not succeed, our intrenchments would give us a safe refuge, where we could hold back the enemy until the promised State troops should join us; then, placing them on the nearest defenses of the place (where there were, or ought to be, seven sea-coast rifles, sent us from Mobile by General Maury), I would attack the Federals in flank with the three Confederate corps. If we were successful, they would be driven against the Chattahoochee below the railroad, where there are no fords, or away from their supplies, as we might fall on their left or right flank. If unsuccessful, we could take refuge in Atlanta, which we could hold indefinitely; for it was too strong to be taken by assault, and too extensive to be invested. This would win the campaign, the object of which the country supposed Atlanta to be.
>
> At Dalton, the great numerical superiority of the enemy made the chances of battle much against us, and even if beaten they had a safe refuge behind the fortified pass of Ringgold and in the fortress of Chattanooga. Our refuge, in case of defeat, was in Atlanta, 100 miles off,

> with three rivers intervening. Therefore victory for us could not have been decisive, while defeat would have been utterly disastrous. Between Dalton and the Chattahoochee we could have given battle only by attacking the enemy intrenched, or so near intrenchments that the only result of success to us would have been his falling back into them, while defeat would have been our ruin.
>
> In the course pursued our troops, always fighting under cover, had very trifling losses compared with those they inflicted, so that the enemy's numerical superiority was reduced daily and rapidly; and we could reasonably have expected to cope with them on equal ground by the time the Chattahoochee was passed. Defeat on the south side of that river would have been their destruction. We, if beaten, had a place of refuge in Atlanta—too strong to be assaulted, and too extensive to be invested. I had also hopes that by breaking of the railroad in its rear the Federal army might be compelled to attack us in a position of our own choosing, or forced into a retreat easily converted into a rout. After we crossed the Etowah, five detachments of cavalry were successfully sent with instructions to destroy as much as they could of the railroad between Chattanooga and the Etowah. All failed, because they were too weak. Captain James B. Harvey, an officer of great courage and sagacity, was detached on this service on the 11th of June and remained near the railroad several weeks, frequently interrupting, but not strong enough to prevent, its use. Early in the campaign the impressions of the strength of the cavalry in Mississippi and east Louisiana given me by Lieutenant-General Polk, just from the command of that department, gave me reason to hope that an adequate force commanded by the most competent officer in America for such service (General N. B. Forrest) could be sent from it for the purpose of breaking the railroad in Sherman's rear. I therefore made the suggestion direct to the President, June 13th and July 16th, and through General Bragg on the 3d, 12th, 16th and 26th of June. I did so in the confidence that this cavalry would serve the Confederacy far better by insuring the defeat of a great invasion than by repelling a mere raid.
>
> I assert that had one of the other lieutenant-generals of the Army (Hardee or Stewart) succeeded me, Atlanta would have been held by the Army of Tennessee.[9]

The success of General Johnston's tenure is borne out by the fact that throughout the campaign to date, the Army of Tennessee under his guidance had sustained 9,972 killed and wounded, while in the same period Sherman's armies lost 31,687 in killed, wounded, and missing.

Atlanta

In 1836, the Georgia General Assembly voted to build the Western and Atlantic Railroad, linking the port of Savannah and the Midwest. It was to run from Chattanooga, Tennessee, to a spot east of the Chattahoochee River. A U.S. Army engineer, Colonel Stephen Harriman Long, recommended the railroad terminate in the vicinity of present-day Atlanta. In 1839, John Thrasher built homes and a general store in this area, which became known as Thrasherville. By 1842, the settlement had six buildings and 30 residents and was called "Terminus," which was changed to Marthasville after the daughter of Governor Wilson Lumpkin. In 1845, the chief engineer of the Georgia

Railroad, J. Edgar Thomson, suggested the name "Atlantica-Pacifica," which was shortened to Atlanta. The city became a manufacturing hub during the Civil War, having four large machine shops, two planning mills, three tanneries, two shoe factories, a soap factory, clothing factories, and was a busy center for cotton distribution.

Atlanta had provided some decided advantages to Joseph Johnston. He was near his base and was no longer troubled by the constant flanking movements by which Sherman had maneuvered him out of strong positions through the threat of interposing between Johnston's army and Atlanta. At Atlanta, the Confederate army had three railroads to get its supplies: the Georgia Railroad from Augusta, the Macon and Western Railroad connecting to the little settlement of Macon to the south and Savannah to the southeast, and the Atlanta and West Point Railroad connecting Atlanta with Montgomery and Mobile to the southwest. Meanwhile, Sherman was solely dependent on the Western and Atlantic Railroad running back to his base at Chattanooga, which could be broken up by cavalry. Sherman could not move against Johnston's communications without exposing his own to depredations. Johnston's army was strongly fortified at Atlanta, which would cost Sherman enormous casualties to assault. Manning the fortifications with State troops would allow Johnston to sally forth with his three corps in a concentrated attack on Sherman's extended line necessitated by investment and "whip him in detail."

"A Lion's Heart and a Wooden Head"

All of this was explained to Hood by Johnston, but Hood was not the right general for the task. While Johnston was deliberate and subtle, Hood was overly pugnacious. Johnston valued the lives of his soldiers, which he considered the Confederacy's most valuable resource, more important than its land and cities, which could be retaken. After Johnston's evacuation of Dalton, Mary Chesnut recorded in her diary on June 4 this quote by Henry P. Brewster, a Texas lawyer and advocate for Hood: "We want a hardened fellow who does not value men's lives."[10] Hood was indeed reckless with the lives of his men, being described by one of the wits in Richmond as having "a lion's heart and a wooden head."[11]

General Hood reflected:

> About 11 o'clock, on the night of the 17th, I received a telegram from the War Office, directing me to assume command of the Army. This totally unexpected order so astounded me, and overwhelmed me with sense of the responsibility thereto attached, that I remained in deep thought throughout the night. Before daybreak I started for General Johnston's

> headquarters, a short distance from which I met Lieutenant General A. P. Stewart, one of my division commanders, who had been recommended by me, and recently promoted to the rank of corps commander to replace General Polk.[12]

Hood had to be helped to mount his horse and strapped into the saddle by two members of his staff. He and Stewart reached Johnston's quarters shortly after dawn, whereupon Hood asked Johnston the reason for the telegrammed order. Johnston replied that he knew nothing of the immediate cause of the order the president had issued to relieve him. Hood insisted that Johnston "Pocket that dispatch, leave me in command of my corps, and fight the battle for Atlanta." However, Johnston responded that he was a soldier, his "first duty was to obey," and he could not think of remaining unless the order was countermanded. After a long conversation with Johnston; Hood—together with Stewart and Hardee—went into the Adjutant General's office and prepared a telegram to President Davis in which they stated that in their judgment, it was dangerous to change commanders at that moment. They requested Davis recall the order until the fate of Atlanta was decided. But Davis would not budge, replying at 5.20 p.m. that same day: "A change of commanders, under existing circumstances, was regarded as so objectionable that I only accepted it as the alternative of continuing in a policy which had proved so disastrous. The order has been executed, and I cannot suspend it without making the case worse than it was before the order was issued."[13] Upon receiving Davis's telegram, Hood, alone, returned to Johnston's headquarters and for a second time urged him "to pocket the correspondence, remain in command, and fight for Atlanta, as Sherman was at the very gates of the city." Johnston again refused to comply with this request.

Hood is a Soldier, Johnston the General

There was much dissatisfaction among the ranking generals with the change in command from Joseph Johnston to John Bell Hood. General Kirby E. Smith knew both men well, being with Johnston at the beginning of the war and having taught Hood at West Point and commanded him in the United States Army prior to secession. Smith made this assessment of the generals in letters to his wife and his mother: "Hood is a soldier, Johnston the General—Hood is bold, gallant, will always be ready to fight but will never know when he should refuse an engagement. Hood is a man of ordinary intellect, Johnston's brain soars above all that surrounds him."[14] In a letter to his wife, General William H. T. Walker wrote: "Hood has 'gone up like a rocket.' It is to be hoped that he will not come down like a stick. He is brave—whether he has the capacity to command armies (for it requires a high order of talent), time will develop."[15]

Johnston had two conversations with Hood concerning his plans to attack the Federal army as it crossed Peachtree Creek. Johnston then decided to leave quietly for Macon with his wife, Lydia. But before he left, several regiments, marching out on the Marietta road to take up positions near Peachtree Creek on the morning of July 19, reached the two-story white house where Johnston had made his headquarters. General Johnston stepped outside. "He stood with his head uncovered," wrote Colonel James C. Nisbet of the 66th Georgia. "We lifted our hats. There was no cheering! We simply passed silently, with heads uncovered. Some of the officers broke ranks and grasped his hand, as tears poured down their cheeks."[16]

In the late afternoon of July 18, Johnston rode to his wife's residence in Atlanta and spent the night there. Early the next morning, he took the train along with Lydia and the Wigfall girls, Luly and Fanny, for Macon, travelling by freight car. The party arrived in Macon about noon on July 20. There they secured a large, roomy, three-story house on the outskirts of Macon.

Major General George Stoneman was dispatched by Sherman with 6,500 cavalry troopers in late July to disrupt the rail lines south of Atlanta. On July 27, one column of this force, comprising about 2,500 men, moved on Macon to cut rail lines and try to release the prisoners at Andersonville, 50 miles to the southwest. The Home Guard reserves and citizens went out to meet the threat; Johnston offered his services and Howell Cobb offered him command, but Johnston thought it best if he acted in an advisory role. However, the Federals turned away from Macon to face Wheeler and his Confederate troopers, who were in hot pursuit. Wheeler caught and surrounded the remnant of Stoneman's command, some seven hundred troopers, who surrendered 28 miles northeast of Macon.

On October 1, Johnston's lease expired and he could not afford to rent another house. William Mackall, who was Johnston's former chief of staff, invited him to move in with his family in Vineville, a small town just outside of Macon, which Johnston accepted. Mackall, who initially retained his job as chief of staff under Hood, had been dismissed by Hood after he refused to shake Bragg's hand at a strategy meeting two days after the battle of Atlanta. He believed Bragg had behaved dishonorably in his relations with Johnston.

Hood Evacuates Atlanta

Meanwhile, Johnston learned of Hood's fight to hold Atlanta. Hood delivered the offensive the administration had called for, but at a cost the Confederacy could not afford. Sherman had lacked a force large enough to invest and encircle Atlanta completely without thinning his lines and allowing Hood to assail his flanks. Nor did he want to assault Atlanta's strong defensive works. Sherman's objective was to cut Atlanta's communications, severing it from its supplies. Hood sought the transfer of Forrest's cavalry to operate against Sherman's communications and to keep the cavalry belonging to his army, to watch the movements of Sherman's army. On July 20, Hood fought the battle of Peachtree Creek, attacking Thomas's Army of the Cumberland as it crossed the creek. The Confederates were stymied and suffered nearly three thousand casualties, while the Federals lost seventeen hundred. Hood blamed the loss on Johnston's policy of retreating and fighting behind fieldworks. On July 22, McPherson's Army of the Tennessee was approaching Atlanta from the east and pushed back Wheeler's cavalry and Cleburne's division. Hood struck the Army of the Tennessee and drove the Federals back a mile or two in the battle of Atlanta, during which Maj. Gen. James B. McPherson was killed. Sherman's losses totaled 3,722, which included 1,733 missing or taken prisoner, while Hood's casualties amounted to seven thousand men. Sherman then decided to cut the remaining rail link supplying Atlanta: the Macon and Western Railroad. Sherman chose Major General Oliver O. Howard as a permanent replacement for McPherson. Howard moved the Army of the Tennessee west of Atlanta to cut the railroad. Opposing him was the recently promoted Lieutenant General Stephen D. Lee, who replaced General Cheatham commanding Hood's old corps. Lee made contact with Howard's troops late on the morning of July 28, precipitating the battle of Ezra Church, in which the Confederates attacked the Federals behind improvised breastworks. Federal casualties were only about six hundred, but the Confederate assaults cost them some five thousand killed, wounded and captured. On August 10, Hood sent Wheeler's cavalry around 4,500 troopers to try to cut Sherman's rail communications, but the attempt was a total failure. Sherman had accumulated sufficient provisions to last him until the railroad was repaired and had opened a second depot at Allatoona. Without half his cavalry, Hood could not ascertain what Sherman was up to. Unbeknown to Hood, Sherman was moving his entire army towards Jonesboro, intending to break the Macon and Western Railroad. The corps of Hardee and Lee, totaling some twenty-four thousand troops, were at Jonesboro and attacked the entrenched Federals on August 31, losing 1,725 men, while the Federals suffered only 179 casualties. Hood had Hardee remain at Jonesboro and ordered Lee's corps back to Atlanta to help defend it. On September 1, the Union army assaulted Hardee's corps behind breastworks, inflicting a thousand casualties while sustaining 1,275 of their own, but forced the Confederates to retreat. Hood evacuated Atlanta that day. In the hasty withdrawal, an ordnance train of five engines and about 80 cars had to be blown up due to gross negligence by the chief quartermaster, who failed to remove them in time.

Johnston believed Hood was too hasty in abandoning Atlanta: "The Federal march to Jonesboro' caused, but did not compel, the abandonment of Atlanta. For if the Southern troops had remained in the place, the enemy would, in a few days, have been forced to return to his railroad. And, besides, Atlanta could have been sufficiently supplied from Macon, through Augusta; but at Jonesboro' the Federal troops could not be fed." In a letter to his brother, Beverly Johnston, Joseph Johnston said that had he been left in command, "it is very unlikely that Atlanta would have been abandoned. At all events ten or twelve thousand soldiers whose lives have been thrown away would have been saved. Nor would I have left Sherman with a force about equal to my own in the heart of Georgia to make such an excursion as our army is now engaged in."[17] In his book *Advance and Retreat*, Hood blamed his failures on Johnston's school of thought, which relied heavily on the use of entrenchments while retreating and fighting at the same time, imperiling, according to Hood, the ardor and spirit of his troops for offensive combat. Hood claimed he was influenced by Robert E. Lee's and "Stonewall" Jackson's mode of warfare, which did not use entrenchments but assailed the enemy with the main body of their army, which he said elevated and inspired the troops.

In mid-September, President Jefferson Davis decided to visit Hood's army in Georgia and make speeches to raise morale in the state. He arrived unannounced in Macon, Georgia, on September 22, during a long, round-about trip to Hood's position south of Atlanta, and spoke at the Baptist Church. There, he said bitter words against Johnston and Governor Brown:

> I know the deep disgrace felt by Georgia by our army falling back from Dalton to the interior of the State, but I was not of those who considered Atlanta lost when our army crossed the Chattahoochee. I resolved that it should not, and I then put a man in command who I knew would strike an honest and manly blow for the city, and many a Yankee's blood was made to nourish the soil before the prize was won.[18]

In private correspondence after this speech, Johnston sarcastically referred to Hood as "the Striker of Manly Blows." President Davis continued his morale-boosting tour, indiscreetly revealing an intended campaign by Hood against Sherman's rear. Davis's addresses were carried to Sherman in newspapers and by spies, whereupon the Federal general said Davis had "lost all sense and reason." Sherman had a transcript sent to Washington, commenting:

"He made no concealment of these vainglorious boasts [to invade Tennessee and Kentucky] and he gave us the full key to his future design."[19]

Hoping to cut Sherman's rail communications with Chattanooga and draw him out of Georgia, Hood took his army across the Chattahoochee River and moved northward in early October. Johnston thought the move foolish, writing to Mansfield Lovell on October 3: "I fear our commanders trust too much to Sherman's ignorance." Johnston believed Hood's move across the Chattahoochee would leave the rest of the state unprotected and allow Sherman "destroy our shops at Columbus, Macon, & Augusta & cut off Genl. Lee's Supplies." Johnston predicted that Sherman would ignore Hood's threat to his rail communications, as "the seas furnishes him as good a base at Charleston, Savannah, Pensacola, or Mobile as he can find in Chattanooga." By mid-October, Hood was at Dalton; Sherman followed Hood and drove him west into Alabama. Sherman halted his pursuit, but sent Maj. Gen. John M. Schofield with a force of twenty-seven thousand to report to Major General George Thomas in Nashville, making a combined army of more than seventy-thousand men to keep an eye on Hood. Sherman returned to Atlanta, put it to the torch, and commenced his march to the sea through Georgia, while Hood continued on his northern march. On November 30, Hood caught up to Schofield at Franklin, Tennessee, and launched a frontal assault which cost him 6,252 casualties, of which 1,750 were killed. Twelve of his generals were casualties—two major generals and 10 brigadiers—with six generals killed, among them Maj. Gen. Patrick R. Cleburne. Federal casualties were 1,222 killed and wounded, with 1,104 missing probably prisoners. Hood pressed on and fought the battle of Nashville on December 15 and 16, where he was assailed and overwhelmed by superior Federal forces under Thomas. The Union force lost about 3,061 killed, wounded, and missing, while the Confederates estimated their losses at 6,400, including 1,500 killed or wounded. The Army of Tennessee was thus incapacitated as a fighting force. The remnants, fewer than eighteen thousand of them, managed to return to Alabama. Colonel Ewell recorded in his journal: "A more triumphal vindication of Genl. Johnston's policy could not be offered."[20] On September 27, Mary Chesnut posted in her diary: "Hood cannot be sufficiently abused."[21] On January 13, 1865, Hood asked to be relieved of command; on January 23, President Jefferson Davis granted his request.

Robert Garlick Hill Kean, Head of the Bureau of War for the Confederacy, jotted down in his diary on November 20, 1864, concerning General Johnston:

> Johnston's report of operations in Georgia, down to the date of his being relieved in July last, is a very strong paper. It puts things in such a light that Mr. Seddon (Secretary of War) said

> to Judge Campbell that if they had been so understood, he would not have been removed. The results in Georgia since his removal have furnished powerful ground for his vindication. He thinks that Bragg was the cause of his removal. I thought differently at the time and supposed that Bragg was wholly innocent of it, but I now hear from Judge Campbell that Bragg had telegraphed from Atlanta to the President that Johnston ought to be removed and Hood put in command, and that Johnston had seen it. The present alarming condition of things in Georgia affords his friends a great triumph."

Just over a week later, on November 30, Kean made another entry in his diary regarding Johnston's report on the Atlanta campaign:

> I have been preparing the correspondence with Johnston, to accompany copies of his report, which has been called for by both houses of Congress. The portion of it conducted with Bragg gave me a new light on the history of the early campaign in Georgia. It shows a mastery of the situation, a sagacity in anticipating the future, and a comprehensive view of the situation on Johnston's part, in strong contrast with Bragg's plans, which Johnston tears to tatters, and his speculations which events prove erroneous. One fact is very striking. Bragg writes the President one letter showing that Johnston was enormously overmatched, and evidently intended to get him (Bragg) "right on the rears." A few days later he writes another in which he represents that Johnston's strength approaches more nearly to equality with the enemy to be opposed than General Lee's, and while he does not say so, implies that Johnston might do better if he would. The impression the whole thing makes on me is, that damaging as Johnston's report is, it would be better for the President to send it in as is than to send the correspondence with it, better at least for Bragg and for the President.[22]

CHAPTER 21

Recalled to Service

In February 1865, General Joseph E. Johnston had taken residence in Lincolnton, North Carolina. By 1865, the Confederacy was in dire straits, with Union forces overrunning what was left of its shrinking domain. On January 14, 1865, Senator Wigfall was instrumental in getting the Confederate Senate to pass a resolution, by a 20–2 vote, to elevate General Robert E. Lee to general-in-chief of all Confederate armies. Additionally, it was resolved that Johnston was to be restored to command of the Army of Tennessee and General Beauregard was to take charge in South Carolina. The House passed the bill by a margin of 63 to 14 four days later. This was also a vote of no confidence in President Davis's conduct of the war. Davis complied with the request to appoint General Lee as general-in-chief but refused to assign Johnston command of the Army of Tennessee. Longstreet advised Lee on February 2 that he had learned from friends that only by restoring General Johnston to the command of the Army of Tennessee could the army's organization, morale, and efficiency be restored:

> This is my own opinion also. I hope, therefore, that you will not think it improper in me to beg that this may be one of your first acts as commander-in-chief. If I was not satisfied in my own mind that this was essential to the preservation of that army, I should not volunteer an opinion upon a matter beyond my proper sphere. I have served under General Johnston, and, so far as I am capable of judging, I am satisfied that he is one of our ablest and best generals. He has not been successful, but you can readily see that no general can be successful if he does not receive the support of the authorities above him.[1]

Memo

To justify his opposition, Davis wrote a memo for Congress of over 4,500 words, reviewing Johnston's wartime career and reasons for his lack of confidence in Johnston's capacity for command. Davis declared: "My opinion of

General Johnston's unfitness for command has ripened slowly and against my inclinations into a conviction so settled that it would be impossible for me again to feel confidence in him as the commander of any army in the field."[2] Davis decided not to send it to Congress, and instead sent a copy to his friend, ex-Senator Phelan of Mississippi, and two copies to Congressman Barksdale of Mississippi. When the memo was divulged after the war, it created much controversy. On February 6, 1864, when the act of Congress was published naming Lee as commander-in-chief, Davis submitted General John Cabell Breckinridge as Secretary of War, replacing Seddon, who had resigned. Breckinridge acted quickly to appoint Brigadier General Isaac St. John as Commissary-General in place of the inept Colonel Northrop. Fifteen senators petitioned Lee to appoint Johnston as commander. Lee refused, replying:

> I entertain a high opinion of Genl Johnston's capacity, but think a continual change of commanders is very injurious to any troops and tends greatly to their disorganization. At this time, as far as I understand the condition of affairs, an engagement with the enemy may be expected any day, and a change now would be particularly hazardous. Genl Beauregard is well known to the citizens of South Carolina, as well as to the troops of the Army of Tennessee, and I would recommend that it be certainly ascertained that a change was necessary before it was made.[3]

Rumors started to circulate that Beauregard's health was "feeble and precarious." On February 19, 1865, Lee informed Breckinridge that Beauregard's health was stated by many sources to be "indifferent" and had no one on duty to replace him. "General J. E. Johnston is the only officer," Lee resumed, "whom I know has the confidence of the army and the people, and if he was ordered to report to me I would place him there on duty."[4] Breckinridge passed the request along to President Davis, who acquiesced to the recall. On February 23, General Johnston received a telegram from the War Department simultaneously with a dispatch from General Lee, who directed him to: "Assume command of the Army of Tennessee and all troops in the Department of South Carolina, Georgia and Florida. [North Carolina was added to his command in early March 1865.] Assign General Beauregard to duty under you as you select. Concentrate all available forces and drive back Sherman."[5] Johnston, not wanting Lee to entertain unrealistic expectations of his circumstances, replied: "It is too late to expect me to concentrate troops capable of driving back Sherman. The remnant of the Army of Tennessee is much divided. So are other troops. I will get information from General Beauregard as soon as practicable. Is any discretion allowed me? I have no staff."[6] Always considerate, Joseph Johnston traveled to Charlotte to meet with Beauregard to ascertain if a subordinate position was agreeable to him. Beauregard affirmed that it was acceptable because of his poor health; hence, on February 25, Johnston assumed command at Charlotte, North Carolina, where he established his first headquarters.

Johnston confided to Wigfall that he wondered if his new assignment was a set-up so that he would be the scapegoat for the Confederacy's collapse. Wigfall wrote to Johnston on February 27:

> You are mistaken. Lee I believe fully sustains you & is now I understand hated by Davis as much as you are. It was out of confidence & kindness & a real desire to obtain the benefit of your ability in this crisis. He does not hesitate to speak of your removal as unfortunate and having caused all of our present difficulties. Lee does not hesitate to say that he was consulted and disapproved of your removal.[7]

Wigfall was correct that there were bad feelings between Robert E. Lee and Jefferson Davis. On February 25, Davis wrote to Lee: "Rumors assuming to be based on your views have affected the public mind, and it is reported obstructs needful legislation. A little further progress will produce panic. If you can spare the time I wish you to come here." Lee requested the material be sent to him for consideration. Perceiving his response to be a slight, President Davis replied in a letter ending with this admonishment: "Rest assured I will not ask your views in answer to measures. Your counsels are no longer wanted in this matter."[8]

The small number of troops in Johnston's command were widely separated and scattered. He issued a general order exhorting all absent soldiers to rejoin the ranks. Johnston appealed to Breckinridge for four months' pay for twenty thousand men, with a portion of it in specie. Breckinridge replied that the government was "almost universally paralyzed for want of means"; there was no money. To his fellow soldiers, Johnston stated that the "confidence in their discipline and valor which he has publicly expressed is undiminished." According to George W. Nichols, author of *The Story of the Great March*, the people of North Carolina wee "delighted with Johnston's restoration for they profess to think him the greatest general in the country. I have never heard but one expression of opinion among the Southerners relative to the respective merits of Johnston and Lee. Johnston is regarded as much superior to Lee, especially as a genius for strategy."[9] Lieutenant General Wade Hampton expressed the same sentiment to diarist Mary Chesnut, who recorded on February 8, 1865: "Hampton says Joe Johnston is equal, if not superior, to Lee as a commanding officer."[10]

General Sherman was marching his army through South and North Carolina to break up the railroads and link up with Grant's army operating against Richmond. Sherman had reached Cheraw, South Carolina, where he halted his army of 53,275 infantry and artillery and a division of 4,391 cavalry, commanded by General Judson Kilpatrick, from March 3–5. Johnston, needing to concentrate his forces, decided North Carolina was the place to make a stand. On March 4, he transferred his headquarters from Charlotte to Fayetteville, North Carolina, where he would be better able to supervise Confederate troops and quickly gather intelligence of the enemy's movements.

Lieutenant General William J. Hardee had moved up from Charleston, South Carolina, to Cheraw by railroad, about a dozen miles from the North Carolina border. Hardee was trying to block Sherman's advance with a force estimated by General Beauregard at twelve thousand; eleven hundred of his troops were South Carolina militia and reserves, and were not expected to leave their state. Remnants of the Army of Tennessee had halted in northeastern Mississippi at Tupelo after Hood's disastrous expedition to Nashville. Upon reaching Tupelo, Beauregard furloughed 3,500 of the most broken-down troops and sent four thousand of his best-equipped men to reinforce Mobile, Alabama. He ordered those remaining on duty to the Carolinas when Sherman's army invaded South Carolina. Troops from the Army of Tennessee were moving to a concentration point at Fayetteville, North Carolina; 1,200 under Lt. Gen. Alexander P. Stewart and 1,900 commanded by Maj. Gen. Benjamin F. Cheatham. Another two thousand under the command of Maj. Gen. Carter L. Stevenson were near Charlotte. Meanwhile, Lt. Gen. Stephen D. Lee had united small parties of the Army of Tennessee at Augusta, some 3,500 men who had come through Georgia, and conducted them to Smithfield, North Carolina, a rendezvous point fixed by Johnston. Johnston's army was assisted by Wheeler's division of Confederate cavalry, about three thousand troopers, and Butler's one thousand or so, all led by Lt. Gen. Wade Hampton. The cavalry observed and impeded the enemy's progress. Another source of manpower was a force under General Braxton Bragg, whom the Federals had forced to abandon Wilmington, North Carolina, and had pulled back to Goldsboro, 100 miles north of Wilmington. General Johnston suggested Robert E. Lee assign them to him, to which Lee complied. Bragg's troops consisted of Major General Robert F. Hoke's division, numbering 4,775 infantry and 782 artillerists, the latter battalion the only artillery Johnston had.

The Army of Tennessee was in ruins, having lost a large part of its artillery either captured, abandoned, or destroyed. Two-thirds of the troops were without small arms, having lost them in Tennessee. They depended on workshops in Alabama and Georgia for rifled muskets, plus what the Ordnance Department was able to procure, but received only a partial supply, leaving thirteen hundred veterans unarmed until the end of the war. The wagon transportation was devastated, with what was left of it moving through Georgia from Mississippi to the Carolinas. Another issue Johnston had to deal with was a scarcity of provisions for his troops. General Lee's army depended for subsistence on the officers of the commissariat in North Carolina, who were instructed by the Commissary-General and the War Department to collect provisions in the state exclusively for the army in Virginia. Rations for sixty thousand men for more than four months had been amassed in the principal railroad depots between Charlotte, Danville, and Weldon, but were not available to Johnston's army. Lee wrote to Johnston on March 5 on this subject: "Endeavor to supply your army by collecting subsistence through the country. That at depots is necessary for the Army of Northern Virginia."[11] Johnston, dependent upon the wagons of his army to collect provisions, appealed to Governor Zebulon Vance of North Carolina for help. From his headquarters at Charlotte, Johnston sent a message to Governor Vance on March 3: "To make a prompt movement to meet the enemy threatening your capital, I need fifty additional good wagons and teams to transport supplies. To meet the emergency will you assist me by having them collected from the vicinity of Raleigh and Smithfield at the earliest moment."[12] Vance acted promptly to provide assistance, in collaboration with Colonel Arthur H. Cole's excellent system of supply, so that the troops were furnished with food until the wagon-train of the Army of Tennessee came up.

Johnston picked Smithfield as a rendezvous point and sent orders to the different units of his army to concentrate there. It was midway between Raleigh and Goldsboro, which were both targeted, so Confederate forces could easily shift to meet these threats. The area around Raleigh was an important source of supplies for Lee's army. General Lee wrote: "I fear I cannot hold my position if road to Raleigh is interrupted. Should you be forced back in this direction both armies would certainly starve."[13] The North Carolina reservists were called out for service under the command of Lt. Gen. Theophilus H. Holmes. Not only were Sherman's forces advancing on a broad front, but Maj. Gen. John M. Schofield was moving up from Wilmington to hook up with Sherman at Goldsboro. Schofield had been ordered to take XXIII Corps (fourteen thousand men) on transports for a trip down the coast to Wilmington. Once there, his command was supplemented by Major General John G. Foster and the Army of the James to a strength of twenty-four thousand. Johnston went to Smithfield, where he was greeted with cheers by his old comrades of the Army of Tennessee. While there, Johnston placed Lieutenant General Stewart in command of the infantry and what remained of the artillery of the Army of Tennessee. Escorted by Captain Bromfield L. Ridley of Stewart's staff, Johnston visited Stewart's headquarters.

Captain Ridley was captivated by Johnston, whom he described as "surprisingly social," adding that he "endeavors to conceal his greatness rather than to impress you with it. I expressed to him the joy the Army of Tennessee manifested, on hearing of his restoration to command. He said that he was equally as much gratified to be with them as they were at his coming but he feared it 'too late to make it the same army.'"[14]

Johnston had Hardee's infantry and Hampton's cavalry impede the progress of the Federals. On March 6, Bragg reported from Goldsboro that Schofield's Federal division of Major General Jacob D. Cox was approaching Kinston. Bragg asked for reinforcements to launch a counterattack. The nearest troops, about two thousand in number, were under Maj. Gen. Daniel Harvey Hill, who, ironically, hated Bragg for having him removed from command after Chickamauga. Johnston ordered Hill to Bragg's assistance, adding: "I beg you to forget the past in this emergency." Hill obeyed the order, though afterward he protested to Johnston: "I hope that it may be possible & consistent with intents of the service to give me another commander than Genl. Bragg. He has made me the scapegoat once & would do it again."[15] Bragg was also uncomfortable with his situation, having played a part in the removal of Johnston at Atlanta. Bragg wrote to Jefferson Davis on March 5: "This military department having been merged by the general-in-chief, as a natural consequence of the present condition, in the command of General Johnston, it fairly terminates the temporary command to which you assigned me. For this and other reasons which present themselves to your mind as forcibly as I could express them, I beg that you will relieve me from the embarrassing position."[16] But he got no relief. The Confederate attack drove Cox's column back, taking three artillery pieces and inflicting a loss of 57 killed, 265 wounded, and 935 captured or missing, while suffering only 134 casualties themselves.

Meanwhile, Hardee and Hampton were falling back to Fayetteville, with all the fighting being done by the cavalry. Hampton surprised the Federal cavalry under Kilpatrick and seized his camp, taking prisoners and releasing the Confederates taken captive by Kilpatrick. After Sherman occupied Fayetteville on March 11, destroying a quantity of valuable machinery at the arsenal there, Hardee withdrew in the direction of Averysboro, where he threw up entrenchments in front of the Federal left wing that consisted of two corps. On the morning of March 16, the Federals attacked him and, after sharp fighting, turned his left flank and forced him to fall back to a stronger position, which he held until nightfall. During the night, Hardee marched toward Smithfield to Elevation. Hardee lost 108 dead and 68 wounded, the Federals 12 officers and 65 men killed and 477 wounded.

As of March 6, Sherman had learned that Johnston was back in command and that he could no longer deal with the Confederate army in the Carolinas in the same manner. "I knew then that my special antagonist, General Jos. Johnston was back, with part of his old army," he wrote later in his memoirs, "that he would not be misled by feints and false reports, and would somehow compel me to exercise more caution than I had hitherto done." Another Federal officer noted in his diary: "The important news is that Johnston has been restored to command. I do not imagine for a moment that this change of Rebel commanders will influence General Sherman in his purpose, yet it will alter the modus operandi, for Johnston cannot be treated with the contempt Sherman shows for Beauregard."[17]

Joseph Johnston realized that both Confederate armies were hopelessly outnumbered, and must avail themselves of the interior lines and combine forces against one or other of their antagonists. On March 1 and again on March 11, Johnston asked the general-in-chief: "Would it be possible to hold Richmond itself with half your army while the other half joined us near Roanoke to crush Sherman? We might then turn on Grant." There is no indication that General Lee replied. Lieutenant General Wade Hampton reflected:

> Under these circumstances, but two alternatives were presented to the Confederate general: one was to transport his infantry by rail rapidly to Virginia, where the re-enforcements he could thus bring to General Lee might enable these two great soldiers to strike a decisive blow on Grant's left flank; the other was to throw his small force on the army confronting him, with the hope of crippling that army, if he could not defeat it.

Hampton believed Johnston contemplated both these options. Major General John B. Gordon, when asked by Lee about a course of action in the present predicament, responded: "Abandon Richmond and Petersburg, unite by rapid marches with General Johnston in North Carolina, and strike Sherman before Grant can join him." Lee stated that the deplorable plight of his army due to starvation stood in the way of such a move.[18]

Bentonville

Joseph Johnston showed remarkable skill in uniting his dispersed army under very adverse conditions. He sent a dispatch about midnight on March 17 to his cavalry commander, Lt. Gen. Wade Hampton. Johnston asked Hampton to "give him his views" as to the disposition of the Federal corps, the practicality of attacking at an advantage, and where the attack could be made. On the early morning of March 18, Johnston received reports from Hampton that Sherman's left and right wings were a day's march apart,

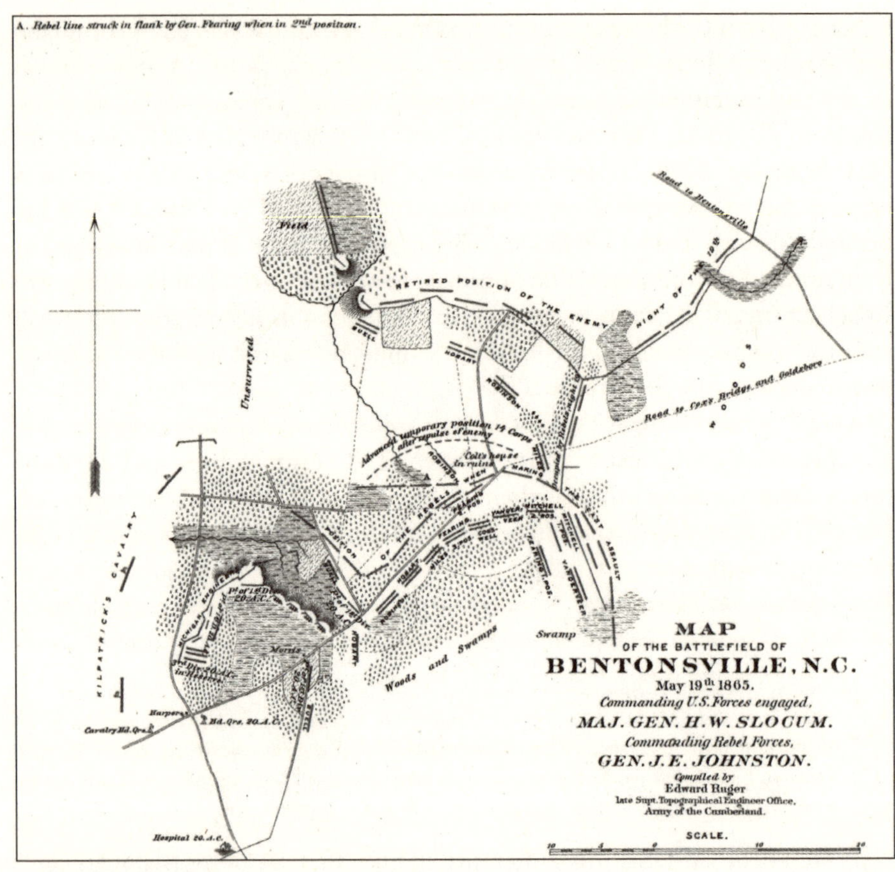

Battle of Bentonsville, May 19, 1865. (Library of Congress)
General Joseph Johnston commanded the Confederate forces and Major General Slocum commanded Union forces. Rebels placed their troops to flank the Union troops

heading for Goldsboro. Sherman's right wing of two corps (Logan's and Blair's) was on a direct road from Fayetteville, having crossed the Black River, while his left wing, commanded by Major General Henry W. Slocum, composed of two corps—XIV Corps (Davis's) and XX Corps (Williams's)—was on the road from Averysboro to Goldsboro via the hamlet of Bentonville. Hampton suggested a spot near Bentonville, about 16 miles from Confederate headquarters at Smithfield, as an admirable one for an attack on the left-hand Federal column. Johnston instructed Hampton to hold the ground and said he would move at once to the position. Johnston then directed Hardee, Stewart, and Bragg to gather at the ambush site as quickly as possible. Bragg's men deployed to the left and right of the road to Goldsboro, while the Army of Tennessee under

Stewart—minus two divisions of Cheatham's corps, which were still on the way—was drawn up farther to the right, parallel to the road. Hardee was to fill the gap between Bragg and Stewart, but because of a deceptive map his arrival was delayed. Hampton placed two batteries of horse artillery, under Captains Halsey and Earle, in the vacant space.

Lieutenant General Hampton threw some light entrenchments across the road manned by Butler's division, but was forced back to the main line of works held by Hoke's infantry, supported by two batteries of artillery, the only artillery Johnston had. The Federals were halted, but the attack was so vigorous that General Bragg believed Hoke would be driven from his position and so applied for reinforcements. Hardee did not reach the field until past noon; Johnston diverted the head of his column, Major General Lafayette McLaws's division, to aid Bragg and the division of Brigadier General William Booth Taliaferro to the right. Lieutenant General Stewart's Army of Tennessee, having constructed breastworks, was also assaulted, but repelled the assailants. Johnston launched his flanking attack around 3.00 p.m. on March 19, Hardee being ordered to take charge of the entire attack. Hardee's troops outflanked two Union brigades on the left wing, shattering XIV Corps. Brigades of XX Corps were brought up in support of the broken XIV Corps. The order of battle of Hardee's troops could not be preserved in the dense thicket, and it was necessary to halt and realign the troops. The Union forces took advantage of this pause and assailed the command of Brigadier General Pettus of the Army of Tennessee, but were quickly repulsed. Night brought a close to the fighting and the Confederates fell back to their original lines from which they had moved to attack, where they maintained a defensive position until March 21. Confederate losses in the three days of conflict were 223 killed, 1,467 wounded, and 653 missing. Johnston believed Federal losses exceeded four thousand. The Confederates secured four pieces of artillery, but only had enough harnessed horses to take three from the field. By the afternoon of March 20, General Sherman arrived with two corps of his other wing, and on the next day sent a corps around Johnston's flank, forcing him to retreat. Johnston withdrew to Smithfield, marching to an encampment near the town. He was reinforced by the arrival of several thousand men of the Army of Tennessee, most of them coming through Georgia and united at Augusta by Lieutenant General S. D. Lee. This brought Johnston's army to 13,635 infantry, 1,033 artillery, and 4,093 of cavalry, according to his return of March 27. Meanwhile, Sherman marched to Goldsboro, where he affected a juncture with Schofield, bringing his army to a strength of nearly eighty thousand men of the three arms. Sherman thought his men now needed "rest and to fix up a little."

CHAPTER 22

Surrender

On April 5, General Johnston learned from a newspaper dispatch that Robert E. Lee had abandoned Richmond and the government was at Danville. Johnston was told that General Lee was concentrating toward Amelia Courthouse; no one reported to Johnston that Lee was driven from his lines around Petersburg by Grant, so he thought Lee sought to unite the two armies in North Carolina. On the morning of April 10, Sherman commenced marching from Goldsboro in the direction of Raleigh. Johnston ordered the Confederate forces to Raleigh, his men being a day's march ahead of the Federals. Hardee's corps, with Butler's division of cavalry, acted as a rearguard on the north side of the Neuse River by the Goldsboro road. Johnston in person, along with Stewart's and Lee's corps, plus Wheeler's division of cavalry, crossed the river at Battle's Bridge and encamped near the bridge that night (14 miles east of Raleigh). About 1.00 a.m., Johnston was awakened to receive a telegram from Danville that an unofficial report had been brought by a scout to President Davis indicating Lee had surrendered at Appomattox Court House in Virginia on Sunday, April 9. The three corps took up the march the next morning and reached Raleigh early in the afternoon.

At 4.30 p.m., Jefferson Davis sent a telegram summoning Johnston to Greensboro' and telling him to place Lieutenant General Hardee in command of his troops. On April 11, Johnston boarded the first train about midnight and travelled all night, arriving at Greensboro' at around 8.00 a.m. on April 12. Johnston joined General Beauregard as his guest at his quarters nearby those of President Davis. Within an hour or two, Johnston and Beauregard were summoned to the president's quarters and found Davis with three cabinet members—Judah P. Benjamin (State), Stephen Mallory (Navy), and John H. Reagan (Postmaster). Davis was eager to continue the war and presented an optimistic plan, claiming that in two or three weeks he could recruit a large army in the field by bringing back into service men who had deserted and gone home and by conscripting those who were previously exempted. Johnston and the other military officers remarked that "men who had left the army when our cause was not desperate, and those who, under the same circumstances, could not be forced into it, would scarcely, in the present desperate condition of affairs, enter the service upon mere invitation."[1] Davis adjourned the conference and the meeting was terminated, the president stating it would be reconvened after the arrival of Major General John C. Breckenridge (Secretary of War) in the course of the afternoon.

General Breckenridge arrived at Greensboro' that night and confirmed the report of Lee's surrender. Generals Johnston and Beauregard conversed about the resources of the belligerents and agreed that the war was lost and the Confederacy overthrown. Johnston had a conversation with Breckenridge, expressing his desire to suggest to President Davis that he should terminate the war. Breckenridge promised Johnston he would be allowed to present his views at the cabinet meeting arranged for the following day. Mallory came to converse with Johnston and was anxious for the general to advise Davis that negotiations to end the conflict should commence. On April 13, the next morning, Generals Johnston and Beauregard were summoned to the president's office at the residence of Colonel John Taylor Wood an hour or two after the meeting of his cabinet opened. Breckenridge had just concluded his report of the surrender of Lee's army. Davis gave a roseate evaluation of the military situation: "Our last disasters are terrible, but I do not think we should regard them as fatal. I think we can whip the enemy yet, if our people will turn out."[2]

After Davis finished, he called on Johnston as the senior officer for his views. Johnston argued:

> I represented that under such circumstances it would be the greatest of human crimes for us to attempt to continue the war; for, having neither money or credit, nor arms but those in the hands of our soldiers, nor ammunition but that in their cartridge boxes, nor shops for repairing arms or fixing ammunition, the effect of our keeping the field would be, not to harm the enemy, but to complete the devastation of our country and ruin of its people. I therefore urged that the President should exercise at once the only function of the government still in his possession, and open negotiations for peace.[3]

Davis listened to Johnston quietly, with his head bowed, nervously folding and unfolding a newspaper to display his agitation. After Johnston finished, Davis asked Beauregard for his opinion. Without hesitation, Beauregard stated: "I concur in all General Johnston has said." All cabinet members except Judah P. Benjamin agreed with Johnston's appraisal. "Well, General Johnston," Davis asked, "what do you propose?" The president claimed that from previous experience, the Government of the United States would not negotiate with him since it did not recognize the Confederacy. Johnston said it was not unusual for military commanders to initiate negotiations upon which treaties of peace were founded, and asked that he be allowed to send a note through the lines to Sherman to arrange terms of an armistice. Davis answered: "Well, sir, you can adopt this course, though I confess I am not sanguine as to ultimate results."[4]

Reluctantly, President Davis dictated a letter, which was written up by Mallory for Johnston to sign:

> The results of the recent campaign in Virginia have changed the relative military condition of the belligerents. I am, therefore, induced to address you in this form, the inquiry whether to stop the further effusion of blood and devastation of property, you are willing to make a temporary suspension of active operations, and to communicate to Lieut.-General Grant, commanding the armies of the United States, the request that he will take like action in regard to other armies, the object being to permit the civil authorities to enter into the needful arrangements to terminate the existing war.[5]

On April 14, the letter, entrusted to Hampton's cavalry, was sent out under a flag of truce toward Raleigh. Sherman sent a reply on the morning of April 16 assenting to a conference regarding an armistice. In a telegraph, Johnston requested Lieutenant General Hampton arrange the time and place of the meeting. Johnston went to Greensboro' to consult and inform Davis of developments, but found the president had left for Charlotte on the 15th with his party, escorted by a small band of cavalry. Upon learning this, Johnston telegraphed Secretary of War Breckinridge: "Your immediate presence is necessary, in order that I should be able to confer with you." Johnston was following the advice of Beauregard, who forewarned that a Cabinet member should be present to witness the proceedings so that Johnston was protected "from the invidious & ungenerous remarks which would certainly be made otherwise" by President Davis and his followers, no matter what terms were agreed on.[6] Upon arriving at Hampton's headquarters, 2 or 3 miles southeast of Hillsboro', Johnston was informed that the meeting was to take place in a rough-hewn wooden cabin owned by James Bennett and his wife, Nancy, at noon on April 17. At the appointed time, Johnston and Sherman met and moved to the house.

President Lincoln Assassinated

The two army leaders entered the house and went to their assigned room. As soon as they were alone, Sherman showed Johnston a telegram from Secretary of War Stanton, announcing the assassination of President Lincoln two days before. After reading it, Johnston said that "in my opinion, the event was the greatest possible calamity to the South." Johnston hoped Sherman did not charge it to the Confederate Government. "I told him," Sherman wrote, "I could not believe that he or General Lee, or the officers of the Confederate army, could possibly be privy to acts of assassination; but I could not say as much for Jeff Davis, George Sanders, and men of that stripe."[7]

Durham Convention

Sherman offered Johnston the same terms that were granted to Robert E. Lee. Johnston declined, stating that his army was not surrounded, instead proposing a partial suspension of hostilities to arrange the terms for a permanent peace. Sherman questioned whether Johnston had sufficient authority to arrange such a peace, but Johnston said that he could secure such authority and it was agreed that they would meet at the same place the next day, April 18. The conference was resumed at 10.00 a.m. the next morning, Johnston being accompanied by Breckinridge in the capacity of a major general, since Sherman did not want to treat with civil authorities of the Confederate Government. An agreement to end the war was reached and signed, in what was to be called the Durham's Station Convention. But it was not to be. On April 24, Sherman received notice that the terms were rejected by the Federal Government due to agitation over Lincoln's assassination. Sherman notified Johnston that hostilities would resume at 11.00 a.m. on April 26 unless the Confederate army surrendered on the terms granted to General Lee. Johnston, realizing that Sherman's message was an ultimatum, asked to meet him again for a conference. They met on April 26 at the house of Mr. Bennett and agreed to the following terms:

1. All acts of war on the part of the troops under General Johnston's command to cease from this date.
2. All arms and public property to be deposited at Greensboro, and delivered to an ordnance officer of the United States Army.
3. Rolls of all officers and men to be made in duplicate; one copy to be retained by the commander of the troops and the other to be given to an officer to be designated by General Sherman; each officer and man to give his individual obligation in writing not to take up arms against the Government of the United States until properly released from this obligation.
4. The side arms of the officers and their private horses and baggage to be retained by them.
5. This being done, all the officers and men will be permitted to return to their homes, not to be disturbed by the United States authorities so long as they observe their obligation and the laws in force where they may reside.

Supplemental Terms

A few days after the convention, supplemental terms were agreed by General Schofield on behalf of Sherman as follows:

> 1. The field transportation to be loaned to the troops for their march to their homes and for subsequent use in their industrial pursuits. Artillery horses may be used in field transportation if necessary.
> 2. Each brigade or separate body to retain a number of arms equal to one seventh of its effective strength, which, when the troops reach the capitals of their States, will be disposed of as the general commanding the department may direct.
> 3. Private horses and other private property of both officers and men to be retained by them.
> 4. The commanding general of the Military Division of West Mississippi, Major-General Canby, will be requested to give transportation by water from Mobile or New Orleans to the troops from Arkansas or Texas.
> 5. The obligations of officers and soldiers to be signed by their immediate commanders.
>
> Naval forces within the limits of General Johnston's command to be included in the terms of this convention.[8]

By these arrangements and through the generosity of Sherman, who furnished them a large amount of rations, the return of the Confederate troops to their homes was made comparatively comfortable, considering the state of the country at the time. On April 30, Johnston announced the result of his negotiations to the governors of Georgia, South Carolina, and Florida in a telegram:

> The disaster in Virginia, the capture by the enemy of all our workshops for the preparation of ammunition and repairing arms, the impossibility of recruiting our little army, opposed by more than ten times its numbers, or of supplying it except by robbing our own citizens, destroyed all hope of successful war. I have therefore made a military convention with General Sherman to terminate hostilities in North and South Carolina, Georgia, and Florida. I made this convention to spare the blood of the gallant little Army committed to me, to prevent further suffering of our people by the devastation and ruin inevitable from the marches of invading armies, and to avoid the crime of waging hopeless war.[9]

Farewell

On May 2, General Johnston issued an emotional general order of farewell to the army:

> Comrades: In terminating our official relations I most earnestly exhort you to observe faithfully the terms of pacification agreed upon, and to discharge the obligations of good and peaceful citizens at your homes as well as you have performed the duties of thorough soldiers in the field. By such a course you will best secure the comfort of your families and

> kindred and restore tranquility to your country. You will return to your homes with the admiration of our people, won by the courage and noble devotion you have displayed in the long war. I shall always remember with pride the loyal support and generous confidence you have given me. I now part with you with deep regret, and bid you farewell with feelings of cordial friendship and with earnest wishes that you may have hereafter all the prosperity and happiness to be found in the world.[10]

CHAPTER 23

Private Citizen

The 58-year-old Joseph Johnston was now a private citizen, preoccupied by the necessity to make a living. Lydia Johnston wrote to her husband's former chief of staff, Ben Ewell, who had been restored to the presidency of William and Mary College. She asked if he knew of any prospects in Richmond: "Engineering he rather prides himself on, but would take anything that would keep the kettle boiling."[1] Johnston was concerned about Lydia's health, which the doctors diagnosed as "neuralgia," which included a wide variety of symptoms, including headaches, tiredness, and general malaise. Throughout their marriage, she had almost constantly contended with one illness after another. Johnston took up residence at a resort a few miles from Danville to help Lydia recover, but there was no improvement in her health, and with Grant's permission they went to Baltimore, Maryland, for a stay with her family. Johnston made an application for amnesty to President Andrew Johnson, without success. He wrote in his petition: "I regret to be unable to advance any special claim for indulgence. Perhaps, however, Your Excellency may think it worth consideration that while as an officer of the United States Army I served faithfully for many years & gave my blood & offered my life in that service many times."[2]

In November 1865, Johnston, along with other ex-Confederates, organized at Richmond, Virginia, the National Express & Transportation Company, under the laws of Virginia, to engage in the business of quick transportation of parcels in the North and South. As the company's president, Johnston traveled frequently. On a trip on a Chesapeake steamer, he met a man who insisted the South "was conquered but not subdued." The general immediately asked the speaker with what command he had served. "Unfortunately, circumstances made it impossible for me to be in the army," the reply came. Johnston cut him off abruptly. "Well, Sir, I was. You may not be subdued, but I am."[3]

The National Express & Transportation Company failed to secure financial backing, so Johnston took a position as president from May 1866 to November 1867 of the Alabama and Tennessee River Rail Road Company, later renamed the Selma, Rome and Dalton Railroad, that ran a line from Selma in Alabama to Blue Mountain, Georgia. The headquarters of the company was in Selma, where Joseph and Lydia Johnston established residence. Johnston held the post from May 1866 to November 1867, and in August 1867 the railroad was reorganized by its directors as the Selma, Rome, & Dalton Railroad. However, the company failed for lack of sufficient capital and Johnston resigned as president. While in Selma, Johnston took interest in the church which had motivated him to be baptized by Bishop Polk; on Good Friday 1867, Bishop Wilmer of Alabama confirmed him at St Paul's Church, where he became a communicant.

In 1868, the London, Liverpool and Globe Insurance Company and the New York Life Insurance Company invited Johnston, based on the recognition and power of his name, to become their manager for the Gulf States, with headquarters at Savannah. Johnston made residence there and pushed the business with the same consciousness, energy, intelligence, and watchfulness which he displayed in his military duties. In the fall of 1868, Johnston sailed to Europe to visit the company's offices in London, Liverpool, and Paris. Upon his return, he organized Joseph E. Johnston and Company, with B. G. Humphreys and Livingston Mims as partners to act as General Agents. Humphreys, who served as an officer throughout the Civil War and had been the first governor of Mississippi after the war, was in charge of the Jackson office. Mims, who was the Chief Quartermaster for Mississippi in the war, directed the Atlanta office. Johnston was responsible for business in Savannah, where he remained for nearly a decade. Within four years, Johnston had more than 120 agents working for him in Georgia, Alabama, and Mississippi. He invited several former reputable Confederate officers to join the firm, who bestowed prestige to the endeavor.

Throughout his life, Joseph Johnston appreciated humorous stories that poked fun at poseurs. One of his favorites, which always made him laugh, concerned the story of an officer who had just returned from an extended trip to Florida. This officer told several friends how he had personally captured an alligator more than 20 feet long. When a diminutive listener voiced some skepticism, the storyteller responded: "Surprised are you?" "O, no," the doubter replied, "I am a liar myself."[4]

Robert E. Lee visited Savannah in the spring of 1870 and met with Johnston. Within a few months, Lee lay dead in Lexington. In 1873, Johnston was influential in raising a large contribution for the monument placed over his old friend, and received a resolution of thanks from the Memorial Association. In the fall of 1873, his brother Beverly Johnston passed on; Joseph was broken hearted. To settle Beverly's estate, the family decided to sell the estate at Panecillo.

A portrait of Robert E. Lee (1807–70) and Joseph E. Johnston taken in April 1870 during Lee's farewell tour of the South. Lee died six months later. The image was sold to raise funds for the Lee Monument in Richmond, Virginia. (Library of Congress)

Narrative of Military Operations

General Johnston turned to writing his memoirs, *Narrative of Military Operations Directed During the Late War Between the States*, which were published in 1874. He wanted to have them published to refute Jefferson Davis's "unsent message" to Congress of February 1865, in which the president disparaged Johnston's fitness for command. Johnston heard of this document on a visit to Jackson, Mississippi, in the winter of 1866–67 and made great efforts to obtain a copy.

In December 1876, Johnston made a second effort to obtain amnesty and remove his political disabilities. Both houses of Congress passed a bill to relieve his handicap and President Grant approved it on February 23, 1877.

Joseph Johnston wanted to return to his native state of Virginia, and at the beginning of 1877 moved from Savannah to Richmond, where he found employment as the Virginia agent for the Home Insurance Company. In 1878, a local Democratic committee was eager for Johnston to be a candidate for Congress. He accepted and was elected to the House of Representatives from the Fourth Virginia District, taking his seat in the 46th Congress on March 4, 1879. Johnston served on the Military Affairs Committee and the Committee on Levees and Improvements of the Mississippi River. He also held appointments as Regent of the Smithsonian Institution and Visitor to the Military Academy at West Point as a member of the congressional oversight delegation. Upon completion of his two-year term, he decided not to run for office again. He retained his home in Washington and maintained legal residence in Richmond, where he voted. In 1884, the Democratic candidate for president, Grover Cleveland, defeated James G. Blaine by the small margin of twenty-nine thousand votes. Cleveland appointed the 76-year-old Johnston as U.S. Railroad Commissioner, a position which required him to travel throughout the country. Johnston's responsibility was to inspect the railroads each summer and present a report in the fall to Secretary of the Interior Lucius Q. C. Lamar, a former Confederate officer from Georgia, who had briefly served on Johnston's staff in 1861. Johnston was in Portland, Oregon, in July 1885, where he received notice to return east to act as one of the pallbearers at Ulysses Grant's funeral. In a great show of unity, Simon Buckner, Philip Sheridan, Sherman, and Johnston carried Grant's coffin to his tomb. In November 1885, Johnston traveled to Trenton, New Jersey, to participate in the funeral of George B. McClellan, an old friend in the prewar days and an adversary in the Peninsula campaign.

Death of Lydia

Lydia's health continued to deteriorate, in spite of trips to health spas and the machinations of doctors. On February 22, 1887, she died at their Washington home, aged 65; they had been married for over 40 years. In reply to a condolence letter a month later, Joseph Johnston lamented that he would "never again hear her sweet voice, the gay tones of which give me happiness." For the rest of his life, he could not bring himself to write or speak her name.[5]

Johnston's tenure as Railroad Commissioner ended in 1888 when Grover Cleveland lost to Benjamin Harrison in the Electoral College, even though Harrison had sixty thousand fewer popular votes. Johnston retired to his home on Connecticut Avenue in Washington in 1889.

He was invited to attend a Confederate memorial ceremony in Atlanta in the spring of 1890, where he was to share an open carriage with Edmund Kirby Smith, drawn by two black horses and escorted by 40 of the Governor's Horse Guard. Just as the parade had begun, someone in the crowd shouted: "That's Johnston! That's Joe Johnston!" The crowd surrounded the carriage, reaching out their hands to the old general. The horses were unhitched and the men took hold of the traces, pulling the carriage the length of the parade route. The carriage stopped in front of the stage door to the opera house, where Johnston was assisted to the ground as the crowd cheered wildly.

CHAPTER 24

Death and Funeral

In the winter of 1891, Johnston was selected as an honorary pallbearer for William Tecumseh Sherman, his antagonist in the Atlanta campaign. Johnston stood at the graveside with his hat in his hands on a cold and wet February afternoon. Another mourner leaned forward to urge him to put on his hat, lest he catch a chill. Though feeble at the time, Johnston declined, declaring: "If I were in his place and he were standing here in mine, he would not put on his hat." Johnston did indeed catch a cold and was confined to his house at No. 1023 Connecticut Avenue, Washington, D.C. He developed an infection and his breathing grew difficult. On the night of March 21, 1891, he peacefully passed away. His funeral was held the next day, when he was laid to rest in the McLane family plot of the Greenmount Cemetery, Baltimore, next to his wife and his nephew, Preston Johnston, whose remains he had brought back from Mexico.[1]

All that marks his last resting place is this simple inscription, selected by himself:

Joseph E. Johnston
Son of
Judge Peter & Mary Johnston, of Va.,
Born at
Longwood, Prince Edward Co., Va.,
February 3, 1807.
Died March 21, 1891.
Brigadier General, U.S.A.
General, C. S. A.[2]

Epitaph

Sam Watkins, an infantryman of the 1st Tennessee Regiment, offered this moving epitaph to General Joseph Eggleston Johnston:

> Old Joe Johnston had taken command of the Army of Tennessee when it was crushed and broken, at a time when no other man on earth could have united it. He found them in rags and tatters, hungry and heart-broken, their morale gone, their pride a thing of the past. Through his instrumentality and skillful manipulations all these had been restored. We had been under his command nearly twelve months. He was more popular with his troops day by day. We had made a long and arduous campaign, lasting four months; not one single day in that four months that did not find us engaged in battle with the enemy. History does not record a single incident of where one of his lines was ever broken—not a single rout. He had not lost a single piece of artillery, he had dealt the enemy heavy blows; he was whipping them day by day, yet keeping his own men intact. His men were in as good spirits and as sure of victory at the end of four months as they were at the beginning. Instead of the army being depleted, it had grown in strength. 'Tis sure he had fallen back, but it was to give his enemy the heavier blows. He brought all the powers of his army into play. Ever on the defensive, 'tis true, yet ever striking his enemy in his most vulnerable part. His face was always to the foe. They could make no movement in which they were not anticipated. Such a man was Joseph E. Johnston, and such his record. Farewell, old fellow! We privates loved you because you made us love ourselves![3]

Conclusion

On July 23, 1879, Henry W. Grady of the *New York Herald* interviewed General James Longstreet regarding the war, a record of which appeared in the August 2 issue of the *Philadelphia Weekly Times*, headed: "General Longstreet: His Reminiscences of the Struggle Between the States, Mistakes of the War and Why the South Was Beaten." The article included the following passage:

> He is a soldier [Longstreet] by instinct, education, practice and habit. There is no man whose opinions on the conduct of the war have more weight with thoughtful and competent people. His opinions are entitled to weight.
>
> Grady: Who do you think was the best general on the Southern side of the war?
>
> Longstreet: I am inclined to think that General Joe Johnston was the ablest and most accomplished man that the Confederate armies ever produced. He never had the opportunity accorded to many others, but he showed wonderful power as a tactician and commander. I do not think that we had his equal for handling an army and conducting a campaign.[1]

General Joseph Eggleston Johnston was a brilliant strategist and tactician but his designs were thwarted by President Davis, who considered himself a superior military genius.

General Longstreet was with Johnston on the Peninsula when Johnston wisely abandoned the Yorktown–Warwick river line and retreated towards Richmond. Although, General Robert E. Lee and President Jefferson Davis were in favor of defending the Peninsula, Johnston realized that his old-fashioned smoothbore guns were no match for the technically advanced rifled guns of General George McClellan and the Federal fleet. The superior rifled cannon, with their longer range and greater accuracy, outgunned the Confederates and would have smashed their defense line. Furthermore, Johnston felt that his army could be outflanked on the Peninsula. Indeed, the Federal fleet could move transports up the York River and place a force in the rear of the Confederates, cutting communication with Richmond. Johnston advocated a concentration of all available forces from Georgia and North and South Carolina to join with the Virginia troops at Richmond in an offensive movement to overwhelm McClellan's army. This good advice was not given the weight it deserved and his plan was not accepted by the Confederate Government.

Johnston pulled back to Richmond and awaited McClellan's approach. McClellan placed Keyes's and Heintzelman's corps south of the Chickahominy River, which had become swollen due to heavy rains. Johnston used this development to his advantage and devised a plan to entrap the two Union corps and destroy them, attacking with the bulk of his army. However, he was wounded by a large fragment of shell before he could consummate his stratagem. Johnston and Longstreet had long discussions concerning Johnston's plans for the battle.

Johnston was inactive until November 1862, when he was assigned a geographical command encompassing a territory between the Blue Ridge Mountains and the Mississippi River. His position was that of a scapegoat who would be blamed for whatever failures President Davis's favorite but ineffective generals would commit.

Johnston was faced with an immediate crisis as General Grant led an army to defeat General Pemberton's forces and seize Vicksburg, Mississippi. Johnston advocated for some of General Holmes's troops in the Trans-Mississippi to join Pemberton to defeat Grant, but this was not carried out due to objections by President Davis.

General Johnston arrived at Jackson, Mississippi, on May 13, 1863, to take command of six thousand troops, a force which was slowly raised to twenty-eight thousand. Johnston ordered General Pemberton to march towards him with all his forces and abandon Vicksburg, which had lost its strategic importance once the Federal fleet had bypassed it. However, Johnston's orders were countermanded by President Davis, who as commander-in-chief superseded Johnston. Davis had sent private telegrams to Pemberton ordering him to hold Vicksburg and Port Hudson at all costs. The foundation of Johnston's strategic theory of the art and science of war was for the concentration of troops to achieve victory, thereby regaining localities and territories lost to attain success on the battlefield. He always believed that saving troops took priority over holding strategic positions. He rejected the notion to hold all points, a policy which favored the advantage the North possessed in its greater numbers of manpower. Robert M. Hughes, Johnston's biographer, wrote:

> Nothing could have suited the South better than an attempt of the North to seize and garrison its cities. Its great extent of territory would then have become its strength, the superior numbers of the enemy would have been dissipated in numerous garrisons, and the

> Southern armies, equal to any moveable forces which its foe could have brought against them, might have faced them with confidence and destroyed them in detail. Under the strategy of President Davis, the extent of Southern territory was a source of weakness; under Johnston's it would have been a bulwark of power.[2]

As Johnston predicted, Grant laid siege to Pemberton's entrapped army at Vicksburg, which surrendered due to starvation. Johnston's military maxim throughout the war was to save the South's manpower. "'Let the place go, and save the garrison,' was his motto from the beginning to the end of the war," Hughes asserted.[3]

Ulysses Grant had great respect for Johnston's military capabilities. John Russell Young, in his account of General Grant's two-year tour around the world from 1877–79, reports him as saying:

> The Southern army had many good generals. Lee, of course, was a good soldier, and so was Longstreet. I knew Longstreet in Mexico. He was a fine fellow, and one of the best of the young officers. I do not know that there was any better than Joe Johnston. I have had nearly all the Southern generals in high command in front of me, and Joe Johnston gave me more anxiety than any of the others. I was never half so anxious about Lee. Take it all in all, the South, in my opinion, had no better soldier than Joe Johnston—none, at least, that gave me more trouble.[4]

After Bragg's resignation of command on December 2, 1863, following his defeat on Missionary Ridge and Lookout Mountain, General Johnston was given command of the Army of Tennessee on December 16 at Dalton, Georgia. Facing Johnston was a Federal army under General Sherman of approximately one hundred thousand men, while Johnston had around fifty-five thousand troops—forty-five thousand infantry, seven thousand cavalry, and three thousand artillery. Johnston quickly realized that the railroad, a technological advancement of the 1840s with its rapid high-lift capacity, was the key to strategic success on the battlefield. He requested that a cavalry force under the gifted Nathan Bedford Forrest be sent to disrupt Sherman's lengthy railroad communications. Johnston reasoned that if Forrest could seize the railroad and inflict permanent damage to it, Sherman would be compelled to attack on Johnston's terms or retreat, since his receipt of daily ammunition and provisions would be interrupted. President Davis felt that Forrest was needed to protect Mississippi and Alabama from raids rather than defeating this major invasion. He recommended Johnston send a strong detachment of cavalry from his own army. However, Johnston needed all the cavalry he had to protect his own communications, hold portions of his lines against Sherman's superior numbers, and provide reconnaissance.

Edward A. Pollard, editor of the *Richmond Examiner* during the Civil War, was generally acknowledged as the ablest and most prolific Southern writer of the period. He had this to say about Johnston's Atlanta Campaign:

> General Johnston was now executing the masterpiece of his military life. He had fought down to Atlanta with far more success and brilliancy than Lee had fought down to Richmond, with more incidents of advantage, and to greatly better effect. His retrograde from Dalton to Atlanta has been described as a future study in military schools, and as exact as a figure in geometry—his plan of campaign being the avoidance of pitched battles and the substitution of flank movements, interspersed with actions between detachments and sometimes rising to a general engagement. He had performed the wonder of conducting an army in retreat through nearly one hundred and fifty miles of intricate country, absolutely without any loss in material or prisoners; he had brought along every thing, every gun, every wagon, every camp-kettle; he had inflicted a loss upon the enemy of forty-five thousand men, more than four times his own; and in pursuance of his plan of reducing the numerical superiority of Sherman's army so as "to cope with it on equal ground by the time the Chattahoochee was passed," he had now that army south of the stream where its defeat would be inevitably its destruction, and where, on the other hand, the Confederates would have a place of refuge in Atlanta, which their commander, writing officially to Richmond had described as "too strong to be assaulted and too extensive to be invested." Never was any situation of the war so advantageous for the Confederates, and so critical and tremulous for the enemy, unable, as he was, to go further, brought to a place which he dared not to assault, and which he was unable to invest and suspended one hundred and forty miles in a hostile country by a single line of communication. The fears of the giddy enemy was excessive, almost to demoralization; the assurances of Johnston were as perfect as human foresight could make them. We repeat that his position in Atlanta was more secure than that of Lee in Richmond. Judging prospective by past events, it was impossible to doubt that he would have held Sherman as well as Lee held Grant. He could at least have done this; and it was probable he would have done more, for if he had succeeded in destroying Sherman's line of land communication, which was obviously easier to reach than that of Grant over water, he might have forced his enemy to retreat, in which surrender or annihilation would be the choice.
>
> One other movement now only remained to complete the discomfiture of the enemy. It was plain and inviting; and it seemed indeed as if all events had been marshalled in favor of Johnston. The defeat by Forrest's cavalry in northern Mississippi of an expedition of the enemy under Sturgis designed to protect and operate in Sherman's rear, left that rear uncovered, and presented the spectacle of an enemy a hundred and forty miles in the interior of Georgia, holding a single line of communication which might be easily destroyed by cavalry. General Johnston at once dispatched to Richmond a request that Forrest's cavalry might be transferred from Mississippi, where it was then roving as an independent command, representing that if it got on Sherman's line, it could destroy it beyond the possibility of further use. He did not doubt that the government would at once see an opportunity so plain and splendid; he was in the highest spirits from all his prospects of advantage in the campaign; he supposed that what he had done was appreciated at Richmond, and that what he proposed would now be ordered with alacrity. To his infinite surprise and alarm, he received an order from Richmond denying his request and prohibiting him from any command of Forrest's cavalry to move it to the rear of Sherman.

On the 17th day of July, General Johnston was standing on the fortification of Atlanta, conversing with his chief engineer. A dispatch was handed to him; there were no marks of importance upon it; he read it without a change of countenance. It was an order removing him from the command of the army; brief, decisive; he should "immediately turn over the command of the army and department of Tennessee to General Hood."

It was a day never to be forgotten, for it contained the doom of the South. On the slight piece of paper that Johnston read silently, looking over the great army that he had hoped to led to victory, that had been his pride, and joy, glory, and that, standing upon the ramparts, he now saw, for the last time, stretched before him, there was written not only his removal, not only this cruel and sneering brevity to himself, but the sentence that murdered tens of thousands of brave soldiers, the message of greatest joy and encouragement to the enemy, the death-warrant of the Southern Confederacy.

"We must," said a Richmond journalist, "think of these things, for these are the causes which produce the effects. It is manifestly absurd to put up and pull down a commander in the field according to the crude views or peevish fancies of a functionary in Richmond. Such conduct of a government would paralyze the greatest military genius, ruin the oldest army, and render success in war absolutely impossible. Now is it not hard, is it not cruelly hard, that the struggle of eight millions, who sacrifice their lives, sacrifice their money, who groan in the excess of exertion, who wrench every muscle till the blood starts with sweat—should come to naught—should end in ruin for us all—in order that the predilections and antipathies, the pitiful personal feelings of a single man may be indulged?"[5]

While Sherman had but one line of communication, Johnston had three railroads leading into Atlanta, any one of which could supply him with ammunition and provisions. Unfortunately for the Southern cause, as the battle for Atlanta was commencing, Jefferson Davis had Johnston removed as commander and replaced him with Hood, who had abundant courage but was overly aggressive to the point of recklessness and lacked the competency of a sound strategist and tactician such as Joseph Johnston.

Lord Wolseley, in a review of the same campaign published in the *Civil War Observer*, stated:

It has always struck me that Sherman's overcautious slowness of movement was here the result of the very high reputation as a leader generally accorded to Johnston, and acknowledged by all the regular officers in the United States army. During this early part of the campaign Sherman seemed rather to aim at the protection of his army from some skillful counter-attack by his active and redoubtable enemy than at any bold, offensive operations of his own. In fact, he was determined to afford Johnston no opportunity for any display of his well-known genius and enterprise. The result was a hesitating slowness of movement. Notwithstanding his great numerical superiority, he hesitated to adopt any vigorous offensive in front of so skillful a tactician. This illustrates very usefully and clearly the power and effect of one of many moral influences always at work in war, not only upon the heart and soul of an army as a whole, but upon the brain, reasoning and actions of individual commanders. The cautious nature of the policy to which Sherman here carefully restricted himself was apparently dictated by the dread that he might omit some precaution, and so give his clever antagonist an opening of which he might be able to take advantage. How often is this the case at chess! A man,

> perhaps a good player, destroys his play by over-caution, the result of the awe with which his antagonist, of great repute as a player, has inspired him.[6]

Edward Pollard believed Johnston could be seen as the "military genius of the Confederacy," and compared him very favorably to Robert E. Lee:

> There was no Confederate commander so remarkable for long foresight and for the most exact fulfillment of prophetic words as Gen. Joseph E. Johnston. He was more profound than Lee; his mind could range over larger fields; at all times of the war his cool, sedate judgments were so in opposition to the intoxicated senses of the Confederate people, that he was rather unpopular than otherwise, and rested his reputation on the appreciative and intelligent, who steadily marked him as the military genius of the Confederacy. It remained for the sequel to justify the reputation of this greatest military man in the Confederacy, who, cooler even than Lee himself, without ardour, made up almost exclusively of intellect, saw more clearly than any other single person each approaching shadow of the war, and prophesied, with calm courage, against the madness of the Administration at Richmond and the extravagant vanity of the people.[7]

Johnston was never adequately supported by the Confederate Government, especially President Jefferson Davis; indeed, they showed dissatisfaction and displeasure at his conduct. Pollard commented on Davis's obvious hatred of Johnston and his unfounded prejudice against "the most sober and safe … most careful and judicious" general the South possessed:

> Unfortunately Mr. Davis had an inveterate and stubborn dislike of Johnston. Perhaps the reader has been already brought to consider him as a ruler, whose private obstinacies were superior to all considerations of the public interest; a nervous, ill-tempered person, making his government a fretful distribution of his personal likes and dislikes. It is said that he hated Johnston for no other reason than his cold and sturdy manners. This commander was remarkable for his plain and business-like communications with the government; he scorned political influence; he had no arts to conciliate Mr. Davis; in manners he was the severe soldier, cold and reticent; he never gratified the vanity of the President by shows of deference, or even pleased popular passion by fulsome and rhetorical language about the war; and yet this stern, almost mute commander, illustrating the severity of military manners, had outlived a short term of unpopularity in the South, was generally esteemed the most sober and safe of Confederate Generals, and to-day is accounted, even beyond Lee, the most careful and judicious spirit in the war.
>
> In all periods of the war there was a parcel of Confederate commanders known as "the President's Pets". The use of such a phrase shows how familiar was public sentiment in the South with the fact that the President was a man of prejudices, and how persistent he was in asserting them.[8]

Colonel Charles Cornwallis Chesney, the eminent English military writer, in an article entitled "Sherman and Johnston, and the Atlanta Campaign," says: "A dictatorial president, puffed up, as his dispatches show, with mistaken belief in his own military judgment, and advised by the very officer whom Johnston had superseded, was, from the moment of the latter's appointment, disposed to interfere with his arrangements and prescribe his strategy."[9] General Johnston was not in the exclusive group of the "President's Pets," and thus was unable to reach his full potential and effectiveness. His sound strategic advice was not heeded, and his strategic plans were thwarted by President Davis, which were the deciding factors that caused the South to lose the war.

Endnotes

Chapter 1

1 Symonds, *Joseph E. Johnston, A Civil War Biography*, 17.
2 Ibid., 18.
3 Govan and Livingwood, *A Different Valor*, 14.

Chapter 2

1 Symonds, *Joseph E. Johnston, A Civil War Biography*, 25.
2 Ibid., 30.
3 Ibid., 34.
4 Ibid., 39–41, also Govan and Livingwood, *A Different Valor*, 16–17, and Ditchfield, *Joseph E. Johnston*, 18–21.
5 Symonds, *Joseph E. Johnston, A Civil War Biography*, 50–51.

Chapter 3

1 Symonds, *Joseph E. Johnston, A Civil War Biography*, 58.
2 Maury, *Recollections of a Virginian*, 34–35.
3 Ibid., 39.
4 Eisenhower, *So Far From God*, 276.
5 Maury, *Recollections of a Virginian*, 40.
6 Eisenhower, *So Far From God*, 295.
7 Ibid., 311.
8 Symonds, *Joseph E. Johnston, A Civil War Biography*, 63.
9 Maury, *Recollections of a Virginian*, 40–41, also Freeman, *R. E. Lee*, Volume I, 266, and Symonds, *Joseph E. Johnston, A Civil War Biography*, 65–66.
10 Govan and Livingwood, *A Different Valor*, 20.
11 Williams, *Beauregard in Mexico*, 79–81, also Symonds, *Joseph E. Johnston, A Civil War Biography*, 69.
12 Hughes, *General Johnston*, 30–31.
13 Ibid., 31–32.
14 Ibid., 32, also Govan and Livingwood, *A Different Valor*, 20.
15 Maury, *Recollections of a Virginian*, 154.
16 Symonds, *Joseph E. Johnston, A Civil War Biography*, 76.

Chapter 4

1 Hughes, *General Johnston*, 36–37.

Chapter 5

1 Govan and Livingwood, *A Different Valor*, 47, also Hughes, *General Johnston*, 51.
2 *Battles and Leaders of the Civil War*, Volume I, 183.
3 Govan and Livingwood, *A Different Valor*, 50.
4 Alexander, *Military Memoirs of a Confederate*, 34–35.
5 *Battles and Leaders of the Civil War*, Volume I, 248.
6 Foote, *The Civil War: A Narrative, Fort Sumter to Perryville*, 78.
7 Johnston, *Narrative of Military Operations*, 48.
8 Symonds, *Joseph E. Johnston, A Civil War Biography*, 119–20.
9 *Battles and Leaders of the Civil War*, Volume I, 248.
10 Alexander, *Military Memoirs of a Confederate*, 38.
11 Johnston, *Narrative of Military Operations*, 52.
12 Govan and Livingwood, *A Different Valor*, 58.
13 Johnston, *Narrative of Military Operations*, 59–64.
14 Hughes, *General Johnston*, 66–67.

Chapter 6

1 *Battles and Leaders of the Civil War*, Volume I, 197.
2 Alexander, *Military Memoirs of a Confederate*, 6.
3 Ibid., 8.
4 Ibid., 53–54.
5 Commager, *The Blue and the Gray*, 65–66.

Chapter 7

1 Johnston, *Narrative of Military Operations*, 71–72, also Govan and Livingwood, *A Different Valor*, 67–68, Hughes, *General Johnston*, 79–85, and *Official Records*, Volume 1, 605–8.
2 Hughes, *General Johnston*, 86.
3 Ibid., 100–101.
4 Johnston, *Narrative of Military Operations*, 96–97.
5 Govan and Livingwood, *A Different Valor*, 95.
6 Symonds, *Joseph E. Johnston, A Civil War Biography*, 140.

Chapter 8

1 Govan and Livingwood, *A Different Valor*, 100–1, also Gallagher, *Fighting for the Confederacy*, 73.
2 Ibid., 103, also Symonds, *Joseph E. Johnston, A Civil War Biography*, 146, 404, note 11, Chapter 11.

Chapter 9

1 Hughes, *General Johnston*, 104, also *Battles and Leaders of the Civil War*, Volume II, 121–22.
2 Alexander, *Military Memoirs of a Confederate*, 59.
3 Johnston, *Narrative of Military Operations*, 111–16.
4 Longstreet, *From Manassas to Appomattox*, 66.
5 Johnson, Bradley Tyler, *A Memoir of the Life and Public Service of Joseph E. Johnston*, 254–55.
6 Gallagher, *Fighting for the Confederacy*, 75.
7 Govan and Livingwood, *A Different Valor*, 118–19.
8 Johnston, *Narrative of Military Operations*, 118.

Chapter 10

1 Alexander, *Military Memoirs of a Confederate*, 66.
2 Sorrel, *Recollections of a Confederate Staff Officer*, 64.
3 *Battles and Leaders of the Civil War*, Volume II, 275–76.
4 *Official Records*, Volume 11, Part I, 275.
5 Gallagher, *Fighting for the Confederacy*, 81.
6 Alexander, *Military Memoirs of a Confederate*, 67–68.
7 Johnston, *Narrative of Military Operations*, 122.
8 Longstreet, *From Manassas to Appomattox*, 77–78.
9 Alexander, *Military Memoirs of a Confederate*, 68.
10 *Official Records*, Volume 11, Part I, 540–41.
11 Gallagher, *Fighting for the Confederacy*, 81.
12 *Battles and Leaders of the Civil War*, Volume II, 276.
13 Gallagher, *Fighting for the Confederacy*, 82–83.
14 Symonds, *Joseph E. Johnston, A Civil War Biography*, 157.

Chapter 11

1 Symonds, *Joseph E. Johnston, A Civil War Biography*, 158.
2 *Battles and Leaders of the Civil War*, Volume II, 206.
3 Ibid., 173–74.
4 Longstreet, *From Manassas to Appomattox*, 84–85
5 Johnston, *Narrative of Military Operations*, 131.
6 Alexander, *Military Memoirs of a Confederate*, 94.

Chapter 12

1 Longstreet, *From Manassas to Appomattox*, 85–86.
2 *Battles and Leaders of the Civil War*, Volume II, 224.
3 Ibid., 212.
4 Alexander, *Military Memoirs of a Confederate*, 72, 75.
5 *Official Records*, Volume 11, Part III, 563, also Longstreet, *From Manassas to Appomattox*, 89.
6 *Official Records*, Volume 11, Part I, 938, also Longstreet, *From Manassas to Appomattox*, 89–90.
7 Ibid., 938.

8 Longstreet, *From Manassas to Appomattox*, 88.
9 Johnston, *Narrative of Military Operations*, 133–34.
10 *Official Records*, Volume 11, Part III, 564, also *Battles and Leaders of the Civil War*, Volume II, 241.
11 *Battles and Leaders of the Civil War*, Volume II, 241–42.
12 Longstreet, *From Manassas to Appomattox*, 90–91.
13 Ibid., 91–92.
14 *Battles and Leaders of the Civil War*, Volume II, 212–13.
15 *Official Records*, Volume 11, Part I, 939–49.
16 Ibid., 230.
17 Longstreet, *From Manassas to Appomattox*, 95.
18 *Official Records*, Volume 11, Part I, 944.
19 Ibid., 944.
20 Longstreet, *From Manassas to Appomattox*, 96.
21 *Battles and Leaders of the Civil War*, Volume II, 214.
22 Ibid., 245.
23 Foote, *The Civil War: A Narrative, Fort Sumter to Perryville*, 449.
24 *Battles and Leaders of the Civil War*, Volume II, 245.
25 Longstreet, *From Manassas to Appomattox*, 99.
26 Johnston, *Narrative of Military Operations*, 138.
27 Symonds, *Joseph E. Johnston, A Civil War Biography*, 172.
28 Johnston, *Narrative of Military Operations*, 140–41.
29 Longstreet, *From Manassas to Appomattox*, 100.
30 *Official Records*, Volume 11, Part I, 934.
31 *Battles and Leaders of the Civil War*, Volume II, 215.
32 Symonds, *Joseph E. Johnston, A Civil War Biography*, 176.
33 Govan and Livingwood, *A Different Valor*, 158–59.
34 Hughes, *General Johnston*, 154–55.
35 Maury, *Recollections of a Virginian*, 151.
36 Hughes, *General Johnston*, 155.
37 *Official Records*, Volume 11, Part I, 940.
38 Ibid., 934–35.
39 *Battles and Leaders of the Civil War*, Volume II, 243.
40 Swinton, *Campaigns of the Army of the Potomac*, 130–31.

Chapter 13

1 Hughes, *General Johnston*, 157–8, also Johnston, *Narrative of Military Operations*, 149.
2 Johnston, *Narrative of Military Operations*, 148–50, also Pollard, *Life of Jefferson Davis With a Secret History of the Southern Confederacy Gathered Behind the Scenes in Richmond*, 300.
3 *Battles and Leaders of the Civil War*, Volume I, 102.
4 Symonds, *Joseph E. Johnston, A Civil War Biography*, 179, also Govan and Livingwood, *A Different Valor*, 165.
5 Johnston, *Narrative of Military Operations*, 150–51.
6 Symonds, *Joseph E. Johnston, A Civil War Biography*, 192, also Govan and Livingwood, *A Different Valor*, 170.
7 Johnston, *Narrative of Military Operations*, 152.

8 *Official Records*, Volume 17, Part II, 809.
9 *Official Records*, Volume 20, Part II, 460.
10 Johnson, *A Memoir of the Life and Public Service of Joseph E. Johnston*, 95.
11 *Official Records*, Volume 10, Part II, 492–93.
12 Hughes, *General Johnston*, 164.
13 Symonds, *Joseph E. Johnston, A Civil War Biography*, 187.
14 Govan and Livingwood, *A Different Valor*, 170.
15 Symonds, *Joseph E. Johnston, A Civil War Biography*, 195.
16 Johnston, *Narrative of Military Operations*, 154–55, also Govan and Livingwood, *A Different Valor*, 174.
17 Hughes, *General Johnston*, 164–65.
18 Symonds, *Joseph E. Johnston, A Civil War Biography*, 197, also Hughes, *General Johnston*, 166.
19 Hughes, *General Johnston*, 169.
20 Govan and Livingwood, *A Different Valor*, 185.
21 *Official Records*, Volume 23, Part II, 729–30.
22 Hughes, *General Johnston*, 158.

Chapter 14

1 *Battles and Leaders of the Civil War*, Volume III, 473, also Johnson, *A Memoir of the Life and Public Service of Joseph E. Johnston*, 101–2, also The Comte De Paris, *History of the Civil War in America*, Volume III, 350–52.
2 Ibid.
3 Ibid.
4 Johnston, *Narrative of Military Operations*, 170–71.
5 Hughes, *General Johnston*, 178.
6 *Official Records*, Volume 24, Part I, 215.
7 Ibid., 215, also Comte De Paris, *History of the Civil War in America*, Volume III, 309–12.
8 Korn, Time-Life Books, *The Civil War, War on the Mississippi*, 115.
9 *Official Records*, Volume 24, Part I, 270.
10 Korn, Time-Life Books, *The Civil War, War on the Mississippi*, 141–42.
11 *Official Records*, Volume 24, Part I, 263.
12 Ibid., 272–73.
13 Johnston, *Narrative of Military Operations*, 188–89.
14 *Battles and Leaders of the Civil War*, Volume III, 513.
15 Pollard, *Life of Jefferson Davis with a Secret History of the Southern Confederacy Gathered Behind the Scenes in Richmond*, 297–99, 305–6.
16 *Official Records*, Volume 24, Part III, 845.
17 Govan and Livingwood, *A Different Valor*, 207.
18 Lord, *The Fremantle Diary*, 93–96.
19 Ibid., 99–100.
20 *Battles and Leaders of the Civil War*, Volume III, 518.
21 Korn, Time-Life Books, *The Civil War, War on the Mississippi*, 142.
22 Johnston, *Narrative of Military Operations*, 190–91
23 *Official Records*, Volume 24, Part I, 219–20.
24 Ibid., 226–27.
25 Korn, Time-Life Books, *The Civil War, War on the Mississippi*, 142.

26 McClure, *Annals of the War*, 415–16.
27 Longstreet, *From Manassas to Appomattox*, 327–28.
28 James Longstreet to Louis T. Wigfall, May 13, 1863, "Wigfall Papers," Library of Congress.
29 Johnston, *Narrative of Military Operations*, 202–4.
30 *Official Records*, Volume 24, Part I, 281.
31 Johnston, *Narrative of Military Operations*, 205.
32 Govan and Livingwood, *A Different Valor*, 225–26.

Chapter 15

1 Hughes, *General Johnston*, 208.
2 Symonds, *Joseph E. Johnston, A Civil War Biography*, 225.
3 Ibid., 221.
4 *Official Records*, Volume 24, Part I, 248–49.
5 Pollard, *Life of Jefferson Davis with a Secret History of the Southern Confederacy Gathered Behind the Scenes in Richmond*, 306.
6 *Battles and Leaders of the Civil War*, Volume III, 472.
7 Longstreet, *From Manassas to Appomattox*, 433–34.
8 Woodward, *Mary Chesnut's Civil War*, 469.
9 *Official Records*, Volume 30, Part IV, 705–6.
10 *Official Records*, Volume 30, Part II, 67–68.
11 *Official Records*, Volume 52, Part II, 538, also Woodward, *Mary Chesnut's Civil War*, 482–83.
12 Wert, *General James Longstreet*, 327, also Longstreet, *From Manassas to Appomattox*, 465.
13 Sorrel, *Recollections of a Confederate Staff Officer*, 200–201.
14 Longstreet, *From Manassas to Appomattox*, 466.
15 Govan and Livingwood, *A Different Valor*, 233.
16 Jones, *A Rebel War Clerk's Diary*, Volume II, 70.
17 *Official Records*, Volume 30, Part IV, 742.
18 Gallagher, *Fighting for the Confederacy*, 307–8.
19 Hughes, *General Johnston*, 212–13.

Chapter 16

1 Govan and Livingwood, *A Different Valor*, 238.
2 Woodward, *Mary Chesnut's Civil War*, 507.
3 Hughes, *General Johnston*,213–14.
4 Johnston, *Narrative of Military Operations*, 262–70.
5 Ibid., 274–75.
6 Symonds, *Joseph E. Johnston, A Civil War Biography*, 249–50.
7 *Battles and Leaders of the Civil War*, Volume IV, 260, also Pollard, *Lee and His Lieutenants*, Volume 1, 393.
8 Symonds, *Joseph E. Johnston, A Civil War Biography*, 250.
9 Ibid., 250, 253.
10 Ibid., 257, also Pollard, *Lee and His Lieutenants*, Volume 1, 393.
11 Govan and Livingwood, *A Different Valor*, 244–45.
12 Ibid., 243, also Symonds, *Joseph E. Johnston, A Civil War Biography*, 252.
13 Pollard, *The Lost Cause*, 540–41.

Chapter 17

1 *Battles and Leaders of the Civil War*, Volume IV, 261–62, also Johnston, *Narrative of Military Operations*, 277–78.
2 *Official Records*, Volume 32, Part II, 752.
3 Longstreet, *From Manassas to Appomattox*, 540.
4 *Official Records*, Volume 32, Part II, 799.
5 *Official Records*, Volume 32, Part I, 476.
6 Ibid., 808–9.
7 *Official Records*, Volume 32, Part III, 592.
8 Ibid., 587.
9 *Official Records*, Volume 52, Part II, 634.
10 Longstreet, *From Manassas to Appomattox*, 543–46.
11 Bailey, Time-Life Books, *The Civil War, Battles for Atlanta*, 30.
12 *Official Records*, Volume 52, Part II, 643.
13 *Battles and Leaders of the Civil War*, Volume IV, 261.
14 *Official Records*, Volume 32, Part III, 684–86.
15 Ibid., 753, 772–74.
16 Johnston, *Narrative of Military Operations*, 299–300.
17 Connolly, *Autumn of Glory*, 309–11, also Govan and Livingwood, *A Different Valor*, 255–57.
18 *Official Records*, Volume 38, Part III, 622–25.
19 Symonds, *Joseph E. Johnston, A Civil War Biography*, 263, 267–68, also Govan and Livingwood, *A Different Valor*, 258.

Chapter 18

1 Foote, *The Civil War: A Narrative, Red River to Appomattox*, 319, also Govan and Livingwood, *A Different Valor*, 259–60.
2 Ibid.
3 *Official Records*, Volume 38, Part IV, 659–61, 669.
4 *Battles and Leaders of the Civil War*, Volume IV, 262.
5 Ibid., 262–63.
6 Hughes, *General Johnston*, 227.
7 Johnston, *Narrative of Military Operations*, 307.
8 *Official Records*, Volume 38, Part III, 721.
9 *Official Records*, Part IV, 684, also Symonds, *Joseph E. Johnston, A Civil War Biography*, 277.
10 McClure, *Annals of the War*, 331.
11 McClure, *Annals of the War*, 331, also Johnston, *Narrative of Military Operations*, 315–16, and Johnson, *A Memoir of the Life and Public Service of Joseph E. Johnston*, 114.
12 Symonds, *Joseph E. Johnston, A Civil War Biography*, 280–81.
13 Johnston, *Narrative of Military Operations*, 309–10.
14 Ibid., 311.
15 Symonds, *Joseph E. Johnston, A Civil War Biography*, 281.
16 Johnston, *Narrative of Military Operations*, 317–18.
17 Ibid., 320–21.
18 Foote, *The Civil War: A Narrative, Red River to Appomattox*, 340–41.
19 Govan and Livingwood, *A Different Valor*, 272.
20 Hattaway and Jones, *How the North Won*, 594–95.

21 *Official Records*, Volume 38, Part III, 622, 983.
22 Ibid., 635.
23 Johnston, *Narrative of Military Operations*, 322.
24 Ibid., 322–23.
25 Ibid., 324, also Symonds, *Joseph E. Johnston, A Civil War Biography*, 294, and *Official Records*, Volume 38, Part III, 991.
26 *Official Records*, Volume 32, Part III, 606–8, 781, also Symonds, *Joseph E. Johnston, A Civil War Biography*, 264.
27 *Official Records*, Volume 38, Part IV, 728, 736.
28 Govan and Livingwood, *A Different Valor*, 277, also Woodward, *Mary Chesnut's Civil War*, 616.
29 *Battles and Leaders of the Civil War*, Volume IV, 269–71.
30 Bailey, Time-Life Books, *The Civil War, Battles for Atlanta*, 61, also Symonds, *Joseph E. Johnston, A Civil War Biography*, 306–7, and *Official Records*, Volume 38, Part IV, 776.
31 *Official Records*, Volume 38, Part IV, 777, 792.
32 Johnston, *Narrative of Military Operations*, 360–63, also *Official Records*, Volume 39, Part II, 688, and *Official Records*, Volume 52, Part II, 687.
33 Hughes, *General Johnston*, 237–38.
34 Pollard, *Life of Jefferson Davis with a Secret History of the Southern Confederacy Gathered Behind the Scenes in Richmond*, 372–74.
35 *Official Records*, Volume 38, Part V, 879.

Chapter 19

1 *Official Records*, Volume 38, Part V, 867–69, 875.
2 Ibid., 876–7, also *Official Records*, Volume 52, Part II, 592, and Dowdey and Manarin, *The Wartime Papers of R. E. Lee*, 821–22.
3 Gordon, *Reminiscences of the Civil War*, 131–32.
4 Johnston, *Narrative of Military Operations*, 348.
5 *Official Records*, Volume 38, Part V, 878.
6 Johnston, *Narrative of Military Operations*, 364.
7 Govan and Livingwood, *A Different Valor*, 312, also Symonds, *Joseph E. Johnston, A Civil War Biography*, 323.
8 *Official Records*, Volume 38, Part V, 879–81, also *Official Records*, Volume 39, Part II, 712–14.
9 Ibid.
10 Ibid., 882–83.

Chapter 20

1 *Official Records*, Volume 38, Part V, 885, 888.
2 Ibid.
3 *Battles and Leaders of the Civil War*, Volume IV, 277.
4 Johnson, *A Memoir of the Life and Public Service of Joseph E. Johnston*, 117.
5 *Battles and Leaders of the Civil War*, Volume IV, 253, 313, also Hughes, *General Johnston*, 251.
6 *Battles and Leaders of the Civil War*, Volume III, 710–11.
7 Hughes, *General Johnston*, 249.
8 Johnston, *Narrative of Military Operations*, 363–64.

9 *Annals of the War, General Joseph E. Johnston, The Dalton–Atlanta Operations*, 339, also *Battles and Leaders of the Civil War*, Volume IV, 275–77.
10 Woodward, *Mary Chesnut's Civil War*, 616.
11 Pollard, *Life of Jefferson Davis With a Secret History of the Southern Confederacy Gathered Behind the Scenes in Richmond*, 379.
12 Hood, *Advance and Retreat*, 126.
13 *Official Records*, Volume 38, Part V, 888.
14 Govan and Livingwood, *A Different Valor*, 321.
15 Bailey, Time-Life Books, *The Civil War, Battles for Atlanta*, 90.
16 Ibid.
17 Govan and Livingwood, *A Different Valor*, 333, also *Annals of the War, General Joseph E. Johnston, The Dalton–Atlanta Operations*, 339–40.
18 Ibid., 329.
19 Ibid., 331.
20 Ibid., 327.
21 Woodward, *Mary Chesnut's Civil War*, 64.
22 Younger, *Inside the Confederate Government: The Diary of Robert Garlick Hill Kean*, 178–80.

Chapter 21

1 *Official Records*, Volume 47, Part II, 1078–79.
2 Ibid., 1311.
3 Foote, *The Civil War: A Narrative, Red River to Appomattox*, 797–98.
4 *Official Records*, Volume 47, Part I, 1044.
5 Hughes, *General Johnston*, 261.
6 Johnston, *Narrative of Military Operations*, 587.
7 Symonds, *Joseph E. Johnston, A Civil War Biography*, 343, also Govan and Livingwood, *A Different Valor*, 346.
8 *Official Records*, Volume 45, Part II, 1256, also Govan and Livingwood, *A Different Valor*, 341.
9 Govan and Livingwood, *A Different Valor*, 438–39.
10 Woodward, *Mary Chesnut's Civil War*, 711.
11 *Official Records*, Volume 47, Part II, 1324.
12 Ibid., 1316.
13 Ibid., 1372.
14 Govan and Livingwood, *A Different Valor*, 354.
15 Symonds, *Joseph E. Johnston, A Civil War Biography*, 346.
16 Govan and Livingwood, *A Different Valor*, 350.
17 Symonds, *Joseph E. Johnston, A Civil War Biography*, 347.
18 Hughes, *General Johnston*, 264, also *Battles and Leaders of the Civil War*, Volume IV, 701, and Gordon, *Reminiscences of the Civil War*, 389–91.

Chapter 22

1 Johnston, *Narrative of Military Operations*, 397.
2 Govan and Livingwood, *A Different Valor*, 361.
3 Johnston, *Narrative of Military Operations*, 398–99.

4 Symonds, *Joseph E. Johnston, A Civil War Biography*, 355.
5 Johnson, *A Memoir of the Life and Public Service of Joseph E. Johnston*, 221–22.
6 Govan and Livingwood, *A Different Valor*, 362.
7 Ibid., 363–64.
8 Hughes, *General Johnston*, 277–79.
9 Ibid.
10 Symonds, *Joseph E. Johnston, A Civil War Biography*, 357.

Chapter 23

1 Symonds, *Joseph E. Johnston, A Civil War Biography*, 359.
2 Govan and Livingwood, *A Different Valor*, 378.
3 Ibid., 378.
4 Symonds, *Joseph E. Johnston, A Civil War Biography*, 386.
5 Ibid., 379.

Chapter 24

1 Symonds, *Joseph E. Johnston, A Civil War Biography*, 380–81.
2 Hughes, *General Johnston*, 289.
3 Ibid., 299–300.

Conclusion

1 *Philadelphia Weekly Times*, Volume III, no. 23, Saturday, August 2, 1879, also *Civil War Times*, April 2010, 32–39.
2 Hughes, *General Johnston*, 302.
3 Ibid., 304.
4 Ibid., 291.
5 Pollard, *Life of Jefferson Davis with a Secret History of the Southern Confederacy Gathered Behind the Scenes in Richmond*, 366–67, 371–72, 375, 380–81.
6 Hughes, *General Johnston*, 293–94.
7 Pollard, *The Lost Cause*, 439–40.
8 Pollard, *Life of Jefferson Davis with a Secret History of the Southern Confederacy Gathered Behind the Scenes in Richmond*, 296–97.
9 Hughes, *General Johnston*, 292.

Bibliography

Alexander, E. P. *Military Memoirs of a Confederate*. New York: Charles Scribner's Sons, 1907; Reprint Edition, Dayton, Ohio: Morningside Bookshop, 1977.

Civil War Times.

Clark, John E., Jr. *Railroads in the Civil War, The Impact of Management on Victory and Defeat.* Baton Rouge: Louisiana State University Press, 2001.

Connelly, Thomas Lawrence. *Autumn of Glory, The Army of Tennessee, 1862–1865*. Baton Rouge: Louisiana State University Press, 1971.

Ditchfield, Christin. *Joseph E. Johnston, Confederate General*. Philadelphia: Chelsea House Publishers, 2002.

Dowdey, Clifford and Louis H. Manarin, eds. *The Wartime Papers of R. E. Lee*. Boston: Little, Brown and Company, 1961.

Eisenhower, John S. D. *So Far From God*. New York: Doubleday, 1989.

Foote, Shelby. *The Civil War: A Narrative*. 3 Volumes. New York: Random House, 1963.

Freeman, Douglas Southall. *R. E. Lee, A Biography*. 4 Volumes. New York: Charles Scribner's Sons, 1949.

Gallagher, Gary W. *Fighting for the Confederacy, The Personal Recollections of General Edward Porter Alexander*. Chapel Hill: The University of North Carolina Press, 1989.

Gordon, John B. *Reminiscences of the Civil War*. New York: Charles Scribner's Sons, 1903.

Govan, Gilbert and James Livingwood. *A Different Valor, Joseph E. Johnston*. New York: Smithmark Publishers Inc., 1995.

Hattaway, Herman and Archer Jones. *How the North Won, A Military History of the Civil War*. Chicago: University of Illinois Press, 1983.

Hood, John Bell. *Advance and Retreat*. Edison, New Jersey: The Blue and Grey Press, 1985

Hughes, Robert M. *Great Commanders, General Johnston*. New York: D. Appleton and Company, 1893.

Johnson, Bradley Tyler. *A Memoir of the Life and Public Service of Joseph E. Johnston, Once the Quartermaster General of the Army of the United States and A General in the Army of the Confederate States of America*. Baltimore: R. H. Woodward & Company, 1891.

Johnston, Joseph Eggleston. *Narrative of Military Operations Directed, During the Late War Between the States*. Bloomington: Indiana University Press, 1959; Millwood, NY: Kraus Reprint, 1981.

Johnson, Robert Underwood and Clarence Clough Buel, eds. *Battles and Leaders of the Civil War*. 4 Volumes. Secaucus, NJ: Castle, 1982.

Jones, Archer. *Civil War Command & Strategy, The Process of Victory and Defeat*. New York: The Free Press, 1992.

Jones, John B. *A Rebel War Clerk's Diary*. 2 Volumes. Philadelphia: J. B. Lippincott & Company, 1866.

Longstreet, James. *From Manassas to Appomattox, Memoirs of the Civil War in America*. Secaucus, NJ: The Blue and Grey Press, 1984.

Lord, Walter. *The Fremantle Diary, Being the Journal of Lieutenant Colonel James Arthur Lyon Fremantle, Coldstream Guards, on his Three Months in the Southern States.* Boston: Little, Brown and Company, 1954.

Maury, Dabney Herndon. *Recollections of a Virginian in the Mexican, Indian, and Civil Wars.* New York: Charles Scribner's Sons, 1894.

McClure, Alexander K., ed. *The Annals of the War Written by Leading Participants North and South.* Washington, D.C.: The Times Publishing Company, 1878; Reprint Edition, Dayton, Ohio: Morningside Bookshop, 1988.

McDonough, James Lee and Jones, James Pickett. *War So Terrible: Sherman and Atlanta.* New York: W. W. Norton & Company, 1987.

Philadelphia Weekly Times.

Pollard, Edward A. *Life of Jefferson Davis with a Secret History of the Southern Confederacy Gathered Behind the Scenes in Richmond.* Philadelphia: National Publishing Company, 1869.

Pollard, Edward A. *The Lost Cause, A New Southern History of the War of the Confederates.* Honolulu, Hawaii: University Press of the Pacific, 1867.

Sorrel, G. Moxley. *Recollections of a Confederate Staff Officer.* New York: The Neale Publishing Company, 1905; Reprint Edition, Dayton, Ohio: Morningside Bookshop, 1978.

Symonds, Craig L. *Joseph E. Johnston, A Civil War Biography.* New York: W. W. Norton & Company, 1992.

Time-Life Books Inc. *The Civil War.* 28 Volumes. Alexandria, Virginia: Time-Life Books, 1985.

United States War Department, *The War of the Rebellion: A Compilation of the Official Records of the Union and Confederate Armies.* 128 Volumes. Washington, D.C.: The Government Printing Office, 1891.

Wert, Jeffry D. *General James Longstreet, The Confederacy's Most Controversial Soldier.* New York: Simon & Schuster, 1993.

"Wigfall Papers," Library of Congress.

Williams, T. Harry. *With Beauregard in Mexico: The Mexican War Reminiscences of P. G. T. Beauregard.* Baton Rouge: Louisiana State University Press, 1956.

Woodward, C. Vann. *Mary Chesnut's Civil War.* New Haven: Yale University Press, 1981.

Younger, Edward, ed. *Inside the Confederate Government: The Diary of Robert Garlick Hill Kean.* New York: Oxford University Press, 1957.

Index

Abercrombie, Brigadier General John, 84, 86–87
Abingdon, 2, 152
  Academy, 2
abolitionism, 5, 26
Adams, President John Quincy, 3
Alabama, 7, 26, 33, 58, 98, 103, 127, 129, 136, 146, 150, 152, 155–56, 164–65, 168, 182, 185, 192–93, 209, 214, 228, 235
Alabama (steamer), 23
Alexander, Captain Edward Porter, 32, 34, 37–38, 51, 53, 59, 61, 65–68, 74, 78, 132, 137, 146, 151
Allatoona, 179–81, 207
American Civil War, 1, 25, 38, 96, 102, 104, 167, 182, 204, 228, 236
Anderson, General J. R., 64, 73
Andersonville, 193, 206
Arkansas, 23, 95–96, 98–100, 102, 110, 113, 167, 187, 225
Army
  3rd Kentucky Mounted Infantry Regiment, 115
  103rd Pennsylvania Regiment, 78
  Alabama Infantry, 146
    9th Alabama Infantry Regiment, 65
    19th Alabama Infantry Regiment, 146
  artillery division
    1st U.S. Artillery, 65, 87
      Battery H, 65
    4th U.S. Artillery, 5
      Company C, 5–7
  cavalry, 1–2, 13, 20, 23, 27, 29, 34, 49, 61–64, 67, 73, 80, 93, 99, 101, 110–11, 120, 125, 137, 143, 146–47, 150, 154, 158–60, 164–76, 179, 181–85, 188, 191–93, 196, 203–7, 214, 216, 219, 221–23, 235–36
    1st Cavalry Regiment, 23
  Coldstream Guards, 120
  Corps of Engineers, 5
  Corps of Topographical Engineers, 7, 11, 13, 22
  Georgia Infantry
    7th Regiment, 30
    8th Regiment, 30
    27th Regiment, 83–85
    66th Regiment, 206
  of Mississippi, 136, 139, 146, 150, 161, 173, 177
    19th Mississippi Regiment, 65
  of Northern Virginia, 38, 44, 49, 53, 57, 132, 193, 199, 215
  of Tennessee, 96, 99, 104–5, 132–34, 136, 138, 139–47, 149, 154, 156, 158, 160, 165, 169, 174, 176, 178, 185, 188, 193–94, 199, 201, 203, 209, 211–19, 232, 235
    1st Tennessee Infantry Regiment, 142, 144, 232
  of the Cumberland, 132, 164, 166, 175, 187, 192, 207
  of the Potomac, 44, 49, 72, 92, 158, 171
Atkinson, Brigadier General Henry, 6
Atlanta, 99, 113, 131, 133–37, 143, 149–50, 155, 161–63, 165–66, 169, 172, 175, 180–89, 191, 193–97, 199, 201–10, 216, 228, 230, 236–38
Atlanta Campaign, 162–63, 201–10, 231, 236–38
Augusta, 8, 156, 193, 197, 204, 208–9, 214, 219

Baker's Creek, 116, 130
Baltimore, 11–12, 227, 231
baptism, 174–75
Barbour, James, 3

Baton Rouge, 111
Beauregard, Brigadier General Gustave, 21, 29–35, 37, 41–44, 113, 152–54, 157, 211–14, 217, 212, 221–23
Beaver Dam Creek, 75, 78
Bee, Brigadier General Barnard, 30, 33
Benjamin, Judah P., 44–47, 221–22
Bentonville, 217–18
Big Black River, 107, 116, 125
Black Hawk, 5–6
Black Hawk War, 6
Blaine, James G., 230
Blue Ridge Mountains, 29, 44–45, 95–96, 234
Bottom's Bridge, 73, 78
Bowen, Brigadier General John S., 112, 126
Bragg, General Braxton, 95, 112–14, 123, 129, 131–38, 139–42, 145–47, 149, 151–56, 159–60, 165, 178, 182, 188, 193–96, 202–3, 206, 210, 214, 216, 218–19, 235
Breckinridge, Major General John Cabell, 103, 132, 144, 212–13, 223–24
Brewster, Colonel Henry P., 179, 204
British Band, the, 6
Brown, Governor Joseph E., 143, 167, 181–88, 194, 208
Bruinsburg, 110–12
Buchanan, President James, 23, 174
Bull Run, 32–33, 113
Bureau of War, 129, 209 *see also* War Department
Burnside, Major General Ambrose, 51, 99, 133, 137

Cadwalader, Major General, 17–18, 20, 23
Calhoun, 149, 173
Calhoun, John C., 3
Camp Creek, 168, 171
Cantey, Brigadier General James, 168
Canton, 115–16, 120–22, 126, 176
Carter, Captain Thomas H., 83–84
Casey, General Silas, 64, 78, 83–84
Cassville, 173–76, 179
Centreville, 30, 32, 34, 44, 46, 53, 56
Charles City, 78–80, 82, 84–85, 91
Charleston, 7, 26, 57, 98, 119, 121, 124, 153, 209, 214
Chattahoochee River, 181, 186, 191–97, 200–203, 208–9, 236
Chattanooga, 95, 98–99, 102–3, 114, 131–35, 137–38, 142, 149, 154–55, 158, 164, 166, 169, 183–84, 202–4, 209
    Battle of, 138 *see also* Missionary Ridge
Cheatham, Major General Benjamin F., 136, 145, 147, 166, 171, 173, 187, 191, 195, 207, 214, 219
Cheraw, 213–14
Chesapeake, 45, 50, 58, 227
Chesney, Colonel Charles Cornwallis, 238
Chesnut, Colonel James, 135
Chesnut, Mary, 133, 135, 139, 179, 204, 209, 213
Chicago, 6
Chickahominy River, 72–73, 75, 78–80, 86, 92–93, 234
Chickamauga, 132–37, 146, 153, 216
    Battle of, 132–37, 146, 153, 216
cholera, 6
Cleburne, Major General Patrick R., 103, 136, 145, 166–69, 180, 185, 195, 207, 209
Cleveland, 158–59, 164–65
Cleveland, Grover, 230
Cobb, Howell, 129, 206
Colquitt, Colonel Peyton H., 115
Confederacy, 25, 37, 41–43, 45–46, 54, 56, 58, 71, 89, 96, 98, 100, 105, 107, 116–20, 122–23, 129, 131–32, 138, 140, 145, 159, 172, 183–88, 200–204, 206, 209, 211, 213, 222–23, 237–38
    Southern, 26, 42, 90, 188, 237
Confederate battle flag, 35
Confederate States of America, 1, 41–44, 86, 96, 183 *see also* Confederacy
Congress, 6–8, 13, 22–23, 41–43, 47, 98, 119, 139–40, 145, 195, 199, 210–12, 229
Cooper, Adjutant General Samuel, 23, 27, 29, 41–42, 98–99, 105, 110, 122, 129, 141, 145, 155, 165, 176, 178, 199
court-martial, 16, 43, 92
Cox, General Jacob D., 201, 216

Dabney, Lieutenant F. Y., 64
Dalton, 137, 139–44, 149–55, 157–59, 164–66, 169–70, 178–79, 182, 192, 196, 202–4, 228, 235–36
Danville, 215, 221, 227

Davis, President Jefferson, 25–26, 32, 34, 41, 43–47, 49–51, 55–60, 71–73, 86, 88–89, 91–92, 96–105, 107, 113–14, 117–19, 127, 129–31, 134–38, 139–146, 149–59, 165, 178–79, 182–89, 192–96, 199–201, 205, 208–9, 211–13, 216–18, 221–24, 229, 233–35, 237–39
Drewry's Bluff, 72–73
Dug Gap, 167–68
Durham, 224

Early, Colonel Jubal, 33–34, 65–67
El Paso, 22
Elzey, Colonel Arnold, 34
Episcopal Church, 12, 134, 170, 182
Etowah, 143, 174, 177–80, 203
Evans, Colonel Nathan G., 32
Ewell, Colonel Benjamin S., 33, 91, 121, 145, 156–57, 209, 227

Fairfax Court House, 41, 44, 56
Fairfield Race Course, 80
Farmville, 1
Fayetteville, 214–16, 218
Florida, 7, 9, 11, 212, 225, 228
Floyd, John B., 25
Foote, Henry S., 47, 98
Force Bill, the, 6–7
Forrest, Brigadier General Nathan Bedford, 101, 164, 171, 173, 175, 182–85, 188, 203, 207, 235–36
Fort Magruder, 61–63, 66
Fort Monroe, 5–7, 50, 53–54, 56
Fort Sumter, 26, 97
Franklin, General William B., 61, 67, 73
Fredericksburg, 49–50, 72, 74, 99, 102
Fremantle, Lieutenant Colonel Arthur James Lyon, 120–21
French and Indian War, 1
French, Major General Samuel, 50, 175, 177–78, 187
Frobel, Colonel B. W., 86
furlough, 45, 143, 158, 214

Gardner, Major General Franklin, 119–20
Garland, Brigadier General Samuel, 78, 83
Georgia, 17, 30, 44, 56–57, 83, 85, 91, 95, 122, 132, 137, 142–43, 150, 153, 156, 159, 161, 164–65, 170–71, 175, 181–88, 192–94, 197, 199, 203–4, 206, 208–10, 212–15, 219, 225, 228, 230, 233, 235–36
Gettysburg, 39, 124, 127, 129, 146
Gist, Brigadier General States Rights, 33, 120
Gloucester Point, 55–57, 59
Gordon, Major General John B., 193, 217
Grand Gulf, 107, 110, 112
Grant, Major General Ulysses S., 95, 98–99, 101–2, 107, 110–17, 120–24, 126, 131, 136–37, 150, 161, 168, 173, 191, 194, 199, 201, 217, 221, 223, 227, 229–30, 234–36
Great Lakes, 6
Greensboro', 221–23
Grenada, 100–1
Grierson, Colonel Benjamin H., 111
Grigsby, Colonel J. Warren, 167–68
Gulf of Mexico, 13, 95
Gulf States, 184, 228

Halleck, General, 122, 131
Hampton, Lieutenant General Wade, 67, 87, 200, 213–19, 223
Hancock, Brigadier General Winfield Scott, 65–67
Hardee, Lieutenant General William Joseph, 101–3, 136–37, 145, 150, 167, 170–78, 180–81, 185, 193, 195–96, 203, 205, 207, 214, 216, 218–21
Harpers Ferry, 26–27
Harvey, Captain James B., 203
Haynes Bluff, 101, 111, 116
Heintzelman, Major General Samuel P., 73, 78–79, 85, 234
Hill, Major General Daniel Harvey "D. H.," 59, 61, 65–67, 74, 78–85, 89, 91, 119, 133–34, 216
Hill, Senator Benjamin H., 186, 188–89
Hindman, Major General Thomas C., 133, 135, 145, 166, 169–71, 176, 185
Holly Springs, 95, 101
Holmes, Major General Theophilus H., 32–33, 45, 49, 51, 91, 95–96, 98–99, 102, 110, 187, 215, 234
Hood, Lieutenant General John Bell, 67–68, 86, 88, 132–33, 145–46, 160, 169–81, 185–86, 191–96, 199–210, 214, 237

Hooker, Brigadier General Joseph, 32, 61, 64–65, 68, 73, 78, 137, 158, 167, 171, 175, 180, 186
horses, 84, 86, 88, 90, 112, 122, 143–44, 146, 151, 156–57, 160, 166–67, 173, 178, 180, 185, 205, 219, 224–25, 230 *see also* Army, cavalry
House of Representatives, 12, 25, 229
Howard, Major General Oliver O., 158, 180, 187, 200, 207
Hudson River, 6
Huger, Major General, 20, 57, 71, 73, 78–85, 91–92
Hurlbut, General Stephan A., 114

Illinois, 6, 23

Jackson (Mississippi), 99–100, 113–18, 120–23, 125–27, 129, 131, 149, 228–29, 234
Jackson, Brigadier General William H., 127, 173–74
Jackson, General Thomas Jonathan "Stonewall," 30, 32–33, 45, 49, 74, 91, 121, 180, 191, 208
Jackson, President Andrew, 6–7, 9–10, 12
Jesup, Quartermaster General Thomas S., 9, 25
Jefferson, Thomas, 2
Johnson, President Andrew, 227
Johnston, Albert Sidney, 23, 25, 41, 44
Johnston, General Joseph Eggleston
  Army of Tennessee *see* Army, of Tennessee
  at Fremantle, 120–23
  Atlanta *see* Atlanta Campaign
  at Richmond, 71
  at Seven Pines, 75–88
  birth, 1, 5
  childhood, 3
  Congress, 229
  command, 95–98, 199–202, 211–17
  death, 231–32
  early military career, 5–18
  fall of Vicksburg, 126–30
  First Manassas, 29–30, 32–35
  feud over the general's rank, 41–47
  forms an army, 125
  leaves the army, 225–26
  memoir *see Narrative of Military Operations Directed During the Late War Between the States*
  Railroad Commissioner, 230
  recall, 211–17
  retreat, 49–51, 61
  siege, 59–60
  strategy, 100, 115, 154–55, 172–73, 234
  surrender, 221
  wounded, 88–91, 105
Johnston, Lydia, 11–12, 71, 90, 97, 129, 165, 174, 186, 206, 227, 230
Johnston, Mary Valentine Wood, 1–3, 231
Johnston, Peter, 1–3, 231
Johnston, Preston, 11, 16, 18–19, 231
Jonesboro, 207–8
Juarez, Benito, 23

Kean, Robert Garlick Hill, 129, 209–10
Kennesaw Mountain, 185–87, 191
Kentucky, 17, 95, 115, 123–24, 131, 146–47, 150, 152, 167–68, 178, 183, 209
Keyes, Major General Erasmus D., 73, 75, 78–79, 81, 84, 91, 234
Kilpatrick, General Judson, 214, 216
Knoxville, 137, 150, 153–55, 158
Kolb's Farm, 185

Lee, "Light Horse Harry," 2
Lee, Robert E., 2–3, 5, 7, 11, 14–19, 25, 41–42, 51, 53, 56–60, 71–72, 86, 98, 120, 123–27, 133–34, 138, 139, 146, 152–53, 157–58, 161, 172, 179, 193–94, 200, 208–17, 221–24, 228–29, 233, 238
Lee, Brigadier General Stephen Dill, 165, 173, 175, 207, 214, 219
Lincoln, President Abraham, 26, 53, 73, 53, 223–24, 226
  assassination of, 223–24
Liverpool, 228
London, 228
Long, Colonel Stephen Harriman, 203
Longstreet, Lieutenant General James, 51, 56–57, 59, 62–67, 73–74, 75, 78–79, 82–86, 89, 91–92, 123–25, 132–37, 142, 150–54, 157, 177, 211, 233–35
Lookout Mountain, 137, 235
Loring, Brigadier General William W., 45, 101, 115, 121, 159, 165, 169–70, 181, 185
Lost Mountain, 181, 185

Louisiana, 11, 95, 107, 110–11, 119, 129, 134, 170, 182, 187, 203
Louisville, 99, 101, 152, 164, 200
Lovell, Major General Mansfield, 145, 190, 209

Mackall, Brigadier General William Whann, 134–37, 139, 145, 168, 175–76, 178, 195, 206
Magruder, Major General John B., 18, 55–59, 61, 63, 65–66, 73, 75, 81, 86
Manassas, 29–32, 49–50, 53
    Battle of First, 29–31, 35, 41, 43, 97, 133
Martin, General William T., 154, 170–71
Martin, Lieutenant Colonel William H., 187
Maryland, 11, 17, 74, 124, 227
Mason, Charles, 5
Maury, Major General Dabney, 14–16, 18, 22, 168, 202
McClellan, Major General George, 27, 44, 49, 53–59, 61, 62, 64, 71–79, 87, 91, 230, 233–34
McClernand, 111, 116
McCook, General Alexander, 176
McDowell, Major General Irwin, 29–32, 34, 50, 72–74, 75, 78
McLane, Robert, 11–12, 23, 231
McLaws, Brigadier General Lafayette, 64, 79–81, 219
McPherson, Lieutenant General James B., 37, 113–16, 158, 164, 166–67, 175, 187, 191–92, 200, 207
Merrimack, 71 *see also Virginia*
Mexican War, 13–23, 145, 201
Mexico, 13–23, 95, 231, 235
Missionary Ridge, 137–38, 141, 147, 149, 158, 184, 235 *see also* Chattanooga, Battle of
Mississippi River, 6–7, 95, 99, 107–11, 117, 132, 229, 234
Mobile, 99, 103–4, 113, 129, 149–50, 157, 168, 182, 191, 193, 202, 204, 209, 214, 225
Montgomery, 26, 58, 97, 99, 113, 129, 195, 204
Moore, Major W. E., 140–41
Murfreesboro, 99, 101, 103, 131, 184

Narrative of Military Operations Directed During the Late War Between the States, 46, 184, 202, 229
Nashville, 95, 99, 101, 131, 133, 153, 158, 161, 164, 183, 209, 214
National Express & Transportation Company, the, 227–28
Navy
    Confederate, 61, 67, 72, 121, 221
    U.S., 10
Negley, General James, 133
New Hope Church, 180
New Smyrna, 191
Newton, Brigadier General John, 67, 167, 187
New York Harbor, 5
New York Herald, 233
Nisbet, Colonel James C., 206
Norfolk, 6–7, 56, 71–72, 82
North Carolina, 46, 51, 91, 95, 152, 157, 211–17, 221
Northrop, Colonel, 41, 212

Ohio, 7, 12, 23, 58, 96, 102, 123, 152, 159, 161, 164, 171, 175, 186–87
Oostanaula River, 171–73
Ordinance of Nullification, 6–7
Osborne's Landing, 1

Pamunkey River, 67, 75
Panecillo, 2, 229
Paris, 228 *see also* Philippe, Comte De Paris
Peachtree Creek, 186, 193, 200, 206–7
Pearl River, 116, 126
Pemberton, Lieutenant General John C., 95–96, 146, 116–19, 122–31, 135–37, 234–35
Pendleton, Brigadier General William N., 33, 146, 155, 157–58
Peninsula, 50, 53–57, 59, 60–61, 63, 66, 104, 113, 230, 233
Petersburg, 1, 73, 199, 217, 221
Philadelphia Weekly Times, 233
Philippe, Comte De Paris, 53, 107, 113
Pierce, President Franklin, 19, 21, 57, 201
Pine Mountain, 181–82, 185
Polk, Lieutenant General Leonidas, 103, 105, 133–35, 139–41, 150, 154, 157, 159–60, 165, 169–82, 192, 196, 203, 205
Polk, President James K., 13
Pollard, Edward A., 118, 127, 131, 147, 188, 236, 238 *see also Richmond Examiner*
Porter, General Fitz-John, 73

Porter, (Rear) Admiral, 110, 117
Port Hudson, 95, 100, 107, 110–11, 113, 116, 118–22, 126, 130, 136, 234
Potomac, 27, 29, 44–45, 49–50, 54, 58, 72, 74, 92
Potomac (steamer), 6
Presstman, Colonel, 181, 185, 191, 199
Prince John *see* Magruder, Major General John B.

Quantico, 45

railroad, 3, 9, 22, 27, 29, 37, 39, 49–50, 74, 85, 87, 98–99, 101, 114, 116, 121–22, 124, 125, 152–54, 162, 164, 169–77, 179–85, 191–92, 197, 200, 202, 207–8, 213–15, 230, 235, 237
  Baltimore and Ohio Railroad, 12
  commissioner, 230
  East Tennessee & Georgia railroad, 164
  Georgia, 203–4
  Macon and Western Railroad, 204, 207
  Manassas Gap Railroad, 29–30
  Mississippi Central, 115
  Nashville, 99, 101
  Selma, Rome and Dalton Railroad, 228
  Western and Atlantic, 131, 137, 143, 149, 164, 203–204, 207
  York River, 80, 83, 86
Randolph, Secretary of War George W., 47, 56–57, 92, 96–97
Rapidan River, 49–51, 53, 132
Rappahannock River, 49–50, 53, 177
Republican Party, 2, 26
Resaca, 149, 166–72, 179
Richmond, 26–29, 32, 37, 39, 41, 45–46, 49–50, 53–57, 59–60, 61, 67, 71–74, 79, 85–86, 90–93, 96–98, 100–105, 117–31, 133, 137–39, 144–47, 149, 151–57, 159, 178–79, 183, 186, 188–89, 197, 199, 204, 213, 217, 221–38
Richmond Examiner, 90, 118, 127, 147, 236
Ridley, Captain Bromfield L., 215–16
Ringgold, 149, 158–59, 164–66, 202
Rocky Face Ridge, 166, 170
Rodes, Brigadier General Robert, 78, 80, 82–85
Rome, 155, 159, 165, 168, 170, 175, 228
Rosecrans, Major General William, 95–96, 99, 101, 123, 131–33
Russell, Sir William Howard, 47

Sale, Colonel John B., 154
San Antonio, 17, 19, 22
San Francisco, 37
Sauks, 5 *see also* Black Hawk
Schaller, Colonel Frank, 129
Schofield, Major General John M., 158, 162, 166–67, 171, 175, 186, 192, 200, 209, 215–16, 219, 225
Scotland, 1
Scott, General Winfield, 6, 8, 13–21, 25, 27, 29, 32
Seddon, Secretary of War James A., 96–97, 104, 113–14, 104, 123–24, 133, 137, 139–40, 155, 178, 200, 209, 212
Sedgwick, Brigadier General John, 61, 67, 87
Selma, 165, 228
Senate Military Affairs Committee, 25, 124
Seven Pines, 75–93, 121
Shenandoah Valley, 32, 50
Sherman, Major General William Tecumseh, 101, 111–16, 122, 125–26, 137, 142, 149–50, 161–89, 191–94, 199–200, 209, 212–19, 221–25, 230, 231, 235–38
Shoup, Brigadier General Francis A., 146, 177, 191
Smith, Brigadier General Morgan, 187
Smith, General Edmund Kirby, 16, 30, 34, 45, 87, 95, 102, 194, 205, 230
Smith, General Persifer, 18
Smith, Major General Gustavus W., 44, 51, 56–57, 61, 67, 73, 75, 79–81, 86–89, 92, 119, 181
Smith, Major Norman W., 156
Snake Creek Gap, 149, 166–71
Sorrel, Lieutenant Colonel Gilbert Moxley, 64, 136
South Carolina, 6–8, 26, 56–57, 84–85, 91, 97, 152, 211–14, 225, 233
Stevenson, Major General Carter L., 99, 101, 115, 126, 145, 166, 171, 185, 214
Stewart, Lieutenant General Alexander P., 136, 145, 166, 171–72, 180, 192, 195–96, 203–5, 214–15, 218–19, 221
St. John, Brigadier General Isaac, 8, 41, 212

Stoneman, Major General George, 64, 170, 206
Stuart, Jeb, 29, 34, 49, 63–64, 67, 74–75, 86
Sudley Springs Ford, 32
Sumner, Colonel "Bull," 20, 23, 61
Sumner, General Edwin V., 73, 87

Taliaferro, Brigadier General William Booth, 219
Taylor, General Richard, 50
Taylor, Major General Zachary, 13, 15
telegraph, 26, 29, 39, 54, 98–99, 104, 111, 114, 120, 122, 130, 135, 154, 164, 173, 194–95, 210, 223
Tennessee, 2, 47, 75, 95–105, 110–11, 114, 123, 129, 131–38, 139–47, 149–61, 164–65, 167–69, 173–78, 182–88, 193–94, 199, 201, 203, 207, 209, 211–15, 218–19, 232, 235, 237 *see also* Army, of Tennessee
tête-du-pont, 191–92
Texas, 11, 13, 22, 68, 97, 124, 146, 179, 186, 204, 225 *see also* El Paso, San Antonio
Trans-Mississippi, 111, 118, 234
Tullahoma, 101, 104, 112–13, 123, 155
Tunnel Hill, 150, 166–69

Vance, Governor Zebulon, 215
Van Dorn, Major General Earl, 101
Vicksburg, 95, 98–100, 107–25, 149–50, 234–35
  fall of, 126–28, 129–37
Virginia, 1–3, 5, 7, 14, 17, 26–27, 32, 37–39, 41–45, 49–51, 57–58, 67, 96, 113, 118, 120, 132–33, 136, 152–58, 174, 179, 193–94, 199, 215, 217, 221, 223, 225, 227, 229, 233 *see also* Abingdon, Farmville
Virginia, 71–72 *see also Merrimack*

Walker, Brigadier General William H. T., 33, 113, 115, 205
Walker, Leroy P., 35, 45
Walker, Major General W. H. S., 132, 145, 166, 169, 171–72
War Department, 29, 41, 45, 95–96, 98, 104, 111, 114, 125, 130, 132, 137–38, 201, 212, 215 *see also* Bureau of War
Warwick River, 55, 233
Washburn, General, 175
Washington, 7–8, 10, 23, 27, 29, 34, 44, 53, 58, 72–74, 79, 81, 152, 159, 208, 230–31
Watkins, Private Sam R., 142–44, 170, 232
weapons
  cannon, 9, 15, 21, 55, 87, 120, 175, 186, 233
    rifled, 56, 59–60, 65, 177, 202, 233
  gunpowder, 20, 38
  mortar, 14–15, 20, 55, 59
  musket, 15, 21, 26, 32, 38, 55, 85–86, 89, 92, 101, 143, 156, 180, 187
    rifled, 26, 38–39, 167, 173, 214
  Napoleons, 64, 87, 156, 171
  Parrott gun, 55, 59, 181
  pistol, 68, 88
  rifle, 35, 39, 59, 78, 84, 89, 126, 156, 164, 172, 191, 202
West Point, 1–6, 11, 25, 32, 53, 61, 64, 67, 95, 145–46, 182, 200–1, 204–5, 229
White Oak Swamp, 80, 84
Whiting, Major Jasper, 29, 67, 73, 79–81, 86–87, 92
Wigfall, Louis T., 97–99, 102, 124, 127, 129–30, 139, 145–46, 157, 160, 186, 188, 206, 211, 213
Wilcox, General, 82, 84–85
William and Mary College, 227
Williamsburg, 54, 61–69, 74, 78–85, 91
  Battle of, 67
Wilmington, 214–15
Wolseley, Lord, 237
Wood, Colonel John Taylor, 222

Yancey, William L., 98
Yazoo River, 116, 125
York River, 50, 53, 55–56, 63, 67–68, 72, 80, 86, 233
Yorktown, 2, 55–57, 59, 61, 64, 239